Savings and Investment Information for Teens

Second Edition

TEEN FINANCE SERIES

Second Edition

Savings and Investment Information for Teens

Tips For A Successful Financial Life

Including Facts About Economic Principles, Wealth Development, Bank Accounts, Stocks, Bonds, Mutual Funds, And Other Financial Tools

◆

Edited by Karen Bellenir

P.O. Box 31-1640, Detroit, MI 48231-1640

Bibliographic Note

Because this page cannot legibly accommodate all the copyright notices, the Bibliographic Note portion of the Preface constitutes an extension of the copyright notice.

Edited by Karen Bellenir

Teen Finance Series

Karen Bellenir, *Managing Editor*
Elizabeth Collins, *Research and Permissions Coordinator*
Cherry Edwards, *Permissions Assistant*
EdIndex, Services for Publishers, *Indexers*

* * *

Omnigraphics, Inc.

Matthew P. Barbour, *Senior Vice President*
Kevin Hayes, *Operations Manager*

* * *

Peter E. Ruffner, *Publisher*

Frederick G. Ruffner, Jr., *Chairman*

Copyright © 2009 Omnigraphics, Inc.

ISBN 978-0-7808-1064-8

Library of Congress Cataloging-in-Publication Data

Savings and investment information for teens : tips for a successful
financial life including facts about economic principles, wealth
development, bank accounts, stocks, bonds, mutual funds, and other financial
tools / edited by Karen Bellenir. -- 2nd ed.
    p. cm. -- (Teen finance series)
  Includes bibliographical references and index.
  Summary: "Provides information for teens about strategies for saving
money, investment options, and economic factors that affect personal wealth.
Includes index, resource information and recommendations for further
reading"--Provided by publisher.
  ISBN 978-0-7808-1064-8 (hardcover : alk. paper) 1. Saving and
investment. 2. Teenagers--Finance, Personal. I. Bellenir, Karen.
  HG4521.S337 2009
  332.02400835--dc22
                                                        2009003482

Printed in the United States

Table of Contents

Part Three: Banks And Bonds

Part Four: Stocks And Mutual Funds

Part Five: If You Need More Information

Preface

About This Book

According to Jump$tart Coalition for Personal Financial Literacy, recent surveys indicate that students are still confused about financial issues and many do not understand basic principles regarding saving and investing their money. In a biennial survey conducted in 2008, high school seniors scored lower than their 2006 counterparts in a national test of financial literacy. Fewer than half correctly answered questions about the best way to save for emergencies, the safety of various savings options, and the impact of inflation, taxes, and finance charges on wealth development.

Savings And Investment Information For Teens, Second Edition provides updated information to help today's young adults learn how to develop the habit of saving money and investing for the future. It explains how the economy works and how factors such as interest rates and inflation impact personal wealth. It offers practical suggestions for developing a financial plan, and it describes the risks and rewards associated with bank accounts, stocks, bonds, and mutual funds. The book concludes with a directory of resources for additional information and suggestions for further reading.

How To Use This Book

This book is divided into parts and chapters. Parts focus on broad areas of interest; chapters are devoted to single topics within a part.

Part One: How The Economy Works describes the basic principles that govern the functioning of the U.S. and global economies. It provides historical information about the use of money and explains the economic factors that influence interest rates, inflation, and consumer prices.

Part Two: Keys To Wealth Development explains the fundamental tools that can be used in saving money and making it grow. It discusses the benefits and risks of different types of investment choices and provides tips for how to understand financial documents and how to work with financial industry professionals. The part also includes cautions against common misunderstandings, frauds, and scams, and it concludes with a chapter about the hazards associated with managing money in an online environment.

Part Three: Banks And Bonds discusses the similarities and differences among banks, thrifts, and credit unions, and it describes the most common investment vehicles used in managing cash, including various types of savings accounts, certificates of deposit (CDs), and bonds. It discusses the benefits, risks, liquidity, and potential for generating returns associated with different savings instruments, and it offers an explanation about which types of accounts are insured by the Federal Deposit Insurance Corporation (FDIC).

Part Four: Stocks And Mutual Funds explains equity investments and the various ways people can own stocks as part of an investment portfolio, including owning individual stocks and purchasing different types of mutual funds. It also explains the special risks associated with investing in foreign stocks, trading in microcap stocks, and day trading.

Part Five: If You Need More Information provides a directory of savings and investment organizations and suggestions for additional reading.

Bibliographic Note

This volume contains documents and excerpts from publications issued by the following government agencies: Federal Deposit Insurance Corporation; Federal Reserve Board; Federal Trade Commission; OnGuard Online; U.S. Department of Labor, Bureau of Labor Statistics; U.S. Department of State; U.S. Department of the Treasury; U.S. Secret Service; and the U.S. Securities and Exchange Commission.

In addition, this volume contains copyrighted documents and articles produced by the following organizations: American Association of Individual

Investors; Department of Banking, State of Connecticut with the Conference of State Bank Supervisors; Federal Reserve Bank of Chicago; Federal Reserve Bank of Minneapolis; Federal Reserve Bank of Philadelphia; Federal Reserve Bank of San Francisco; Financial Industry Regulatory Authority, Inc.; Investment Company Institute; Investopedia, ULC; Motley Fool; North American Securities Administrators Association; NYSE Group, Inc./NYSE Euronext; VISA; and the Young Americans Center for Financial Education.

Full citation information is provided on the first page of each chapter. Every effort has been made to secure all necessary rights to reprint the copyrighted material. If any omissions have been made, please contact Omnigraphics to make corrections for future editions.

Acknowledgements

In addition to the organizations who have contributed to this book, special thanks are due to research and permissions coordinator, Liz Collins; permissions assistant, Cherry Edwards; editorial assistant, Nicole Salerno; and prepress technician, Elizabeth Bellenir.

Part One

How The Economy Works

Chapter 1

The History Of Money

Consider this problem: You catch fish for your food supply, but you're tired of eating it every day. Instead you want to eat some bread. Fortunately, a baker lives next door. Trading the baker some fish for bread is an example of barter, the direct exchange of one good for another.

However, barter is difficult when you try to obtain a good from a producer that doesn't want what you have. For example, how do you get shoes if the shoemaker doesn't like fish? The series of trades required to obtain shoes could be complicated and time consuming.

Early societies faced these problems. The solution was money. Money is an item, or commodity, that is agreed to be accepted in trade. Over the years, people have used a wide variety of items for money, such as seashells, beads, tea, fish hooks, fur, cattle, and even tobacco.

Coins

Most early cultures traded precious metals. In 2500 BC the Egyptians produced metal rings for use as money. By 700 BC, a group of seafaring people called the Lydians became the first in the Western world to make coins. The

About This Chapter: This chapter includes text from "The History of Money," reprinted with permission from the Federal Reserve Bank of Minneapolis, www.minneapolisfed.org. © date unknown; accessed May 2008.

Lydians used coins to expand their vast trading empire. The Greeks and Romans continued the coining tradition and passed it on to later Western civilizations. Coins were appealing since they were durable, easy to carry, and contained valuable metals.

During the 18th century, coins became popular throughout Europe as trading grew. One of the most widely used coins was the Spanish 8-reale. It was often split into pieces or bits to make change. Half a coin was four bits, a quarter was two bits, a term still used today.

Coins containing precious metals are an example of "commodity money." The item was traded because it held value. For example, the value of the coin depended upon the amount of gold and silver it contained.

Paper Currency

The Chinese were the first to use paper money, beginning in the T'ang Dynasty (618–907 AD). During the Ming Dynasty in 1300 AD, the Chinese placed the emperor's seal and signatures of the treasurers on a crude paper made from mulberry bark.

Representative money is tokens or pieces of paper that are not intrinsically valuable themselves, but can be

♣ **It's A Fact!!**
The Functions Of Money

Medium Of Exchange: Acts as a go-between to make it easier to buy and sell goods or services or pay debts. Allows buyers and sellers to avoid the difficulties associated with barter exchanges of goods and services.

Store Of Value: Allows people to transfer the purchasing power of their present money income or wealth into the future, ideally without a loss of value. Stores purchasing power between the time money is earned and the time it is spent.

Unit Of Account: Serves as a way to measure and compare the value of goods and services in relation to one another. When comparing prices, individuals can determine if one good is a better buy than another. It also allows people to keep accurate financial records.

Source: Excerpted from "Benjamin Franklin and the Birth of a Paper Money Economy," © 2006. Reprinted with permission from the Federal Reserve Bank of Philadelphia, www.philadelphiafed.org.

exchanged for a specific commodity, such as gold or silver. In 1715 Maryland, North Carolina, and Virginia issued a "tobacco note" which could be converted to a certain amount of tobacco. This type of money was easier to make large payments and carry than coin or tobacco leaves.

In the late 1800s, the U.S. government issued gold and silver certificates.

Fiat money is similar to representative money except it can't be redeemed for a commodity, such as gold or silver. The Federal Reserve notes we use today are an example of fiat money. In 1967 Congress authorized the U.S. Treasury to stop redeeming silver certificates in silver dollars or bullion beginning the following year. By 1970 silver was removed from the production of coins. The old coins were gradually removed from circulation and replaced with new copper-cored coins that were faced or "clad" with layers of

---

♣ It's A Fact!!

Electronic Money

Thirty years ago, some predicted we were on the verge of a cashless society. Paper currency and checks would join the Edsel and the black-and-white television as antiquated symbols of the past. Consumers would embrace a new alternative for making payments: electronic money. As it turned out, consumers have been reluctant to give up on currency and checks.

In recent years, however, consumers seem to be changing their minds. Cash and checks are still widely used. Currency is used for the vast majority of payments, mainly for smaller purchases. And checks are the payment choice for about 10 percent of transactions each year. But the percentage of transactions done electronically is growing dramatically. The important role of electronic payments can be seen by looking at the value of payment transactions. Electronic payments account for more than 90 percent of the dollar value of transactions.

Source: Excerpted from "Electronic Money," reprinted with permission from the Federal Reserve Bank of Chicago, www.chicagofed.org. © 2008.

an alloy of 75 percent copper and 25 percent nickel—the same alloy used in nickels.

People are willing to accept fiat money in exchange for the goods and services they sell only because they are confident it will be honored when they buy goods and services. The Federal Reserve is responsible for maintaining the integrity of U.S. currency by setting monetary policy—controlling the amount of money in circulation—to keep prices stable. If prices remain stable, people have confidence that the dollar they use to buy goods and services today will buy a similar amount in the future.

Chapter 2

The American Experience With Money

The Beginnings...And Beyond

From the earliest times when commodities such as tobacco and beaver pelts were used as money, to the present when credit and debit cards are commonplace, money has always played a central role in the American experience.

Early in our history, our monetary system consisted of numerous foreign coins and paper currencies issued by the thirteen colonies and the Continental Congress. More than two hundred years later, we now have a single national currency and privately owned banks chartered by state and federal governments. Furthermore, a central bank, the Federal Reserve, has replaced gold as the regulator of the value of our money.

The evolution from a decentralized system to a more centralized system has been marked by controversy and slowed by a general suspicion of banking power. Each change has involved extensive legal debate focusing on the rights of state and federal governments and the freedom of the individual.

Another important dimension of our nation's economic development is the role of gold. Once a cornerstone of the financial system, gold has gradually

About This Chapter: "Money Matters: The American Experience with Money," reprinted with permission from the Federal Reserve Bank of Chicago, www.chicagofed.org. © 2008.

but perceptibly become less important, both as a medium of exchange and as a regulator of the money supply. This process was driven by the nature of gold itself as well as by the changing needs of our modern and complex economy.

The Constitution And Money

The framers of the Constitution were apparently undecided about the form of financial system they should establish. Some preferred a centralized system with most of the power residing in the federal government. These framers wanted a national currency and a single federally chartered bank with branches throughout the country.

> ### ✎ What's It Mean?
> Gold Standard: A monetary system in which currencies are defined in terms of a given weight of gold.
>
> Source: Excerpted from "An Outline of the U.S. Economy, Glossary of Economic Terms," by Christopher Conte and Albert R. Karr, U.S. Department of State, 2001.

Others involved in developing the Constitution envisioned a decentralized financial system with principal authority resting in the states. They preferred that each state charter its own banks, and each bank issue its own bank notes—that is, its own paper currency. There would be no uniform national currency and no central bank.

After long debate, the framers of the Constitution permitted the federal government "to coin money, (and) regulate the value thereof and of foreign coins..." They also declared that "no state shall...coin money, [nor] emit bills of credit [that is, paper currency]..." Significantly, no mention was made of a national currency nor federally chartered banks.

The Constitution specified little involvement for the federal government in our financial system. Congress was expressly permitted only the right to mint metal coins, regulate the percentage of precious metal in those coins, and determine the metallic content of the many kinds of foreign coins that circulated throughout the states. In other words, Congress' involvement in the financial system focused on the intrinsic value of coins, which was determined by the amount of precious metal in the coin.

Fear Of Paper

Many of the framers of the Constitution opposed paper money largely because of their experience during the Revolutionary War. In 1775 the Continental Congress faced the problem of fighting a war without the means to pay for it. The British blockade of our ports limited trade, reducing revenues from tariffs, and European nations were reluctant to lend us money. Left with little alternative, the Continental Congress authorized $2 million of Continental currency. This was the first of many issuances. In total, between 1775 and the adoption of the Constitution in 1787, Congress authorized the printing of about $242 million in "Continentals."

Congress promised to pay the holders of the currency the face value of the bills in gold or silver or in Spanish coins, widely circulated at the time. However, Congress did not have enough gold or silver to make payment. In reality, there was no "backing" for the Continentals; that is, there was no mechanism, except the authority of the Continental Congress, to fix the value of Continentals or to limit the amount that could be issued. As a result, Congress issued more Continentals than the economy could handle without inflation.

The colonies experienced a rapid increase in inflation as the government printed money without restraint. The resulting oversupply of money undermined the purchasing power, and therefore value, of the Continentals.

To support the faltering currency, Congress declared that any person convicted of refusing Continentals at face value was an enemy of the country and should be "precluded from all trade...with the inhabitants of these colonies."

Despite such efforts to maintain the Continental's value, people paying in these notes were charged more than people paying with foreign coin of gold and silver. In other words, Continentals were discounted.

Although the printing of Continentals was an emergency measure that helped to win the war, this episode illustrated the perils of issuing too much currency.

Eventually, in 1790, Congress began redeeming the currency at a rate of 100 Continentals to the dollar measured in Spanish coins, which contained gold and silver. By using gold and silver as currency, the founding fathers sought to maintain the value of money by limiting the amount in the economy. The upper limit was set by the amount of gold and silver that could be produced domestically or acquired from other nations. There was no such upper limit under the "paper standard" of Continental currency.

To set this limit, the founding fathers could have used any commodity with the desirable properties of money. Gold and silver were good choices because they were durable; easy to recognize, store, move, divide, and standardize; and, most importantly, relatively scarce.

✎ What's It Mean?

Continental Dollar: Paper currency issued by the Continental Congress to finance the Revolutionary War. The currency was not redeemable on demand for gold or silver. Congress issued so much of this currency during the war that inflation became rampant and destroyed its value, which led people to use the phrase: "Not worth a Continental."

Source: Excerpted from "Benjamin Franklin and the Birth of a Paper Money Economy," © 2006. Reprinted with permission from the Federal Reserve Bank of Philadelphia, www.philadelphiafed.org.

The U.S. Mint

As the U.S. moved away from paper currency, Congress passed the Coinage Act in 1792, ordering Alexander Hamilton, the first Secretary of the Treasury, to establish the U.S. Mint. The Mint cast coins free of charge from gold or silver brought in by individuals. The ratio of silver to gold was fixed at 15 to one, reflecting their relative values at the time. In other words, 15 silver coins could be exchanged for one gold coin. Most coins were fullbodied, meaning their intrinsic value was equal to their face value.

This was our first attempt to adopt by law a bimetallic standard in which both gold and silver were declared legal tender. Free and unlimited coinage of both metals was allowed. Unfortunately, this bimetallic standard for determining the value of money was difficult, if not impossible, to maintain.

The market price of silver began to fall, and it became apparent that fixing the intrinsic value of coins was not something done once, for all time. Because the value of the silver in a coin no longer equaled the coin's face value, the 15 to one ratio no longer reflected a balance among the two metals. People sought to exchange silver coins for gold coins. The value of the gold in the coins increased in relation to the face value of the coins. People began hoarding gold coins for their gold content rather than circulating them at face value.

In fact, until 1834 gold tended to leave the country principally because it was valued at a higher rate in France and England than it was here. In an attempt to slow or stop this outflow of gold, the Mint in 1834 changed the ratio of silver to gold to 16 to one. This change overvalued gold and caused a return flow to the United States. Silver coins in turn tended to stop circulating.

Thus the intrinsic worth of gold and silver actually restricted their ability to act as a medium of exchange since people frequently tended to hoard them rather than circulate them.

Bank Of The United States

While most agreed that Congress should not authorize paper money, there was a significant controversy about Congress' right to charter a bank that could issue its own bank notes.

Thomas Jefferson and Alexander Hamilton represented the opposing viewpoints. Jefferson felt that only states could charter banks. Because the Constitution did not expressly grant the power to Congress, he reasoned that federally chartered banks were unconstitutional.

Hamilton, however, felt that federally chartered banks were not only constitutional but also necessary. He reasoned that since the Constitution established a government, it granted that government the right to establish institutions necessary for its operation.

♣ **It's A Fact!!**

Thomas Jefferson and Alexander Hamilton disagreed on the proper role of the federal government in the financial system. Jefferson favored a more decentralized government and believed that only states could charter banks under the Constitution. Hamilton felt that the federal government had the power to charter banks because the Constitution granted the government the right to establish institutions necessary for its operations. In a far-reaching decision, Supreme Court Chief Justice John Marshall followed Hamilton's reasoning and ruled in *McCulloch vs. Maryland* that the Second Bank of the United States was constitutional.

Source: © 2008 Federal Reserve Bank of Chicago.

Although these two leaders raised the issue, the constitutionality of federally chartered banks was not resolved at that time. Without determining constitutionality, Hamilton convinced Congress and President Washington in 1791 to establish the Bank of the United States with a twenty-year charter.

The Bank is now referred to as the first central bank in the United States principally because of its national scope and services to the federal government. However, it did little to affect the total supply of money in the economy, as a modern central bank would do. The Bank did aid the government in obtaining emergency loans, facilitated the payment of taxes, and served as receiver and disburser of public funds. In addition, it issued bank notes and made them fully redeemable in coin.

The Bank was a commercial success and provided financial stability. However, in 1811 Congress did not renew the charter chiefly because of the question of the Bank's constitutionality. Once again, as in 1791 when the Bank was chartered, no constitutional test was brought before the Supreme Court.

Second Bank Of The United States

In 1812, the nation was at war with the British, and again without a national bank to help finance it. This time, as an emergency measure, the Treasury issued a small number of interest-bearing notes, which were retired soon after the war.

The problems of financing the war, the inflation as a result of the war, and the varying values of the many state bank notes, combined to change Congressional sentiment about a federally chartered bank. In 1816 Congress approved the charter of the Second Bank of the United States, larger in assets than the First Bank and, as it turned out, more controversial.

After some initial years of difficulty the Second Bank helped bring about financial stability and economic prosperity. Like the First Bank, it issued nationally uniform paper currency, redeemable for coin.

The Second Bank, however, is remembered more for its legal and political difficulties than for its financial successes. To promote the soundness of the financial system, the Second Bank required that all state-chartered banks redeem their notes for an equal value in gold or silver coins. The measure was made in an effort to prevent the overissuance of notes and the resulting devaluation.

Many state-chartered banks, however, did overissue currency. To meet the Second Bank's requirements, they had to reduce the amount of their paper notes outstanding. Many states felt the Second Bank was usurping their constitutional authority. Resentment spread until Maryland and Ohio retaliated by taxing local branches of the Second Bank. The resulting case, *McCulloch vs. Maryland,* was brought before the U.S. Supreme Court in 1819. This case became the first test of the constitutionality of federally chartered banks and nationally issued paper currency.

In one of its most important cases, the Supreme Court unanimously decided that the Bank and its currency were constitutional and that the state tax was unconstitutional. Following Hamilton's rather than Jefferson's reasoning, Chief Justice John Marshall's far-reaching decision stated that the Constitution granted the federal government the powers "necessary and proper" for carrying out its operations, unless the power was clearly withheld by the Constitution.

A landmark decision, *McCulloch vs. Maryland* created the doctrine of "implied powers" that has become the cornerstone of American constitutional law. The decision became the legal safeguard not only for the Second Bank of the United States and its notes, but also for paper money later issued by Congress.

Despite its financial success and legal support, however, Congress did not renew the Bank's charter. Two factors led to the Bank's demise. In 1832 the directors of the Bank made some politically unwise loans to members of Congress. In addition, President Andrew Jackson, a Westerner, distrusted the Eastern monied class, symbolized in his eyes by the Second Bank. The combination of the loans and Jackson's attitudes helped make the Bank a political issue in the presidential election of 1832.

With Jackson's reelection, the fate of the Bank was sealed. Jackson vetoed the bill to renew the Bank's charter, and Congress could not override the veto. In 1833 the federal government removed all deposits from the Bank. In 1836 when the Bank's federal charter expired, it was granted a state charter in Pennsylvania but soon went out of business.

The Free Banking Period

With the demise of the Second Bank, states took over principal control of currency and banking, as some of the framers of the Constitution envisioned. Since each state administered its own system according to its own laws, banking standards were uneven throughout the country.

State-chartered banks issued paper money, which was redeemable for gold or silver. This redemptive quality, or backing by gold and silver, set the limit on the amount of notes that could be printed. While many banks did not overissue notes, some issued more paper money than they had gold and silver to back it. As a result, people became suspicious of unfamiliar notes, frequently accepting them only at less than face value. To compound these problems, even the best managed banks tended to discontinue redemption in gold and silver during a crisis. The difficulties were magnified by a dramatic surge in the number of banks, which tripled between 1837 and 1860.

Despite these problems, people still looked to gold to regulate the money supply. They rejected the possibility of a flexible or discretionary system managed in an intelligent, non-political, non-inflationary way. Instead, many thought that impersonal, inflexible gold was a flawed, but acceptable alternative. This feeling about gold was confirmed in the minds of many by the Civil War experience with paper currency that could not be redeemed for gold and silver.

National Currency And National Banks

A serious and recurring problem with gold was its inflexibility. When the economy needed more money to finance expenditures, gold coins and gold-backed currency often could not provide the necessary funds. Thus, it is not surprising that we abandoned gold during the Civil War.

When the Confederacy attacked Fort Sumter in 1861, the United States once again found itself at war without a national currency or federally chartered banks to help finance it. Learning from its experience with the First and Second Banks, Congress did not establish a single publicly owned bank that issued its own bank notes. Rather it established a system of federally chartered, privately owned banks and a national currency.

♣ It's A Fact!!

At one time, more than 10,000 different bank notes were in circulation.

Source: © 2008 Federal Reserve Bank of Chicago.

In the early stages of the war the Treasury tried to finance its spending by borrowing money, that is by selling government bonds in exchange for gold and silver. However, it soon became apparent that war spending was far greater than revenues raised from bond sales. In response, the Treasury began paying for purchases by issuing a variety of paper notes, collectively called greenbacks. These paper notes, most of which were not redeemable for gold, became the principal source of financing the war.

Many types of paper currency were issued during this period, including the greenback demand notes, interest-bearing notes, and gold certificates. However, United States notes, first issued in 1862, were historically the most significant. Congress declared the new notes legal tender, meaning they had to be accepted in payment of debt. They were not redeemable for gold or silver coins, as were the First and Second Banks' notes, but were backed by bonds issued by the federal government.

As the government printed more and more notes, the economy experienced a sharp inflation, which pushed the dollar price of gold above its official price. Gold was withdrawn from the nation's banks and hoarded. Once again, the intrinsic value of gold detracted from its ability to circulate.

As a result of this large issuance, the value of a paper dollar decreased to 35 cents in gold. During this period the term "inflation" was used for the first time.

There was soon a cry for a return to gold. Many thought that governments could not be trusted voluntarily to restrain the issuance of money. They felt that our money could only retain its purchasing power if we limited its supply with the nondiscretionary restraint of gold.

National Currency And The Constitution

As the nation struggled with inflation, some questioned whether the federal government had the power to charter banks and issue a national currency. While the new national currency issued by federally chartered banks solved many problems for the government, it added another kind of note for people to carry in addition to the state-chartered bank notes already in circulation. To eliminate these other notes, Congress in 1865 issued a 10 percent tax on state bank notes. These notes soon became too expensive to circulate, and U.S. notes became the dominant medium of exchange.

The question as to whether Congress had the right to impose the so-called death tax on state bank notes was answered in *Veazie Bank vs. Fenno* (1869). The Supreme Court upheld the tax, stating that Congress has the power "to secure a sound and uniform currency for the country" and "to restrain by suitable enactments the circulation as money of any notes not issued under its own authority."

Eighty years after the adoption of the Constitution and in response to the needs of a growing and struggling country, we acknowledged that the federal government, not state governments, had exclusive power over the country's currency.

This decision did not end the constitutional problems facing a national currency, however. The Court still had to decide the more difficult question about the status of legal tender.

United States notes were issued as an emergency provision to help finance the war, but many, even some in Lincoln's administration, viewed them as unconstitutional. Shortly after the war the question as to whether U.S. notes were legal tender was brought before 17 state supreme courts. In 16 cases those courts found in favor of the legal tender status of U.S. notes. In the other case, *Hepburn vs. Griswold*, the Kentucky Supreme Court decided that U.S. notes could not be considered legal tender. Therefore U.S. notes could not be used to make payment for contracts made before Congress declared these notes legal tender.

If left to stand, this ruling would have significant financial implications. Inflation had increased the intrinsic value of gold and silver coins beyond their face value. As a result, creditors wanted debts repaid in coin, while debtors preferred repaying in depreciated legal tender notes.

The case was appealed before the Supreme Court of the United States in 1867. *Hepburn vs. Griswold* (1870 and 1871) was heard twice before the U.S. Supreme Court under extraordinary circumstances. In 1867 when it was first heard, there were only seven justices rather than the nine mandated by the

---

✎ What's It Mean?

Fiat Paper Money (or Fiat Currency): Paper currency that has value because the government has decreed that it is a "legal tender" for making tax payments and often for discharging other debts and payments as well. Fiat money does not represent a claim on some other form of money or commodity such as gold and silver.

Legal Tender Laws: Government laws that decree that creditors are required to accept an asset (such as paper money or coins) in settlement of debts and that the government will accept the asset in payment of taxes. When paper money and coins are a legal tender and people use them to settle a debt, the obligation is considered to be paid in full.

Source: Excerpted from "Benjamin Franklin and the Birth of a Paper Money Economy," © 2006. Reprinted with permission from the Federal Reserve Bank of Philadelphia, www.philadelphiafed.org.

Constitution. After two years of deliberation and a great deal of emotion, the Court decided by a four to three vote that all contracts made before U.S. notes were declared legal tender were not bound by the legal tender laws. In addition, the opinion implied that all contracts written afterward were not bound by those laws. In effect, the Court said that the notes were not legal tender.

President U. S. Grant, recognizing the implications of this ruling, quickly filled the two remaining Supreme Court justice positions with people who favored legal tender laws. In 1871 *Hepburn vs. Griswold* was reheard. This time by a vote of five to four the Court found legal tender laws constitutional. The ruling was based on the understanding that U.S. notes were necessities of warfare. The Court found that a means of self-preservation could not be withheld from a government.

♣ **It's A Fact!!**
The right of Congress to issue paper currency and declare it legal tender in times of peace was established in *Juilliard vs. Greenman* (1884). Noting that the Constitution granted Congress the right to make all laws necessary and proper for carrying out its powers, the Court ruled Congress has the authority to issue its own currency.

Source: © 2008 Federal Reserve Bank of Chicago.

A Return To Gold...

As the legality of national notes was debated, the government returned to the gold standard in an effort to stabilize prices after the inflationary Civil War years. To do this, Congress had to remove greenbacks from circulation.

The reduction in the money supply initiated a recession and began one of the most intense and dramatic struggles in the history of American money—a struggle, in essence, about how our money should be valued.

The lines were clearly drawn. On the one side, the hard-money advocates, generally representing big business and banking groups of large Eastern cities, favored the gold standard. On the other side, the easy-money advocates, generally representing small business and small town and farming groups of the West, favored easier money and credit and abandoning the gold standard.

The controversy continued intermittently for 30 years. Advocates of easy money organized their own political party, the Greenback Party, and entered candidates in three presidential campaigns. However, their lack of success can be attributed at least partially to national sentiment favoring gold.

When the government removed paper money after the war, prices fell, eventually coming fairly close to pre-war levels. Congress then passed the Resumption Act, directing the Treasury to redeem any paper money presented for redemption after January 1, 1879. The money was to be redeemed in coin, at pre-Civil War gold parity. With the greenback a lost cause, the easy-money bloc turned to silver coins as a means of increasing the money supply.

And Maybe Silver...

Silver coins had not been circulated widely since 1834 because the official ratio of gold to silver was 16 to one. Since the price of silver was higher in the open market than at the Mint, mine owners sold their silver to bullion dealers.

In an effort to align the law with reality, Congress ended the coinage of silver dollars in 1873, although it authorized a new silver coin—the trade dollar—which had a higher silver content and was intended for foreign commerce. At about the same time, however, miners discovered large new deposits of silver. Silver miners and others in the easy money bloc interested in an expanded money supply decried the "Crime of '73" and demanded a return to the old silver dollar. Joining the crusade were farmers and other debtors who would have benefited from an expanded money supply.

Responding to the outcry Congress passed the Bland-Allison Act in 1878, which authorized the Treasury to purchase silver and issue silver certificates for the first time. The easy money bloc achieved another victory in 1890 when Congress passed the Sherman Silver Purchase Act, which required to Treasury to purchase 4.4 million ounces of silver each month using a legal tender Treasury note. To make the notes more acceptable, the Treasury redeemed them in gold. There were immediate problems. People exchanged the notes for gold and hoarded the gold or used it to purchase imports.

The Treasury's gold holdings fell rapidly, severely decreasing the money supply and setting off the Panic of 1893 and a sharp recession. Congress quickly repealed the Sherman Silver Purchase Act, ending the panic, but the recession lasted for years.

...But Finally Gold

The easy-money bloc's attacks on gold continued throughout the recession, culminating in the presidential election of 1896. The hard-money advocate William McKinley defeated easy-money advocate William Jennings Bryan, famous for his "Cross of Gold" speech at the Democratic National Convention. Bryan's losses in 1896 and again in 1900 marked the end of the free silver movement. Fulfilling his campaign promise, McKinley signed the Gold Standard Act in 1900. The act officially ended bimetallism and established gold as the single legal standard.

While the gold standard provided a means of limiting the money supply, the economy was marked by periodic financial panics, inflations, and recessions through much of the nineteenth century. It became clear that the gold standard was sometimes too inflexible. We needed a monetary authority that would be disciplined enough to increase or decrease the flow of money based on the needs of the economy.

Federal Reserve And Elastic Currency

In response to the problems in our economy and financial system, Congress in 1913 created the Federal Reserve System. The Federal Reserve (Fed), our nation's central bank, is a network of 12 regional Reserve Banks supervised by a Board of Governors in Washington, D.C.

Congress gave the Fed responsibility for providing an elastic currency, that is, a currency that could increase and decrease to accommodate the needs of the economy. To expand the currency, the central bank made loans to banks and provided them currency, Federal Reserve notes, to meet their customers' demands. These loans helped prevent runs on banks and kept many banks from closing. Congress tried to prevent overissuance by requiring that Federal Reserve notes be backed by gold and certain kinds of securities representing loans to manufacturers and farmers.

For the first time in our history we had a monetary authority that could influence the money supply to the benefit of the economy. The amount of money in the economy no longer would be determined solely by the supply of gold or wartime needs. With the Federal Reserve System, Congress created a viable alternative to gold.

Gradually we relied more and more on the Fed's discretionary authority and eventually eliminated the gold backing of money. The initial break came with World War I.

The Break With Gold

In 1914, shortly after President Woodrow Wilson signed the Federal Reserve Act, World War I broke out, severing international relations. Countries refused to ship gold to one another in payment for international debt. Gold tended to accumulate in the treasury vaults of the world, particularly in the safe haven of the United States.

Because of this war-time breakdown, gold gradually lost much of its monetary importance. Gold certificates and gold coins still circulated, but much of our gold was concentrated in the Treasury's vaults. Monetary gold became a reserve backing for the money supply and a means of settling international transactions.

The final break with gold, which came in the early 1930s during Franklin Roosevelt's administration, created the need for new criteria and standards to replace gold's automatic operation. Congress had already laid this groundwork two decades before with the Federal Reserve Act.

From its inception, the Fed had been charged by Congress not only with providing an elastic currency, but also with maintaining stability in our financial system and promoting a healthy economy. With the break from gold, the Federal Reserve assumed the primary responsibility for influencing the money supply to encourage a healthy, growing economy.

This responsibility requires the Fed to maintain the long-term purchasing power of money as well as foster high employment and economic growth. In the long run, the Federal Reserve seeks to achieve reasonable price stability, which in turn, sets the stage for a healthy, growing economy. However, the Federal Reserve must also consider the performance of the economy in the short and intermediate terms, and avoid the boom and bust cycles that plagued the U.S. economy in the late 1800s.

Faced with all these goals simultaneously, the Fed seeks an acceptable balance among them. In practice it is not always clear what is in the best short-term and long-term interest of the economy. Difficult decisions have to be made. While the gold standard provided little flexibility, the Fed operates with discretion. This discretion allows it to respond to the changing needs of the economy to foster a healthy, growing economy with price stability.

Chapter 3

The Federal Reserve System And How It Affects You

The Fed...to some the name evokes images of money stacks; to others it is just a dim memory from an economics class. To most, the overall picture is unclear—a hazy image that needs to be focused. Even the language associated with the Federal Reserve may seem as mysterious as an alchemist's formula. The Federal Open Market Committee (FOMC), the discount window, open market operations—what exactly do they mean? What does the Fed do and how does it affect us?

Put most simply, the Federal Reserve System is the central bank of the United States. Congress created the Federal Reserve through a law passed in 1913, charging it with a responsibility to foster a sound banking system and a healthy economy. This remains, today, the broad mission of the Fed and its component parts: the 12 Federal Reserve Banks nationwide, each serving a specific region of the country; and the Board of Governors in Washington, D.C., set up to oversee the Fed System.

To accomplish its mission, the Fed serves as a banker's bank and as the government's bank, as a regulator of financial institutions, and as the nation's

About This Chapter: From "The Fed: Our Central Bank," reprinted with permission from the Federal Reserve Bank of Chicago, www.chicagofed.org. © 2008.

money manager, performing a vast array of functions that affect the economy, the financial system, and ultimately, each of us.

A Bank For Banks

Each of the 12 Fed Banks provides services to financial institutions that are similar to the services that banks and thrifts provide to businesses and individuals. By serving as a "banker's bank" the Fed helps assure the safety and efficiency of the payments system, the critical pipeline through which all financial transactions in the economy flow.

Each day the Fed processes millions of payments in the form of both paper checks and electronic transfers. So when you cash a check or have money electronically transferred, there is a good chance that a Fed Bank will handle the transfer of funds from one financial institution to another. Each of the Fed Banks offers these and other services, on a fee basis, to the depository institutions in its Federal Reserve District. Institutions can choose to use the Fed's services or those offered by other competitors in the marketplace.

Together, the 12 Fed Banks process more than one-third of the checks written in the U.S., a total that exceeds $14 trillion annually. And the dollar volume transferred through the Federal Reserve's electronic network is far greater, over $343 trillion or many times our nation's gross national product.

Another important Federal Reserve responsibility is servicing the nation's largest banking customer—the U.S. government. As the government's bank or fiscal agent, the Fed processes a variety of financial transactions involving trillions of dollars.

> ♣ **It's A Fact!!**
> **Federal Reserve Bank Branches**
>
> • Boston
>
> • New York
>
> • Philadelphia
>
> • Cleveland
>
> • Richmond
>
> • Atlanta
>
> • Chicago
>
> • Saint Louis
>
> • Minneapolis
>
> • Kansas City
>
> • Dallas
>
> • San Francisco
>
> Source: Federal Reserve Bank of Chicago, 2008.

Just as an individual might keep an account at a bank, the U.S. Treasury keeps a checking account with the Federal Reserve through which incoming federal tax deposits and outgoing government payments are handled. As part of this service relationship, the Fed sells and redeems U.S. government securities such as savings bonds and Treasury bills, notes, and bonds.

♣ **It's A Fact!!**

The average $1 bill circulates for approximately 18 months before being destroyed.

Source: Federal Reserve Bank of Chicago, 2008.

The Federal Reserve also issues the nation's coin and paper currency. The U.S. Treasury, through its Bureau of the Mint and Bureau of Engraving and Printing, actually produces the nation's cash supply; the Fed Banks then distribute it to financial institutions. The currency periodically circulates back to the Fed Banks where it is counted, checked for wear and tear, and examined for counterfeits. If the money is still in good condition, it is eventually sent back into circulation as institutions order new supplies to satisfy the public's need for cash. Worn-out bills, however, are destroyed by shredding.

Supervisor And Regulator

As part of its mandate to foster a sound banking system, the Federal Reserve supervises and regulates financial institutions.

As a regulator, the Fed formulates rules that govern the conduct of financial institutions. As a supervisor, the Federal Reserve examines and monitors institutions to help ensure that they operate in a safe and sound manner and comply with the laws and rules that apply to them. The Fed's supervisory duties are carried out on a regional basis. Each of the Reserve Banks is responsible for monitoring bank holding companies (organizations that own one or more banks) and state member banks (banks that are chartered by the state and are members of the Federal Reserve System) based in its District.

The Federal Reserve also helps to ensure that banks act in the public's interest by ruling on applications from banks seeking to merge or from bank

♣ It's A Fact!!
The Fed's Structure

The Federal Reserve System

- The nation's central bank

- A regional structure with 12 districts

- Subject to general Congressional authority and oversight

- Operates on its own earnings

Board Of Governors

- Seven members serving staggered 14-year terms

- Appointed by the U.S. President and confirmed by the Senate

- Oversees System operations, makes regulatory decisions, and sets reserve requirements

Federal Open Market Committee

- The System's key monetary policy-making body

- Decisions seek to foster economic growth with price stability by influencing the flow of money and credit

- Comprised of the seven members of the Board of Governors and the Reserve Bank presidents, five of whom serve as voting members on a rotating basis

Federal Reserve Banks

- 12 regional banks with 25 branches

- Each independently incorporated with a nine-member board of directors from the private sector

- Set discount rate, subject to approval by Board of Governors

- Monitor economy and financial institutions in their districts and provide financial services to the U.S. government and depository institutions

holding companies seeking to buy a bank or engage in a non-banking activity. In making these rulings, the Fed takes into consideration how the transaction would affect competition and the local community. The Federal Reserve also implements laws—such as Truth-in-Lending, Equal Credit Opportunity, and Home Mortgage Disclosure—meant to ensure that consumers are treated fairly in financial dealings.

Another way the Fed helps maintain a sound banking system is as the "lender of last resort." A financial institution experiencing an unexpected drain on its deposits, for example, can turn to its Reserve Bank if it is unable to borrow money elsewhere. This loan from the Fed would not only enable the institution to get through temporary difficulties, but most importantly, would prevent problems at one institution from spreading to others. The basic interest rate charged for these loans is called the discount rate.

Money Manager

The most important of the Fed's responsibilities is formulating and carrying out monetary policy. In this role, the Fed acts as the nation's "money manager." It works to balance the volume of money and credit and their price—interest rates—with the needs of the economy. Simply stated, too much money in the economy can lead to inflation, while too little can stifle economic growth. As the nation's money manager, the Fed seeks to strike a balance between these two extremes.

To achieve this goal, the Fed works to control money at its source by affecting the ability of financial institutions to "create" checkbook money through loans or investments. The control lever that the Fed uses in this process is the "reserves" that banks and thrifts must hold.

In general, depository institutions are subject to rules requiring that a certain percentage of their deposits be set aside as reserves and not used for loans or investments. These reserves determine the amount of money an institution can create through lending and investing. Through reserves, then, the Fed indirectly affects the flow of money and credit through the economy by controlling the raw materials that institutions use to create money. The Fed's action triggers a chain of events that affects interest rates and the levels of prices, employment, and overall growth in the economy. The Fed has three tools for affecting reserves:

- **Reserve Requirements:** Altering the percentage of deposits that institutions must set aside as reserves can have a powerful impact on the flow of money and credit. Lowering reserve requirements can lead to more money being injected into the economy by freeing up funds that were previously set aside. Raising the requirements freezes funds that financial institutions could otherwise pump into the economy. The Fed, however, seldom changes reserve requirements because such changes can have a dramatic effect on institutions and the economy.

♣ **It's A Fact!!**

Myths And Facts

Here are a few facts to help dispel some myths about the Federal Reserve System, how it affects people's lives, and how it works:

MYTH: The Federal Reserve System is a branch of the military.

FACT: President Woodrow Wilson signed the Federal Reserve Act on December 23, 1913, to establish the Federal Reserve as an independent central bank for the United States. The Federal Reserve is not associated with any branch of the military.

MYTH: The Fed has little to do with the lives of ordinary citizens.

FACT: The Federal Reserve affects the economic and financial decisions of virtually everyone—from a family buying a house, to a business expanding its operations, to a consumer choosing a sound financial institution. In the global economy, the Federal Reserve's actions have significant economic and financial effects around the world.

MYTH: Actions of the Fed hurt rather than help people.

FACT: Federal Reserve policies seek to help people and businesses by fostering a sound banking system and a growing economy, with maximum sustainable employment and stable prices. The Fed's monetary policy actions affect the overall level of prices, economic growth, and employment in the

- **Discount Rate:** An increase in the discount rate can inhibit lending and investment activity of financial institutions by making it more expensive for institutions to obtain funds or reserves. But, if funds are readily available from sources other than the Fed's "discount window," a discount rate change won't directly affect the flow of money and credit. Even so, a change in the discount rate can be an important signal of the Fed's policy direction.

- **Open Market Operations:** The most flexible, and therefore most important, of the monetary policy tools is open market operations—the purchase and sale of government securities by the Fed. When the Fed

country. Monetary policy cannot target specific industries or regions within the country.

MYTH: Controlling inflation puts people out of work.

FACT: Stable prices help create jobs and raise incomes. Fluctuating prices distort consumer and investment decisions, thereby adversely affecting employment and growth in the economy.

MYTH: The Fed sets interest rates at whatever level it pleases.

FACT: The Fed influences short-term interest rates in the economy to achieve its goals of stable prices, maximum sustainable employment, and steady economic growth.

MYTH: The Fed is so powerful, it can ignore economic conditions in other countries.

FACT: Global interdependence, through international trade and investments and exchange rate fluctuations, compels the Fed to consider economic conditions in other countries in its monetary policy decisions.

Source: © 2007. Reprinted from the Federal Reserve Bank of San Francisco website, www.frbsf.org. The opinions expressed do not necessarily reflect the views of the management of the Federal Reserve Bank of San Francisco, or of the Board of Governors of the Federal Reserve System.

wants to increase the flow of money and credit, it buys government securities; when it wants to restrict the flow of money and credit, it sells government securities.

As with the other tools, the Fed's open market operations affect the supply of money through the reserves of depository institutions. If, for example, the Federal Reserve wished to increase the supply of money and credit, it might purchase $1 billion in government securities from a securities dealer. The Federal Reserve would pay for the securities by adding $1 billion to the account that the security dealer's bank keeps at the Fed, and the bank would in turn credit the security dealer's account for that amount. While the dealer's bank must keep a certain percentage of these new funds in reserve, it can lend and invest the remainder. As these funds are spent and re-spent, the stock of money and credit will eventually increase by much more than the original $1 billion addition.

The procedure is reversed to decrease the money supply. If the Fed were to sell $1 billion in government securities to a dealer, that amount would be deducted from the reserve account of the dealer's bank. The bank, in turn, would deduct $1 billion from the account of the dealer. The end result—less money flowing through the economy.

The Fed's Checks And Balances

The Federal Reserve's policy-making process highlights the careful way in which it was structured to incorporate broad participation and a system of checks and balances. Authority for each of the Fed's policy tools is vested in a different component of the Federal Reserve System. The authority to change reserve requirements, for example, is held by the Board of Governors. Changes in the discount rate are initiated by the boards of directors of the individual Reserve Banks, subject to approval by the Federal Reserve Board of Governors. Open market operations, the System's most important tool, are directed by a group that brings together the Federal Reserve Board and Banks—the Federal Open Market Committee (FOMC).

The FOMC, the Fed's most important policy-making body, is made up of all seven members of the Board of Governors and the presidents of the

🖎 What's It Mean?

Central Bank: A country's principal
monetary authority, responsible for
such key functions as issuing currency and regulating the supply of
credit in the economy.

Federal Reserve Bank: One of the 12
operating arms of the Federal Reserve System, located throughout the
United States, that together with
their 25 branches carry out various
functions of the U.S. central bank
system.

Federal Reserve System: The principal monetary authority (central
bank) of the United States, which
issues currency and regulates the supply of credit in the economy. It is
made up of a seven-member Board
of Governors in Washington, D.C.,
12 regional Federal Reserve Banks,
and their 25 branches.

Source: Excerpted from "An Outline
of the U.S. Economy, Glossary of
Economic Terms," by Christopher
Conte and Albert R. Karr, U.S. Department of State, 2001.

Reserve Banks. At any point in time, only five of the 12 presidents serve as voting members. The president of the New York Fed, which handles the open market securities transactions on behalf of the System, serves as a permanent voting member, while the other presidents rotate annually. Although only five presidents vote, all 12 participate fully in each FOMC meeting, bringing grass-roots, first-hand information, and views about the economy to the decision-making process.

This broad participation in the policy process is just one example of the checks and balances built into the Fed System. Like those who guided the formation of the American system of government, the framers of the Federal Reserve System were concerned about vesting too much power, especially money power, in the hands of too few. Therefore, they gave the Fed a number of contrasting elements:

It is a central bank, but it is decentralized with a system of regional Reserve Banks responsive to local needs. It is a public institution with a public purpose, but it has some private features—directors, "stockholders," and selling services. It is governmental, but it is independent within government. On the one hand, it was created by and reports to Congress; its highest officials, the members of the Board of Governors, are appointed by the President and confirmed by the Senate; and its earnings ultimately are returned to the U.S.

Treasury. On the other hand, the Fed operates on its own earnings rather than Congressional appropriation; the Board of Governors terms are long and staggered, limiting the President's influence; and unlike some other nations' central banks, it is separate from the Treasury.

With this complicated system of checks and balances, the Federal Reserve is the unmistakable offspring of the American political process. Congress created the System in 1913 in an effort to respond to the needs of a growing U.S. economy, and to avoid the cyclical pattern of booms and busts that had characterized much of the 1800s. By the early 1900s, there was general consensus that the country needed a central bank, but little agreement on how to structure it. As a result, the creation of the Federal Reserve turned into a legislative tug-of-war marked by frequent disagreement, occasional suspicion, but in the end, compromise. Eventually, the Fed—basically a creature borne of compromise—emerged with a structure designed to reconcile the needs, fears, and prejudices of many different interests.

This complicated structure, no doubt, can be confusing. But it ensures that the Fed's decisions are broadly based and properly insulated from narrow and partisan interests. In the end, this structure helps the Fed accomplish its overall mission: fostering a sound financial system and a healthy economy.

Chapter 4

Small Businesses And Corporations In The U.S. Economy

Americans have always believed they live in a land of opportunity, where anybody who has a good idea, determination, and a willingness to work hard can start a business and prosper. In practice, this belief in entrepreneurship has taken many forms, from the self-employed individual to the global conglomerate.

In the 17th and 18th centuries, the public extolled the pioneer who overcame great hardships to carve a home and a way of life out of the wilderness. In 19th-century America, as small agricultural enterprises rapidly spread across the vast expanse of the American frontier, the homesteading farmer embodied many of the ideals of the economic individualist. But as the nation's population grew and cities assumed increased economic importance, the dream of being in business for oneself evolved to include small merchants, independent craftsmen, and self-reliant professionals as well.

The 20th century, continuing a trend that began in the latter part of the 19th century, brought an enormous leap in the scale and complexity of economic activity. In many industries, small enterprises had trouble raising

About This Chapter: Excerpted from "An Outline of the U.S. Economy, Chapter 4: Small Business and the Corporation," by Christopher Conte and Albert R. Karr, U.S. Department of State, 2001. Despite the older date of this document, the information it provides still offers basic descriptions of small businesses and corporations.

sufficient funds and operating on a scale large enough to produce most efficiently all of the goods demanded by an increasingly sophisticated and affluent population. In this environment, the modern corporation, often employing hundreds or even thousands of workers, assumed increased importance.

Today, the American economy boasts a wide array of enterprises, ranging from one-person sole proprietorships to some of the world's largest corporations.

Small Business

Even today, the U.S. economy is by no means dominated by giant corporations. Fully 99 percent of all independent enterprises in the country employ fewer than 500 people. These small enterprises account for 52 percent of all U.S. workers, according to the U.S. Small Business Administration (SBA). Some 19.6 million Americans work for companies employing fewer than 20 workers, 18.4 million work for firms employing between 20 and 99 workers, and 14.6 million work for firms with 100 to 499 workers. By contrast, 47.7 million Americans work for firms with 500 or more employees.

✎ What's It Mean?

Free Enterprise System: An economic system characterized by private ownership of property and productive resources, the profit motive to stimulate production, competition to ensure efficiency, and the forces of supply and demand to direct the production and distribution of goods and services.

Market Economy: The national economy of a country that relies on market forces to determine levels of production, consumption, investment, and savings without government intervention.

Mixed Economy: An economic system in which both the government and private enterprise play important roles with regard to production, consumption, investment, and savings.

Source: U.S. Department of State, 2001.

Small businesses are a continuing source of dynamism for the American economy. They produced three-fourths of the economy's new jobs between 1990 and 1995, an even larger contribution to employment growth than they made in the 1980s. They also represent an entry point into the economy for new groups. Women, for instance, participate heavily in small businesses. Small firms also tend to hire a greater number of older workers and people who prefer to work part-time.

A particular strength of small businesses is their ability to respond quickly to changing economic conditions. They often know their customers personally and are especially suited to meet local needs. Small businesses—computer-related ventures in California's "Silicon Valley" and other high-tech enclaves, for instance—are a source of technical innovation. Many computer-industry innovators began as "tinkerers," working on hand-assembled machines in their garages, and quickly grew into large, powerful corporations. Small companies that rapidly became major players in the national and international economies include the computer software company Microsoft; the package delivery service Federal Express; sports clothing manufacturer Nike; the computer networking firm America OnLine; and ice cream maker Ben & Jerry's.

Small-Business Structures

The Sole Proprietor: Most businesses are sole proprietorships—that is, they are owned and operated by a single person. In a sole proprietorship, the owner is entirely responsible for the business's success or failure. He or she collects any profits, but if the venture loses money and the business cannot cover the loss, the owner is responsible for paying the bills—even if doing so depletes his or her personal assets.

Sole proprietorships have certain advantages over other forms of business organization. They suit the temperament of people who like to exercise initiative and be their own bosses. They are flexible, since owners can make decisions quickly without having to consult others. By law, individual proprietors pay fewer taxes than corporations. And customers often are attracted to sole proprietorships, believing an individual who is accountable will do a good job.

This form of business organization has some disadvantages, however. A sole proprietorship legally ends when an owner dies or becomes incapacitated, although someone may inherit the assets and continue to operate the business. Also, since sole proprietorships generally are dependent on the amount of money their owners can save or borrow, they usually lack the resources to develop into large-scale enterprises.

The Business Partnership: One way to start or expand a venture is to create a partnership with two or more co-owners. Partnerships enable entrepreneurs to pool their talents; one partner may be qualified in production, while another may excel at marketing, for instance. Partnerships are exempt from most reporting requirements the government imposes on corporations, and they are taxed favorably compared with corporations. Partners pay taxes on their personal share of earnings, but their businesses are not taxed.

States regulate the rights and duties of partnerships. Co-owners generally sign legal agreements specifying each partner's duties. Partnership agreements also may provide for "silent partners," who invest money in a business but do not take part in its management.

♣ It's A Fact!!

Many small businesses fail. But in the United States, a business failure does not carry the social stigma it does in some countries. Often, failure is seen as a valuable learning experience for the entrepreneur, who may succeed on a later try. Failures demonstrate how market forces work to foster greater efficiency, economists say.

Source: U.S. Department of State, 2001.

A major disadvantage of partnerships is that each member is liable for all of a partnership's debts, and the action of any partner legally binds all the others. If one partner squanders money from the business, for instance, the others must share in paying the debt. Another major disadvantage can arise if partners have serious and constant disagreements.

Franchising And Chain Stores: Successful small businesses sometimes grow through a practice known as franchising. In a typical franchising arrangement, a successful company authorizes an individual or small group of entrepreneurs to use its name and products in exchange for a percentage of the sales revenue. The founding company lends its marketing expertise and reputation, while the entrepreneur who is granted the franchise manages individual outlets and assumes most of the financial liabilities and risks associated with the expansion.

While it is somewhat more expensive to get into the franchise business than to start an enterprise from scratch, franchises are less costly to operate and less likely to fail. That is partly because franchises can take advantage of economies of scale in advertising, distribution, and worker training.

Corporations

Although there are many small and medium-sized companies, big business units play a dominant role in the American economy. There are several reasons for this. Large companies can supply goods and services to a greater number of people, and they frequently operate more efficiently than small ones. In addition, they often can sell their products at lower prices because of the large volume and small costs per unit sold. They have an advantage in the marketplace because many consumers are attracted to well-known brand names, which they believe guarantee a certain level of quality.

Large businesses are important to the overall economy because they tend to have more financial resources than small firms to conduct research and develop new goods. And they generally offer more varied job opportunities and greater job stability, higher wages, and better health and retirement benefits.

Nevertheless, Americans have viewed large companies with some ambivalence, recognizing their important contribution to economic well-being but worrying that they could become so powerful as to stifle new enterprises and deprive consumers of choice. What's more, large corporations at times have shown themselves to be inflexible in adapting to changing economic conditions. In the 1970s, for instance, U.S. auto-makers were slow to recognize that rising gasoline prices were creating a demand for smaller, fuel-efficient cars. As a result, they lost a sizable share of the domestic market to foreign manufacturers, mainly from Japan.

In the United States, most large businesses are organized as corporations. A corporation is a specific legal form of business organization, chartered by one of the 50 states and treated under the law like a person. Corporations may own property, sue or be sued in court, and make contracts. Because a corporation has legal standing itself, its owners are partially sheltered from responsibility for its actions. Owners of a corporation also have limited financial liability; they are not responsible for corporate debts, for instance. If

---

♣ It's A Fact!!

How Corporations Raise Capital

Large corporations could not have grown to their present size without being able to find innovative ways to raise capital to finance expansion. Corporations have five primary methods for obtaining that money.

Issuing Bonds: A bond is a written promise to pay back a specific amount of money at a certain date or dates in the future. In the interim, bondholders receive interest payments at fixed rates on specified dates. Holders can sell bonds to someone else before they are due.

Corporations benefit by issuing bonds because the interest rates they must pay investors are generally lower than rates for most other types of borrowing and because interest paid on bonds is considered to be a tax-deductible business expense. However, corporations must make interest payments even when they are not showing profits. If investors doubt a company's ability to meet its interest obligations, they either will refuse to buy its bonds or will demand a higher rate of interest to compensate them for their increased risk. For this reason, smaller corporations can seldom raise much capital by issuing bonds.

Issuing Preferred Stock: A company may choose to issue new "preferred" stock to raise capital. Buyers of these shares have special status in the event the underlying company encounters financial trouble. If profits are limited, preferred-stock owners will be paid their dividends after bondholders receive their guaranteed interest payments but before any common stock dividends are paid.

Selling Common Stock: If a company is in good financial health, it can raise capital by issuing common stock. Typically, investment banks help companies issue stock, agreeing to buy any new shares issued at a set price if the

a shareholder paid $100 for 10 shares of stock in a corporation and the corporation goes bankrupt, he or she can lose the $100 investment, but that is all. Because corporate stock is transferable, a corporation is not damaged by the death or disinterest of a particular owner. The owner can sell his or her shares at any time, or leave them to heirs.

The corporate form has some disadvantages, though. As distinct legal entities, corporations must pay taxes. The dividends they pay to shareholders,

public refuses to buy the stock at a certain minimum price. Although common shareholders have the exclusive right to elect a corporation's board of directors, they rank behind holders of bonds and preferred stock when it comes to sharing profits.

Investors are attracted to stocks in two ways. Some companies pay large dividends, offering investors a steady income. But others pay little or no dividends, hoping instead to attract shareholders by improving corporate profitability—and hence, the value of the shares themselves. In general, the value of shares increases as investors come to expect corporate earnings to rise. Companies whose stock prices rise substantially often "split" the shares, paying each holder, say, one additional share for each share held. This does not raise any capital for the corporation, but it makes it easier for stockholders to sell shares on the open market. In a two-for-one split, for instance, the stock's price is initially cut in half, attracting investors.

Borrowing: Companies can also raise short-term capital—usually to finance inventories—by getting loans from banks or other lenders.

Using Profits: As noted, companies also can finance their operations by retaining their earnings. Strategies concerning retained earnings vary. Some corporations, especially electric, gas, and other utilities, pay out most of their profits as dividends to their stockholders. Others distribute, say, 50 percent of earnings to shareholders in dividends, keeping the rest to pay for operations and expansion. Still other corporations, often the smaller ones, prefer to reinvest most or all of their net income in research and expansion, hoping to reward investors by rapidly increasing the value of their shares.

Source: U.S. Department of State, 2001.

unlike interest on bonds, are not tax-deductible business expenses. And when a corporation distributes these dividends, the stockholders are taxed on the dividends. (Since the corporation already has paid taxes on its earnings, critics say that taxing dividend payments to shareholders amounts to "double taxation" of corporate profits.)

Many large corporations have a great number of owners, or shareholders. A major company may be owned by a million or more people, many of whom hold fewer than 100 shares of stock each. This widespread ownership has given many Americans a direct stake in some of the nation's biggest companies.

But widely dispersed ownership also implies a separation of ownership and control. Because shareholders generally cannot know and manage the full details of a corporation's business, they elect a board of directors to make broad corporate policy. Typically, even members of a corporation's board of directors and managers own less than 5 percent of the common stock, though some may own far more than that. Individuals, banks, or retirement funds often own blocks of stock, but these holdings generally account for only a small fraction of the total. Usually, only a minority of board members are operating officers of the corporation. Some directors are nominated by the company to give prestige to the board, others to provide certain skills or to represent lending institutions. It is not unusual for one person to serve on several different corporate boards at the same time.

Corporate boards place day-to-day management decisions in the hands of a chief executive officer (CEO), who may also be a board's chairman or president. The CEO supervises other executives, including a number of vice presidents who oversee various corporate functions, as well as the chief financial officer, the chief operating officer, and the chief information officer (CIO). The CIO came onto the corporate scene as high technology became a crucial part of U.S. business affairs in the late 1990s.

As long as a CEO has the confidence of the board of directors, he or she generally is permitted a great deal of freedom in running a corporation. But sometimes, individual and institutional stockholders, acting in concert and backing dissident candidates for the board, can exert enough power to force a change in management.

Chapter 5

Strong Dollar, Weak Dollar: Foreign Exchange Rates And The U.S. Economy

Strong is good. Weak is bad. These generalizations sound simple enough, but they can be confusing when talking about money. Is a "strong" U.S. dollar always good? Is a "weak" dollar always bad? This chapter explores how the U.S. dollar and foreign currencies affect each other and how their interaction affects you and the economy.

Understanding Foreign Exchange

The terms strong and weak, rising and falling, strengthening and weakening are relative terms in the world of foreign exchange (sometimes referred to as "forex"). Rising and falling, strengthening and weakening all indicate a relative change in position from a previous level. When the dollar is strengthening, its value is rising in relation to one or more other currencies. A strong dollar will buy more units of a foreign currency than previously. One result of a stronger dollar is that the prices of foreign goods and services drop for U.S. consumers. This may allow Americans to take the

About This Chapter: "Strong Dollar, Weak Dollar: Foreign Exchange Rates and the U.S. Economy," reprinted with permission from the Federal Reserve Bank of Chicago, www.chicagofed.org. © 2008.

Strengthening Dollar

Advantages

- Consumer sees lower prices on foreign products/services.

- Lower prices on foreign products/services help keep inflation low.

- U.S. consumers benefit when they travel to foreign countries.

- U.S. investors can purchase foreign stocks/bonds at "lower" prices.

Disadvantages

- U.S. firms find it harder to compete in foreign markets.

- U.S. firms must compete with lower priced foreign goods.

- Foreign tourists find it more expensive to visit U.S.

- More difficult for foreign investors to provide capital to U.S. in times of heavy U.S. borrowing.

Weakening Dollar

Advantages

- U.S. firms find it easier to sell goods in foreign markets.

- U.S. firms find less competitive pressure to keep prices low.

- More foreign tourists can afford to visit the U.S.

- U.S. capital markets become more attractive to foreign investors.

Disadvantages

- Consumers face higher prices on foreign products/services.

- Higher prices on foreign products contribute to higher cost-of-living.

- U.S. consumers find traveling abroad more costly.

- Harder for U.S. firms and investors to expand into foreign markets.

long-postponed vacation to another country or buy a foreign car that used to be too expensive.

U.S. consumers benefit from a strong dollar, but U.S. exporters are hurt. A strong dollar means that it takes more of a foreign currency to buy U.S. dollars. U.S. goods and services become more expensive for foreign consumers who, as a result, tend to buy fewer U.S. products. Because it takes more of a foreign currency to purchase strong dollars, products priced in dollars are more expensive when sold overseas.

A weak dollar also hurts some people and benefits others. When the value of the dollar falls or weakens in relation to another currency, prices of goods and services from that country rise for U.S. consumers. It takes more dollars to purchase the same amount of foreign currency to buy goods and services. That means U.S. consumers and U.S. companies that import products have reduced purchasing power.

At the same time, a weak dollar means prices for U.S. products fall in foreign markets, benefiting U.S. exporters and foreign consumers. With a weak dollar, it takes fewer units of foreign currency to buy the right amount of dollars to purchase U.S. goods. As a result, consumers in other countries can buy U.S. products with less money.

Ideally, the dollar and all nations' currencies should be valued at a level that is neither too high nor too low. Such a level would help sustain long-term economic growth and stability both here and abroad. However, this ideal is difficult to reach since many factors affect the value of a nation's money. Some of the factors are complex, but many are quite simple.

The Value Of A Currency

The value of a currency can be viewed from a domestic as well as an international perspective. Domestically, we use measures such as the Consumer Price Index (CPI) to measure changes in the purchasing power of the dollar over time. When the CPI increases, we say that the dollar is buying less—the value or purchasing strength of the dollar is going down. If the CPI is relatively stable, we say that the value of the dollar is stable. For some products with falling prices, we can even say that the purchasing power of the dollar is increasing.

Even when the dollar may be stable domestically, the value of the dollar could rise or fall as measured by another country's currency. In those cases, a currency is a commodity. It is something that has a price and is bought and sold to be used. The medium of exchange used to purchase this commodity is the currency of another country. The dollar, in that perspective, is purchased by foreign citizens who will, in turn, use it to purchase U.S. goods and services or dollar-denominated assets such as Treasury securities, corporate or municipal bonds, or stock.

Almost every international exchange of goods and services requires the exchange of one currency for another. Less frequently, some countries will barter goods, or settle payments in gold. But most international transactions involve foreign exchange. The individual, firm or government of another country that wants to buy U.S. products needs dollars. This is because the dollar is legal tender in this country and transactions tend to be denominated in dollars.

♣ **It's A Fact!!**

An interesting aspect of foreign exchange is that a currency may be strengthening but still may not be strong relative to its historical position. For example, if the dollar were to rise from 85 yen to the dollar to 88 yen, it is strengthening. However, because the dollar historically is worth more than 100 yen, it is still not "strong." Likewise, a dollar that falls to 175 yen from 185 yen is weakening, but certainly not weak by historical comparison.

The dollar, of course, is not the only currency that is bought and sold, but it is among the most popular. Other important currencies include the euro, the Japanese yen, and the German deutschmark (sometimes referred to as the d-mark).

The Forex Market

In most cases, the buying and selling of currencies takes place in the forex market. The currencies of most advanced and many developing economies are traded in this market. The forex market does not involve sending large loads of currency from one country to another. Typically it involves electronic balances. Dollar-denominated balances in computers in the U.S. or other countries are traded for computer-housed balances around the world that are denominated in yen, euros, d-marks, or any of dozens of other commonly traded moneys. In short, when "currency" is traded, paper and metal are not the usual media of exchange. Foreign exchange exists mainly in the world of cyberspace.

Not all currencies are traded on forex markets. Currencies that are not traded are avoided for reasons ranging from political instability to economic uncertainty. Sometimes a country's currency is not exchanged for the simple reason that the country produces very few products of interest to other countries.

Unlike the commodities or stock markets, the forex market has no central trading floor where buyers and sellers meet. Most of the trades are completed by commercial banks and forex dealers in the U.S. and abroad using telephones and computers.

The forex market operates worldwide, 24 hours a day. Traders in Australia and the Far East begin trading in Hong Kong, Singapore, Tokyo, and Sydney at about the time most workers in San Francisco are going home for supper the previous evening. As the business day in the Far East closes, trading in Middle Eastern financial centers has been going on for a couple of hours, and the trading day in Europe is just beginning. By the time the New York business day gets going in full force, it is almost time for early afternoon tea in London. Some of the large U.S. banks and brokerage houses have an early shift to minimize the time difference of five to six hours with Europe. To complete the circle, West Coast financial institutions extend "normal banking hours" so they can trade with New York or Europe on one side, and with Hong Kong, Singapore, or Tokyo on the other.

In each case, financial institutions, corporations, or even interested individuals buy and sell money. They use one currency to purchase another. In many cases, they are buying money as part of doing business in the country that issues that currency. But in other cases, firms or individuals may buy one currency in one market to sell it in another and profit from the difference in

♣ It's A Fact!!
Two Is Better Than One

It is often possible to see two different national currencies accepted in one country. In some foreign countries, the U.S. dollar is the "currency of choice" because individuals have misgivings about the soundness of the domestic currency. In other cases, accepting two currencies depends on location. For example, in areas near the Canadian border, U.S. currency is sometimes fully acceptable in Canadian shops and Canadian currency is used (often at the official exchange rate) in U.S. establishments. But generally speaking, these areas tend to be small and in close proximity to the borders. Usually the decision to accept a foreign currency is made by local establishments as a convenience to border-crossing tourists.

price. This speculating on price differences is called arbitrage. In an age of virtually instant communication, this is especially challenging because the differences in price may last only a few seconds.

The forex market is distinguished here from the forex futures market, which has several trading floors, principally the International Monetary Market, a division of the Chicago Mercantile Exchange. The futures market in forex was developed to help reduce risk for international firms and financial institutions. The market was designed to "guarantee" exchange rates at a future date in order to facilitate international transactions. Prior to the development of forex futures, there could be a significant amount of risk in entering into a long-term contract with firms in other countries. One of the largest sources of risk was the inability to guarantee the relative value of the currencies involved at the date of delivery.

Price Determined By Supply And Demand

The forex market is essentially governed by the law of supply and demand and is generally not regulated by any government or coalition of governments.

This is true in the U.S., where participation in the forex market is not regulated. The prices set for each country's money is determined by the desire of those trading to acquire more of it or to hold less of it. Each individual acts on the belief that he or she will benefit from the transaction.

According to the law of supply, as prices rise for a given item (in this case money), the quantity of the item that is supplied will increase; conversely, as the price falls, the quantity provided will fall. The law of demand states that as the price for an item rises, the quantity demanded will fall. As the price for an item falls, the quantity demanded will rise. It is the interaction of these basic forces that results in the movement of currency prices in the forex market.

For example, if French investors saw an opportunity in the U.S., they might be willing to pay more francs in order to get dollars to invest in the U.S. If the dollar moved from five francs per dollar to six francs per dollar, the dollar "strengthened against the franc." In other words, a dollar could buy more francs. We could also state the same movement in francs. In the example above, the franc would move from 20¢ per franc to approximately 16¢ per franc. The franc "weakened against the dollar" because a franc could buy fewer dollars.

How do changes in a currency's value affect a country's domestic economy? To show the effects, we can look at the U.S. economy during the 1990s. The dollar was quite strong in relation to other currencies during most of that period. Dollars were in high demand for a number of reasons. Among these was the desire of foreign citizens to buy U.S. financial securities such as Treasury notes and bonds, corporate bonds, and other U.S. assets. Part of the reason for this was the general attractiveness of U.S. government securities; another was because U.S. financial markets were booming through much of the period.

Many sectors of the U.S. economy were borrowing heavily during this period. Government, corporations, and individuals were relying on credit. This created strong demand for money to lend to borrowers. Typically, money saved by consumers is used to help meet such demand. Unfortunately, savings rates in the U.S. were low. Consequently, the money for U.S. borrowing had to come from somewhere. Funds from abroad helped to meet the demand. This rise in demand increased the price of dollars relative to other currencies. This, in turn, made it more attractive for investors to hold dollars.

At the same time, the Federal Reserve kept inflation under control. This made the dollar attractive because of its stability. These trends combined to raise the cost of the dollar for foreign investors. The relatively high rates of return in U.S. financial markets enabled investors to earn better profits than could be found in their own financial markets. The increased demand for U.S. investments helped to make the dollar stronger. In addition to attractive rates, foreigners were

♣ It's A Fact!!

Factors Contributing To A Strong Currency

- Higher interest rates in home country than abroad
- Lower rates of inflation
- A domestic trade surplus relative to other countries
- A large, consistent government deficit crowding out domestic borrowing
- Political or military unrest in other countries
- A strong domestic financial market
- Strong domestic economy/weaker foreign economies
- No record of default on government debt
- Sound monetary policy aimed at price stability

Factors Contributing To A Weak Currency

- Lower interest rates in home country than abroad
- Higher rates of inflation
- A domestic trade deficit relative to other countries
- A consistent government surplus
- Relative political/military stability in other countries
- A collapsing domestic financial market
- Weak domestic economy/stronger foreign economies
- Frequent or recent default on government debt
- Monetary policy that frequently changes objectives

eager to invest in the United States because this country was, and still is, seen as a comparatively stable, safe haven where investments are secure.

Effects On An Economy

The decisions of citizens to invest in another country can have a significant effect on their domestic economy. In the case of the U.S., the desire of foreign investors to hold dollar-denominated assets helped finance the U.S. government's large budget deficit and supplied funds to private credit markets. According to the laws of supply and demand, an increased supply of funds—in this case funds provided by other countries—tends to lower the price of those funds. The price of funds is the interest rate. The increase in the supply of funds extended by foreign investors helped finance the budget deficit and helped keep interest rates below what they would have been without foreign capital.

The rising demand for dollar-denominated assets also had a negative effect on the U.S. economy. The stronger dollar increased the attractiveness of foreign goods in the U.S. Many price-conscious U.S. consumers responded by purchasing more imports and fewer domestic goods. This did help keep inflation under control. But at the same time, U.S. exports were more expensive to foreigners who tended to buy fewer U.S. goods. As a result, the trade deficit widened as U.S. exports decreased and U.S. imports increased.

When a currency becomes too strong or too weak, it tends to distort international competition. As we have seen, the strong dollar of the 1990s distorted the competitiveness of U.S. producers in relation to foreign producers. Even though foreign producers may not have used their resources as efficiently as their U.S. counterparts, they still might have been able to sell their products at lower prices than U.S. goods.

Many U.S. companies responded to this increased competition by streamlining their processes and increasing productivity. In the long run, increased productivity benefited these companies and the U.S. economy. However, some producers could not make sufficient adjustments and found that their products could not compete in either U.S. or international markets.

A Different Lesson From The '90s

The reason a currency weakens may not have much to do with problems in that country's economy. Sometimes, a currency weakens simply because of external factors. While most of the 1990s saw a strong U.S. dollar, the U.S. faced a different situation briefly during the middle of the decade.

During the autumn of 1995, the U.S. dollar began to weaken significantly against both the Japanese yen and the German d-mark. The U.S. economy was still recovering from the 1990–91 recession, although many were concerned about the weakness of the recovery. When the dollar began to fall, this increased investors' and consumers' concern about the strength of the recovery. There were even calls for the Treasury to direct the Federal Reserve to buy dollars and sell yen and d-marks in an attempt to strengthen the dollar.

However, the dollar was not falling because the U.S. economy was weak. Rather, the rising value of the other currencies reflected improving economic conditions within those countries. In Germany, the continued reunification of East and West, while presenting problems, was viewed as an opportunity to reach a large population that previously had not had access to Western goods and services. High interest rates in the reunified Germany were also an attraction to investors.

A different scenario was unfolding in Japan. Despite low interest rates, deflation was actually making "real" Japanese interest rates fairly attractive. Real interest rates are usually calculated by subtracting the rate of inflation from the interest rate quoted. Thus, a four percent interest rate in an economy with three percent inflation converts to a real rate of interest of only one percent (4 percent - 3 percent = 1 percent). Negative inflation (commonly called deflation) essentially adds that rate to the market interest rate. An interest rate of two percent in an economy with three percent deflation yields a real rate of interest of five percent.

Thus, the reason the dollar "weakened" during the fall of 1995 had less to do with weakness in the U.S. economy than with positive opportunities in the economies of Germany and Japan.

In reaction, many of those hurt by foreign imports called for government assistance to limit foreign competition. This assistance came in the form of tariffs, quotas, subsidies and embargoes. This sentiment of protectionism is potentially one of the most harmful outgrowths of changes in the relative strengths of currencies. If one government passes laws setting up protective barriers, other countries would likely retaliate with protective measures of their own. International trade would slow, and people in all nations would then lose the benefits of better quality, lower prices, and a broader selection of products.

Stable Dollar

A strong currency can have both a positive and a negative impact on a nation's economy. The same holds true for a weak currency. Currencies that are too strong or too weak not only affect individual economies, but tend to distort international trade and economic and political decisions worldwide. This is compounded by the fact that individual consumers can benefit from changes in the value of a currency, while producers in the same country are hurt. But the value of a currency alone does not dictate trade flows. Many other factors are involved, such as the quality of the product. Nevertheless, changes in currency values can have a dramatic effect. Ideally, currency values should be relatively stable and at a level that can sustain long-term economic growth both here and abroad.

Bretton Woods And Fixed Rates

If shifts in exchange rates can cause problems, why not fix rates between countries? Under a fixed-rate system, a dollar would always be worth the same amount of pounds, lira, yen or d-marks. This idea is not new. Through most of the modern era the world was on a fixed-rate system. The most recent version is referred to as the Bretton Woods System.

In 1944, the industrialized countries of the world met in Bretton Woods, New Hampshire, to discuss the state of the international economy in the post-WW II era. The heart of the discussion evolved around a plan to fix the rate of exchange for all foreign currencies to the U.S. dollar. The dollar would, in turn, be tied to gold for purposes of international settlement at a set price.

This meant that a pound, lira, yen, etc., would always yield a fixed number of dollars. And an ounce of gold would always cost a set number of dollars.

The hope was that the U.S. dollar would provide stability for international trade. This stability would, in turn, translate to a solid base upon which the war-torn economies of Europe and Asia could rebuild. One disadvantage of this system was that participating nations would need to take actions that would affect their domestic economy—such as increasing or decreasing the money supply—in order to maintain their exchange rate.

The Bretton Woods Agreement, as it came to be called, started to unravel in the early 1960s. The U.S. had enjoyed a period of prosperity for most of the period since the end of World War II. Because the U.S. dollar was not convertible to gold domestically, but was considered "as good as gold" internationally, the growing U.S. economy (and money supply) meant that excess dollars easily found their way overseas.

But, in order to maintain the value of their currencies relative to the dollar, other countries had to expand their money supplies just as quickly in order to maintain the agreed upon ratios of foreign currencies to dollars. This increase in foreign currencies introduced higher inflation to those nations. The U.S. was, in essence, exporting inflation.

By the late 1960s, the now resurgent countries of Europe and Asia recognized one of the sources of their inflation problems. They were reluctant to increase their domestic money supply to keep pace with the U.S., so they began to return excess dollars, demanding gold in payment at the agreed-upon rate of exchange. This led to an outflow of gold from the U.S. Eventually the U.S. holdings of gold became dangerously low. By 1971, President Nixon was forced to close the "gold window" by no longer exchanging dollars for gold at the agreed-upon rate. Since that time, exchange rates have been allowed to "float," with rates determined by the supply of and demand for currencies.

Chapter 6

What Determines Interest Rates?

Interest rates can significantly influence people's behavior. When rates decline, homeowners rush to buy new homes and refinance old mortgages; automobile buyers scramble to buy new cars; the stock market soars, and people tend to feel more optimistic about the future.

But even though individuals respond to changes in rates, they may not fully understand what interest rates represent, or how different rates relate to each other. Why, for example, do interest rates increase or decrease? And in a period of changing rates, why are certain rates higher, while others are lower?

To answer these questions, we must separate movements in the general level of interest rates from differences in individual rates. As we can see in Figure 6.1, rates rose steadily from 1979 to 1981 and generally fell after that, with a few upward turns to break the downward trend. Because interest rates tend to move together, we can characterize certain periods as times of high or low interest rates. For example, in 1981 the general level of interest rates was higher than the general level in 1993.

As we also can see in the figure, however, individual rates tend to differ, even though they are moving in the same general direction. Thus a 30-year

About This Chapter: "Points of Interest: What Determines Interest Rates?" reprinted with permission from the Federal Reserve Bank of Chicago, www.chicagofed.org. © 2008.

Treasury bond may have a higher rate than a three-month certificate of deposit. Similarly, a mortgage loan may have a lower rate than an automobile loan.

These similarities and differences are not determined by luck, coincidence, a world conspiracy of money barons, or even the Federal Reserve. Rather, they are determined by strong, impersonal economic forces in the marketplace, which reflect the personal choices of millions of individual borrowers and lenders.

This chapter is intended to help you better understand interest rates and how they are influenced by these economic forces. The first section, Levels Of Interest, examines the forces that determine the general level of rates. This section discusses basic factors of supply and demand for funds and the function of banks and other similar institutions in meeting the needs of savers and borrowers. It also examines other factors such as fiscal policy and the actions of the Federal Reserve System.

The second section, Different Interests, examines the variations among individual rates, explaining why a six-month Treasury bill may have one rate, business loans another, and home mortgages still a third. This section discusses the unique characteristics of each credit transaction, such as risk, rights, and tax considerations, and how these factors affect the decision-making process of borrowers and lenders.

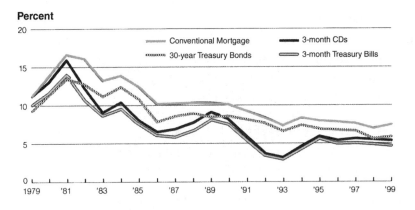

Figure 6.1. Interest Rate Trends

Levels Of Interest

The Price Of Credit

To understand the economic forces that drive (and sometimes are driven by) interest rates, we first need to define interest rates. An interest rate is a price, and like any other price, it relates to a transaction or the transfer of a good or service between a buyer and a seller. This special type of transaction is a loan or credit transaction, involving a supplier of surplus funds, that is, a lender or saver, and a demander of surplus funds, that is, a borrower.

In a loan transaction, the borrower receives funds to use for a period of time, and the lender receives the borrower's promise to pay at some time in the future.

The borrower receives the benefit of the immediate use of funds. The lender, on the other hand, gives up the immediate use of funds, forgoing any current goods or services those funds could purchase. In other words, lenders loan funds they have saved—surplus funds they do not need for purchasing goods or services today.

Because these lenders/savers sacrifice the immediate use of funds, they ask for compensation in addition to the repayment of the funds loaned. This compensation is interest, the price the borrower must pay for the immediate use of the lender's funds. Put more simply, interest rates are the price of credit.

> ✎ **What's It Mean?**
>
> Financial Opportunity Costs: Involve monetary values of decisions made. For example, the purchase of an item with money from your savings means you will no longer obtain interest on those funds.
>
> Time Value Of Money: Can be used to measure financial opportunity costs using interest calculations. For example: Spending $1,000 from a savings account paying 4 percent a year means an opportunity cost of $40 in lost interest. Calculation: $1,000 x .04 (4 percent) x 1 year = $40. Over 10 years, that $40 a year (saved at 4 percent) would have a value of over $80 when taking into account compound interest.
>
> Source: From *Practical Money Skills for Life*, a financial literacy program from Visa, http://www.practicalmoneyskills.com. © 2008 Visa. All rights reserved. Reprinted with permission.

Supply And Demand

As with any other price in our market economy, interest rates are determined by the forces of supply and demand, in this case, the supply of and demand for credit. If the supply of credit from lenders rises relative to the demand from borrowers, the price (interest rate) will tend to fall as lenders compete to find use for their funds. If the demand rises relative to the supply, the interest rate will tend to rise as borrowers compete for increasingly scarce funds. The principal source of the demand for credit comes from our desire for current spending and investment opportunities.

The principal source of the supply of credit comes from savings, or the willingness of people, firms, and governments to delay spending. Depository institutions such as banks, thrifts, and credit unions, as well as the Federal Reserve, play important roles in influencing the supply of credit.

The Source Of Demand

Consumption: At one time or another, virtually all consumers, businesses, and governments demand credit to purchase goods and services for current use. In these loans, borrowers agree to pay interest to a lender/saver because they prefer to have the goods or services now, rather than waiting until some time in the future when, presumably, they would have saved enough for the purchase. To describe this preference for current consumption, economists say that borrowers have a high rate of time preference. Expressed simply, people with high rates of time preference prefer to purchase goods now, rather than wait to purchase future goods—an automobile now rather than an automobile at some time in the future, a current vacation opportunity rather than a future opportunity, and present goods or services rather than those in the future.

Although lenders/savers generally have lower rates of time preference than borrowers, they too tend to prefer current goods and services. As a result, they ask for the payment of interest to encourage the sacrifice of immediate consumption. As a lender/saver, for example, one would prefer not to spend $100 now only if the money was not needed for a current purchase and one could receive more than $100 in the future.

Investment: In the use of funds for investment, on the other hand, time preference is not the sole factor. Here consumers, businesses, and governments borrow funds only if they have an opportunity they believe will earn more—that is, create a larger income stream—than they will have to pay on the loan, or than they will receive in some other activity.

♣ **It's A Fact!!**

What borrowers are willing to pay depends principally on time preferences for current consumption and on the expected rate of return on an investment.

Source: Federal Reserve Bank of Chicago, © 2008.

Say, for example, a widget manufacturer sees an opportunity to purchase a new machine that can reasonably be expected to earn a 20 percent return, that is, produce income from the manufacture of widgets equal to 20 percent of the cost of the machine. The manufacturer will borrow funds only if they can be obtained at an interest rate less than 20 percent.

The Source Of Supply

The supply of credit comes from savings—funds not needed or used for current consumption. When we think of savings, most of us think of money in savings accounts, but this is only part of total savings.

All funds not currently used to purchase goods and services are part of total savings. For example, insurance premiums, contributions to pension funds and social security, funds set aside to purchase stocks and bonds, and even funds in our checking accounts are savings.

Since most of us use funds in checking accounts to pay for current consumption, we may not consider them savings. However, funds in checking accounts at any time are considered savings until we transfer them out to pay for goods and services.

Most of us keep our savings in financial institutions like insurance companies and brokerage houses, and in depository institutions such as banks, savings and loan associations, credit unions, and mutual savings banks. These financial institutions then pool the savings and make them available to people who want to borrow.

This process is called financial intermediation. This process of bringing together borrowers and lenders/savers is one of the most important roles that financial institutions perform.

Bank's And Deposit Creation

Depository institutions, which for simplicity we will call banks, are different from other financial institutions because they offer transaction accounts and make loans by lending deposits. This deposit creation activity, essentially creating money, affects interest rates because these deposits are part of savings, the source of the supply of credit.

Banks create deposits by making loans. Rather than handing cash to borrowers, banks simply increase balances in borrowers' checking accounts. Borrowers can then draw checks to pay for goods and services. This creation of checking accounts through loans is just as much a deposit as one we might make by pushing a ten-dollar bill through the teller's window.

♣ It's A Fact!!
The Federal Reserve System has the responsibility of monitoring and influencing the total supply of money and credit.

Source: Federal Reserve Bank of Chicago, © 2008.

With all of the nation's banks able to increase the supply of credit in this fashion, credit could conceivably expand without limit. Preventing such uncontrolled expansion is one of the jobs of the Federal Reserve System (the Fed), our central bank and monetary authority.

The General Level Of Rates

The general level of interest rates is determined by the interaction of the supply and demand for credit. When supply and demand interact, they determine a price (the equilibrium price) that tends to be relatively stable. However, we have seen that the price of credit is not necessarily stable, implying that something shifts the supply, the demand, or both. Let's examine several factors that influence these shifts.

Expected Inflation: As we have already seen, interest rates state the rate at which borrowers must pay future dollars to receive current dollars. Borrowers and lenders, however, are not as concerned about dollars, present or future, as they are about the goods and services those dollars can buy, the purchasing power of money.

Inflation reduces the purchasing power of money. Each percentage point increase in inflation represents approximately a one percent decrease in the quantity of real goods and services that can be purchased with a given number of dollars in the future. As a result, lenders, seeking to protect their purchasing power, add the expected rate of inflation to the interest rate they demand. Borrowers are willing to pay this higher rate because they expect inflation to enable them to repay the loan with cheaper dollars.

If lenders expect, for example, an eight percent inflation rate for the coming year and otherwise desire a four percent return on their loan, they would likely charge borrowers 12 percent, the so-called nominal interest rate (an eight percent inflation premium plus a four percent "real" rate).

Borrowers and lenders tend to base their inflationary expectations on past experiences which they project into the future. When they have experienced inflation for a long time, they gradually build the inflation premium into their rates. Once people come to expect a certain level of inflation, they may have to experience a fairly long period at a different rate of inflation before they are willing to change the inflation premium.

The effect of an inflation premium can be seen in Figure 6.2. Although the figure tracks the consumer price index or CPI and the constant maturity three-year Treasury note rate, one could use almost any inflation measure and interest rate and see a similar pattern. As inflation rose through the late 1970s, it came to be "expected" by lenders as well as borrowers. This "inflation expectation" can be seen by the fact that investors in Treasury notes were demanding a relatively high inflation premium in the early 1980s, even after inflation reached its apex. This was partially due to the fact that relatively high levels of inflation were fresh in the memories of borrowers and lenders, and there was uncertainty as to how serious policymakers would be in pursuing lower levels of inflation. In 1984, for example, it took only a slight increase in inflation to cause a relatively rapid increase in interest rates.

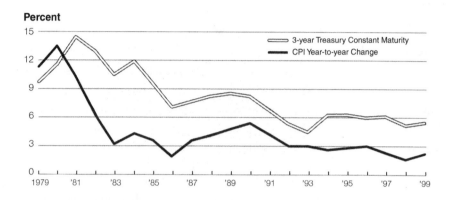

Figure 6.2. Effect Of Inflation Premium

For most of the 1980s, inflation was relatively low and interest rates continued their downward trend with the gap between rates and inflation narrowing. As the memory of high inflation receded, so did pressure for a high inflation premium, as indicated by the relatively modest rise in rates when inflation flared in 1990. Inflationary expectations had been reduced, a goal sought by many monetary policymakers. Indeed, former Fed Chairman Alan Greenspan has stated that price stability would be achieved when the expectation of future price changes plays no role in the decision-making of businesses and households.

Economic Conditions: All businesses, governmental bodies, and households that borrow funds affect the demand for credit. This demand tends to vary with general economic conditions.

When economic activity is expanding and the outlook appears favorable, consumers demand substantial amounts of credit to finance homes, automobiles, and other major items, as well as to increase current consumption. With this positive outlook, they expect higher incomes and as a result are generally more willing to take on future obligations. Businesses are also optimistic and seek funds to finance the additional production, plants, and equipment needed to supply this increased consumer demand. All of this makes for a relative scarcity of funds, due to increased demand.

On the other hand, when sales are sluggish and the future looks grim, consumers and businesses tend to reduce their major purchases, and lenders, concerned about the repayment ability of prospective borrowers, become reluctant to lend. As a result, both the supply of and demand for credit may fall. Unless they both fall by the same amount, interest rates are affected.

Federal Reserve Actions: As we have seen, the Fed acts to influence the availability of money and credit by adjusting the level and/or price of bank reserves. The Fed affects reserves in three ways: by setting reserve requirements that banks must hold, as we discussed earlier; by buying and selling government securities (usually U.S. Treasury bonds) in open market operations; and by setting the "discount rate," which affects the price of reserves banks borrow from the Fed through the "discount window."

These "tools" of monetary policy influence the supply of credit, but do not directly impact the demand for credit. Because the Fed directly affects only one side of the supply and demand relationship, it cannot totally control interest rates. Nevertheless, monetary policy clearly does affect the general level of interest rates.

Fiscal Policy: Federal, state and local governments, through their fiscal policy actions of taxation and spending, can affect either the supply of or the demand for credit. If a governmental unit spends less than it takes in from taxes and other sources of revenue, as many have in recent years, it runs a budget surplus, meaning the government has savings. As we have seen, savings are the source of the supply of credit. On the other hand, if a governmental unit spends more than it takes in, it runs a budget deficit, and must borrow to make up the difference. The borrowing increases the demand for credit, contributing to higher interest rates in general.

Interest Rate Predictions

The level of interest rates influences people's behavior by affecting economic decisions that determine the well-being of the nation: how much people are willing to save, and how much businesses are willing to invest.

With so many important decisions based on the level of interest rates, it is not surprising that people want to know which way rates are going to move. However, with so many diverse elements influencing rates, it is also not surprising that people are not able to predict the direction of these movements precisely.

Even though we are not able to predict accurately and consistently how interest rates will move, these movements are clearly not random. To the contrary, they are strictly controlled by the most calculating master of all— the economic forces of the market.

Different Interests

As we have seen, certain factors affect the general level of interest rates. But why do the rates vary for different transactions? For example, on a typical day at a local financial institution, a lending officer might approve a $20,000 loan to the local school board for emergency repairs on the school's furnace and charge the board eight percent interest for the use of the funds. Later, the banker might approve a used-car loan for $4,000, at 11 percent interest, to be paid in three years, and a small business loan for $17,000, at 8.5 percent interest, for a term of four years.

Meanwhile, the bank's investment officer submits a bid for a two-year Treasury note on which the bank wants to receive six percent interest, and purchases a 15-year general obligation municipal bond issued by the local city government. The bank will receive eight percent interest on this bond. At the next desk, the new accounts officer opens an interest-paying checking account, which will pay a customer 1.5 percent interest.

Credit Transactions

As different as all these transactions may at first appear, they are the same in one respect—they all involve borrowing and lending funds. Each transaction has a lender, who exchanges funds for an asset in the form of an IOU or credit, and a borrower who exchanges the IOU for funds. Because credit, the IOU, is being bought and sold, these are called credit transactions. Most of us can easily see that the loan officer is providing credit—the bank is lending money to the school board, the person buying the used car, and the business-person.

The other transactions are also credit transactions, although we generally think of them in different terms. We usually refer to the purchase of a Treasury note or a municipal bond as making an investment, but they are credit transactions because the bank is loaning money to the federal and city governments. By investing in the note and bond, the bank makes funds available directly to the government (or indirectly by replacing the previous holder of the government's debt). The bank, in return, receives interest payments from the government.

When the new accounts officer opened the checking account for the customer, the bank gained the use of funds. This, too, is a credit transaction in which the customer is the lender and the bank is the borrower. To compensate for the use of funds, the bank pays interest.

Degrees Of Interest

Although all the transactions at the bank that morning were credit transactions, they all involved different interest rates, different prices of credit. As with other prices in a free market system, interest rates are determined by many factors. As we've seen, some factors are more or less the same for all credit transactions. General economic conditions, for example, cause all interest rates to move in the same direction over time.

Other factors vary for different kinds of credit transactions, causing their interest rates to differ at any one time. Some of the most important of these factors are different levels and kinds of risk, different rights granted to borrowers and lenders, and different tax considerations.

Levels Of Risk

Risk refers to the chance that something unfavorable may happen. If you go skydiving, the risks you assume are obvious. When you purchase a financial asset, say by lending funds to a corporation by purchasing one of its bonds, you also take a risk—a financial risk. Something unfavorable could happen to your money—you could lose all of it if the company issuing the security goes bankrupt, or you could lose part of it if the asset's price goes down and you have to sell before maturity.

Different people are willing to accept different levels of risk. Some people will not go skydiving under any circumstances, while others will go at the drop of a hat. In credit transactions, too, people are willing to accept different levels of risk. However, most people risk averse; that is, they prefer to increase risks with their money unless they receive increased compensation.

To illustrate, let's say we have choice of buying two debt securities, which are bonds or IOUs issued by corporations or governments seeking to borrow funds. One security pays (meaning, we will receive) a certain five percent interest, while the other has a 50 percent chance of paying eight percent interest and a 50 percent chance of paying two percent. Which security should we buy? If we are risk averse investors/lenders, we would choose the security

♣ **It's A Fact!!**

Even though lenders are willing to accept different levels of risk, they want to be compensated for taking the risk. Therefore, as securities differ in level of risk, their interest rates tend to differ. Generally, interest rates on debt securities are affected by three kinds of risk:

- Default risk
- Liquidity risk
- Maturity risk

Source: Federal Reserve Bank of Chicago, © 2008.

paying the certain five percent, because would not view the uncertainty return on the second security as advantage.

If, on the other hand, the second security has a 50 percent chance paying 15 percent interest and 50 percent chance of paying two percent, we might be inclined to buy it because we might consider the higher potential return to be worth the risk.

Default Risk

For any number of reasons, even the most well-intentioned borrowers may not be able to make interest payments or repay borrowed funds on time. If borrowers do not make timely payments, they are said to have defaulted on loans. When borrowers do not make interest payments, lenders' returns (the interest they receive) are reduced or wiped out completely; when borrowers do not repay all or part of the principal, the lenders' return is actually negative.

All loans are subject to default risk since borrowers may die, go bankrupt, or be faced with unforeseen problems that prevent payments. Of course, default risk varies with different people and companies; nevertheless, no one is free from risk of default.

While investors/lenders accept this risk when they loan funds, they prefer to reduce the risk. As a result, many borrowers are compelled to secure their loans; meaning, they give the lender some assurances against default. Frequently, these assurances are in the form of collateral, some physical object the lender can possess and then sell in the event of default. For automobile loans, for example, the car usually serves as collateral. Other assurances could include a cosigner, another person willing to make payment if the original borrower defaults. Generally speaking, because secured loans are comparatively less risky, they carry a lower interest rate than unsecured loans.

As a borrower, the federal government offers firm assurances against default. As a result of the power to tax and authority to coin money, payments of principal and interest on loans made to (or securities purchased from) the U.S. government are, for all practical purposes, never in doubt, making U.S. government securities virtually default-risk free. Since investors tend to be

✎ **What's It Mean?**

Capacity: Capacity represents the future ability to service the loan, that is, make principal and interest payments. Income, job stability, regular promotions, and raises are all indicators to be considered.

Capital: Capital represents current financial condition. Is the borrower currently debt-free, or relatively so in comparison with assets? They may represent a party with "thrifty" habits, who can take on additional debt without imposing an undue burden on other assets.

Character: Character represents the borrower's history with previous loans. A history containing bankruptcies, repossessions, consistently late or missed payments, and court judgments may indicate a higher risk potential for the lender.

Source: Federal Reserve Bank of Chicago, © 2008.

risk averse and U.S. government securities are all but free from default risk, they generally carry a lower interest rate than securities from corporations.

Similarly, other types of borrowers represent different levels of risk to the lender. In each case, the lender needs to evaluate what are commonly called "the three Cs" of character, capital, and capacity.

Liquidity Risk

In addition to default risk, liquidity risk affects interest rates. If a security can be quickly sold at close to its original purchase price, it is highly liquid; meaning, it is less costly to convert into money than one that cannot be sold at a price close to its purchase price. Therefore, it is less risky than one with a wide spread between its purchase price and its selling price.

To illustrate, let's say that we have a choice between purchasing an infrequently traded security of an obscure company, and a broadly traded security of a well-known company, which we know we can sell easily at a price close to our purchase price. If we are risk averse, we would choose the security from the well-known company if both were paying the same interest rate.

To encourage us to buy its security, the obscure company must pay a higher rate to compensate us for the difficulty we will experience if we want to sell.

Maturity Risk

Credit transactions usually involve lending/borrowing funds for an agreed upon period of time. At the end of that time the loan is said to have matured and must be repaid. The length of maturity is a source of another kind of risk—maturity risk.

Long-term securities are subject to more risk than short-term securities because the future is uncertain and more problems can arise the longer the security is outstanding. These greater risks usually, but not always, result in higher rates for long-term securities than for short-term securities.

To illustrate, let's examine U.S. government securities—Treasury bills (with original maturities of one year or less), Treasury notes (with original maturities of two to ten years), and Treasury bonds (with original maturities of over ten years). These securities are quite similar, except in length of maturity. As we have seen, U.S. government securities are virtually default-risk free, and because there is such a large and active market for them, they are also virtually liquidity-risk free.

If default and liquidity were the only kinds of risk in holding government securities, we would be inclined to think that they all would have the same interest rate. However, because of maturity risk, short-term Treasury bills usually pay less (have a lower interest rate) than longer-term Treasury notes and bonds.

Different Rights

Risk is not the only reason credit transactions can have different rates of interest. As we have seen, certain assurances, such as securing loans, also affect rates. Typically, borrowers write these assurances into their debt securities specifying the rights of both borrower and lender. Because these rights differ, debt securities tend to pay different rates of interest. Let's look at some of these rights in the more common debt securities.

Coupon And Zero-Coupon Bonds: Most debt securities promise to re-pay the amount borrowed (the principal) at the end of the length of the loan, and also pay interest at specified times, such as every six months, throughout the term of the loan. Some of these bonds are issued with attached coupons, which lenders can clip and send every six months or year to collect the interest that is due.

Zero-coupon bonds, however, make no interest payments throughout the life of the loan. Rather than pay interest, these bonds are sold at a price well below their stated face value. Although not usually thought of in such terms, a savings bond is like a zero-coupon bond in that it renders one payment at maturity.

Even though zero-coupon bonds make no interest payments, investors/lenders still need to know the return on these bonds so they can compare it to the return on a coupon bond or other alternative investment. To figure the return, or yield, investors compare the difference between their purchase price and selling price.

Since zero-coupon bonds provide lenders no compensation until the end of the loan period, borrowers issuing these bonds tend to pay a higher rate than borrowers issuing coupon bonds.

Call Provisions: Some bonds are callable after a specified date; that is, the borrower has the right to pay off part or all of it before the scheduled maturity

♣ It's A Fact!!

Convertible Bonds: Some borrowers sell bonds that can be con-verted into a fixed number of shares of common stock. With convertible bonds, a lender (bondholder) can become a part owner (stockholder) of the company by converting the bond into the company's stock. Because investors generally view this right as desirable, borrowers can sell convertible bonds at a lower interest rate than they would otherwise have to pay for a similar bond that was not convertible.

Source: Federal Reserve Bank of Chicago, © 2008.

date. Unlike convertible bonds which give certain rights to the lenders, call provisions give borrowers certain rights, the right to call the bond. As a result, borrowers must pay a higher interest rate than on similar securities without a call provision.

Of course, borrowers will call (redeem) only when it is to their benefit. For example, when the general level of interest rates falls, the borrower can call the bonds paying high rates of interest and reborrow funds at the lower rate.

As partial compensation to the lender, the borrower often has to pay a penalty to call a bond. Naturally, a borrower will call a bond only if the advantages of doing so outweigh the penalty. In other words, interest rates would have to fall sufficiently to compensate for the penalty before a borrower would call a bond.

Municipal Bonds: Municipal bonds are debt securities issued by local and state governments. Usually these governmental bodies issue either general obligation bonds or revenue bonds.

General obligation bonds, the more common type, are issued for a wide variety of reasons, such as building schools and providing social services. They are secured by the general taxing power of the issuing government.

Revenue bonds, on the other hand, are issued to finance a specific project—building a tollway, for example. The interest and principal are paid exclusively out of the receipts that the project generates.

Both kinds of municipal bonds are considered safe. However, because general obligation bonds are secured by the assets of the issuing government and the power of that government to tax, they are usually considered safer than revenue bonds, whose payments must come out of receipts of the specific project for which the bond is issued. As a result, general obligation bonds usually pay a lower rate of interest than revenue bonds.

Efficient Allocation

With so many different interest rates and so many different factors affecting them, it may seem that borrowing and lending would be hopelessly

complicated and ineffi-
cient. In reality, however,
the variety of interest
rates reflects the effi-
ciency of the market in
allocating funds.

In analyzing invest-
ment opportunities, lend-
ers look for an interest
rate high enough to ac-
count for all their risks,
rights, and taxes, as we
have discussed. If the
project will not pay that
rate, they will look for
other investments. For
their part, borrowers will
undertake only projects
with returns high enough
to cover at least the cost
of borrowed funds.

The market, then,
serves to assure that only
worthwhile projects will
be funded with borrowed
funds. In other words,
market forces and differ-
ences in interest rates
work together to foster
the efficient allocation of
funds.

♣ It's A Fact!!
Tax Considerations

In addition to the level and kinds of risk and
the different rights granted by different debt securities, taxes also play a significant role in affecting rates of return.

To illustrate, let's say you borrow $1,000 for a
year at 10 percent interest. At the end of the year,
you pay the $1,000 principal plus $100 interest.
However, if the lender is in a 25 percent tax
bracket, the lender will pay $25 in taxes on that
$100. Thus, the lender's actual after-tax yield is
reduced from 10 percent to 7.5 percent.

Different debt securities carry different tax
considerations. Corporate bonds (loans to corporations) are subject to local, state, and federal taxes.
U.S. government securities are subject to federal
taxes, but exempt from local and state taxes. Municipal bonds are exempt from federal taxes, and
in some states, exempt from local taxes.

Taking taxes into consideration, a lender will
receive more after-tax interest income from a
municipal bond paying 10 percent than from a
corporate bond paying the same rate. This special tax-exempt status of municipal bonds enables
state and local governments to raise funds at a
relatively lower interest cost.

On the other hand, for corporations to attract
lenders, they must pay a higher rate of interest to
compensate for taxes.

Source: Federal Reserve Bank of Chicago,
© 2008.

Chapter 7
Inflation And
The Consumer Price Index

What Is Inflation?

Inflation means that the general level of prices of goods and services is increasing. When inflation is rapid, the prices of goods and services can increase faster than consumers' income, and that means the amount of goods and services consumers are able to purchase goes down. In other words, the purchasing power of money has declined. With inflation, a dollar buys less and less over time.

The Federal Open Market Committee (FOMC) tries to keep inflation low and stable in the long run because that helps the economy to keep growing over long periods of time. When inflation is low and stable, businesses and households can make better spending and investment plans because they do not have to worry about high inflation decreasing the purchasing power of their money.

About This Chapter: "What Is Inflation?" is excerpted from the Federal Reserve Kids Page (www.federalreserve.gov/kids), Federal Reserve Board of Governors, May 2007; "The Consumer Price Index" is excerpted from "Frequently Asked Questions," Bureau of Labor Statistics, August 2008.

✎ What's It Mean?

Inflation is defined as a sustained increase in the general level of prices for goods and services. It is measured as an annual percentage increase. As inflation rises, every dollar you own buys a smaller percentage of a good or service.

The value of a dollar does not stay constant when there is inflation. The value of a dollar is observed in terms of purchasing power, which is the real, tangible goods that money can buy. When inflation goes up, there is a decline in the purchasing power of money. For example, if the inflation rate is 2% annually, then theoretically a $1 pack of gum will cost $1.02 in a year. After inflation, your dollar can't buy the same goods it could beforehand.

There are several variations on inflation:

<u>Deflation:</u> Deflation is when the general level of prices is falling. This is the opposite of inflation.

<u>Hyperinflation:</u> Hyperinflation is unusually rapid inflation. In extreme cases, this can lead to the breakdown of a nation's monetary system. One of the most notable examples of hyperinflation occurred in Germany in 1923, when prices rose 2,500% in one month!

<u>Stagflation:</u> Stagflation is the combination of high unemployment and economic stagnation with inflation. This happened in industrialized countries during the 1970s, when a bad economy was combined with Organization of the Petroleum Exporting Countries (OPEC) raising oil prices.

In recent years, most developed countries have attempted to sustain an inflation rate of 2–3%.

Source: Excerpted from "Inflation: What Is Inflation?" and reprinted with permission from Investopedia ULC. © 2008 Investopedia.com.

The Consumer Price Index

What is the CPI?

The Consumer Price Index (CPI) is a measure of the average change over time in the prices paid by urban consumers for a market basket of consumer goods and services.

Whose buying habits does the CPI reflect?

The CPI reflects spending patterns for each of two population groups: all urban consumers and urban wage earners and clerical workers. The all urban consumer group represents about 87 percent of the total U.S. population. It is based on the expenditures of almost all residents of urban or metropolitan areas, including professionals, the self-employed, the poor, the unemployed, and retired people, as well as urban wage earners and clerical workers. Not included in the CPI are the spending patterns of people living in rural nonmetropolitan areas, farm families, people in the Armed Forces, and those in institutions, such as prisons and mental hospitals.

Is the CPI a cost-of-living index?

The CPI frequently is called a cost-of-living index, but it differs in important ways from a complete cost-of-living measure. The Bureau of Labor Statistics (BLS) has for some time used a cost-of-living framework in making practical decisions about questions that arise in constructing the CPI. A cost-of-living index is a conceptual measurement goal, however, and not a straightforward alternative to the CPI. A cost-of-living index would measure changes over time in the amount that consumers need to spend to reach a certain utility level or standard of living. Both the CPI and a cost-of-living index would reflect changes in the prices of goods and services, such as food and clothing, that are directly purchased in the marketplace; but a complete cost-of-living index would go beyond this role to also take into account changes in other governmental or environmental factors that affect consumers' well-being. It is very difficult to determine the proper treatment of public goods, such as safety and education, and other broad concerns, such as health, water quality, and crime, that would constitute a complete cost-of-living framework.

What goods and services does the CPI cover?

The CPI represents all goods and services purchased for consumption by the reference population. BLS has classified all expenditure items into more than 200 categories, arranged into eight major groups. Major groups and examples of categories in each are as follows:

- Food and beverages (breakfast cereal, milk, coffee, chicken, wine, full service meals, snacks)

- Housing (rent of primary residence, owners' equivalent rent, fuel oil, bedroom furniture)

- Apparel (men's shirts and sweaters, women's dresses, jewelry)

- Transportation (new vehicles, airline fares, gasoline, motor vehicle insurance)

- Medical care (prescription drugs and medical supplies, physicians' services, eyeglasses and eye care, hospital services)

- Recreation (televisions, toys, pets and pet products, sports equipment, admissions)

- Education and communication (college tuition, postage, telephone services, computer software and accessories)

- Other goods and services (tobacco and smoking products, haircuts and other personal services, funeral expenses)

♣ **It's A Fact!!**

It is important to understand that the Bureau of Labor Statistics bases the consumer price index (CPI) market baskets and pricing procedures on the experience of the relevant average household, not of any specific family or individual. It is unlikely that your experience will correspond precisely with either the national indexes or the indexes for specific cities or regions.

Source: Bureau of Labor Statistics, August 2008.

Also included within these major groups are various government-charged user fees, such as water and sewerage charges, auto registration fees, and vehicle tolls. In addition, the CPI includes taxes (such as sales and excise taxes) that are directly associated with the prices of specific goods and services. However, the CPI excludes taxes (such as income and Social Security taxes) not directly associated with the purchase of consumer goods and services.

The CPI does not include investment items, such as stocks, bonds, real estate, and life insurance. (These items relate to savings and not to day-to-day consumption expenses.)

For each of the more than 200 item categories, using scientific statistical procedures, the Bureau has chosen samples of several hundred specific items within selected business establishments frequented by consumers to represent the thousands of varieties available in the marketplace. For example, in a given supermarket, the Bureau may choose a plastic bag of golden delicious apples, U.S. extra fancy grade, weighing 4.4 pounds to represent the Apples category.

How are CPI prices collected and reviewed?

Each month, BLS data collectors called economic assistants visit or call thousands of retail stores, service establishments, rental units, and doctors' offices, all over the United States, to obtain information on the prices of the thousands of items used to track and measure price changes in the CPI. These economic assistants record the prices of about 80,000 items each month, representing a scientifically selected sample of the prices paid by consumers for goods and services purchased.

During each call or visit, the economic assistant collects price data on a specific good or service that was precisely defined during an earlier visit. If the selected item is available, the economic assistant records its price. If the selected item is no longer available, or if there have been changes in the quality or quantity (for example, eggs sold in packages of ten when they previously were sold by the dozen) of the good or service since the last time prices were collected, the economic assistant selects a new item or records the quality change in the current item.

The recorded information is sent to the national office of BLS, where commodity specialists who have detailed knowledge about the particular goods or services priced review the data. These specialists check the data for accuracy and consistency and make any necessary corrections or adjustments, which can range from an adjustment for a change in the size or quantity of a packaged item to more complex adjustments based upon statistical analysis of the value of an item's features or quality. Thus, commodity specialists strive to prevent changes in the quality of items from affecting the CPI's measurement of price change.

❖ It's A Fact!!

Causes Of Inflation

Economists wake up in the morning hoping for a chance to debate the causes of inflation. There is no one cause that's universally agreed upon, but at least two theories are generally accepted:

Demand-Pull Inflation: This theory can be summarized as "too much money chasing too few goods." In other words, if demand is growing faster than supply, prices will increase. This usually occurs in growing economies.

Cost-Push Inflation: When companies' costs go up, they need to increase prices to maintain their profit margins. Increased costs can include things such as wages, taxes, or increased costs of imports.

Costs Of Inflation

Almost everyone thinks inflation is evil, but it isn't necessarily so. Inflation affects different people in different ways. It also depends on whether inflation is anticipated or unanticipated. If the inflation rate corresponds to what the majority of people are expecting (anticipated inflation), then we can compensate and the cost isn't high. For example, banks can vary their interest rates and workers can negotiate contracts that include automatic wage hikes as the price level goes up.

Problems arise when there is unanticipated inflation:

Is the CPI the best measure of inflation?

Inflation has been defined as a process of continuously rising prices or equivalently, of a continuously falling value of money.

Various indexes have been devised to measure different aspects of inflation. The CPI measures inflation as experienced by consumers in their day-to-day

- Creditors lose and debtors gain if the lender does not anticipate inflation correctly. For those who borrow, this is similar to getting an interest-free loan.

- Uncertainty about what will happen next makes corporations and consumers less likely to spend. This hurts economic output in the long run.

- People living off a fixed-income, such as retirees, see a decline in their purchasing power and, consequently, their standard of living.

- The entire economy must absorb repricing costs ("menu costs") as price lists, labels, menus and more have to be updated.

- If the inflation rate is greater than that of other countries, domestic products become less competitive.

People like to complain about prices going up, but they often ignore the fact that wages should be rising as well. The question shouldn't be whether inflation is rising, but whether it's rising at a quicker pace than your wages.

Finally, inflation is a sign that an economy is growing. In some situations, little inflation (or even deflation) can be just as bad as high inflation. The lack of inflation may be an indication that the economy is weakening. As you can see, it's not so easy to label inflation as either good or bad—it depends on the overall economy as well as your personal situation.

Source: Excerpted from "Inflation: What Is Inflation?" and reprinted with permission from Investopedia ULC. © 2008 Investopedia.com.

living expenses; the Producer Price Index (PPI) measures inflation at earlier stages of the production process; the Employment Cost Index (ECI) measures it in the labor market; the BLS International Price Program measures it for imports and exports; and the Gross Domestic Product Deflator (GDP Deflator) measures inflation experienced by both consumers themselves as well as governments and other institutions providing goods and services to consumers. Finally, there are specialized measures, such as measures of interest rates.

The "best" measure of inflation for a given application depends on the intended use of the data. The CPI is generally the best measure for adjusting payments to consumers when the intent is to allow consumers to purchase at today's prices, a market basket of goods and services equivalent to one that they could purchase in an earlier period.

Part Two
Keys To Wealth Development

Chapter 8

Develop A Financial Plan

Define Your Goals

To end up where you want to be, you'll need a roadmap, a financial plan. To get started on your plan, you'll need to ask yourself what are the things you want to save and invest for. Here are some possibilities:

- A home
- A car
- An education
- A comfortable retirement

- Your children
- Medical or other emergencies
- Periods of unemployment
- Caring for parents

Make your own list and then think about which goals are the most important to you. List your most important goals first.

Decide how many years you have to meet each specific goal, because when you save or invest you'll need to find a savings or investment option that fits your time frame for meeting each goal.

About This Chapter: This chapter includes "Define Your Goals," U.S. Securities and Exchange Commission (SEC), April 3, 2006; "Goal Setting," reprinted with permission from the Young Americans Center for Financial Education (www.yacenter.org), and "Make a Financial Plan," SEC, October 8, 2004.

♣ It's A Fact!!
It's Not Too Early To Learn About Retirement Plans

Retirement Plans: What They Are And How They Work

- Plans that help individuals set aside money to be used after they retire.
- Federal income tax not immediately due on money put into a retirement account, or on the interest it makes.
- Income tax paid when money is withdrawn.
- Penalty charges apply if money is withdrawn before retirement age, except under certain circumstances.
- Income after retirement is usually lower, so tax rate is lower.

Types

- **Individual Retirement Account (IRA):** Allows a person to contribute up to $3,000 of pre-tax earnings per year. Contributions can be made in installments or in a lump sum.
- **Roth IRA (also called the IRA Plus):** While the $3,000 annual contribution to this plan is not tax-deductible, the earnings on the account are tax-free after five years. The funds from the Roth IRA may be withdrawn after age 59, if the account owner is disabled, for educational expenses, or for the purchase of a first home.
- **401(k):** Allows a person to contribute to a savings plan from his or her pre-tax earnings, reducing the amount of tax that must be paid. Employer matches contributions up to a certain level.
- **Keogh Plan:** Allows a self-employed person to set aside up to 15% of income (but not more than $35,000 per year).

IRAs—An Example Of Return On Investment

Contributions made only between ages of 22–30 (9 years):

- $2,000 contributed each year
- Total investment of $18,000
- At an interest rate of 9%, by age 65 will have $579,471

Contributions made only between ages of 31–65 (35 years):

- $2,000 contributed each year
- Total investment of $70,000
- At an interest rate of 9%, by age 65 will have $470,249

Many tools exist to help you decide how much you'll need to save for various needs. For example, the Ballpark Estimate (available online at http://www.choosetosave.org/ballpark), a single-page worksheet created by the American Savings Education Council, can help you calculate what you'll need to save each year for retirement. The Financial Industry Regulatory Authority has a college savings calculator (available online at http://apps.finra.org/investor_Information/Calculators/1/collegecalc.aspx), and the Social Security Administration has a benefits calculator (available online at http://www.ssa.gov/planners/calculators.htm) to estimate your potential benefit amounts.

> ✔ **Quick Tip**
>
> People who write down their goals are much more likely to achieve them than people who don't write them down.
>
> Source: Young Americans Center for Financial Education (www.yacenter.org).

To save more, you'll need to figure out your current finances and where you can achieve real savings.

Goal Setting

Goals are the foundation for plans of action. They often are personal, but can be professional as well. It is good to set both long-term and short-term goals. A long-term goal might be saving money to go to college.

Setting and achieving goals can be easy if you set SMART goals.

SMART goals have five characteristics:

- Goals must be **Specific**: Example—Get out of debt is too broad, while pay off your credit card is specific.

- Goals must be **Measurable**: Example—Paying an extra $20 a month towards your credit card is measurable—you can see each month that you are working towards your goal.

- Goals must be **Attainable**: Example—If you pay an extra $20 a month, can you reach your goal?

- Goals must be **Realistic:** Example—Is it possible to pay off your credit card?
- Goals must be **Time bound:** Example—Paying off your credit card has no time frame, but paying off your credit card in the next 18 months has a deadline.

Our priorities influence our goals, what we do with our time, and even how we spend our money. We have many goals and a limited amount of time in which to accomplish them. Therefore, it is important that we develop a plan to help us achieve our goals.

Financial planning is an ongoing process that changes over time, especially when major changes happen in one's life, such as going to college or buying a home.

Make A Financial Plan

Figuring Out Your Finances

Sit down and take an honest look at your entire financial situation. You can never take a journey without knowing where you're starting from, and a journey to financial security is no different.

You'll need to figure out on paper your current situation—what you own and what you owe. You'll be creating a "net worth statement." On one side of the page, list what you own. These are your "assets." And on the other side list what you owe other people, your "liabilities" or debts.

Your Net Worth Statement

Assets

- Cash
- Checking account
- Savings
- Cash value of life insurance
- Investments
- Personal property
- Other

Liabilities

- Credit cards
- Bank loans
- Car loans
- Personal Loans

Subtract your liabilities from your assets. If your assets are larger than your liabilities, you have a "positive" net worth. If your liabilities are greater than your assets, you have a "negative" net worth. You'll want to update your "net worth statement" every year to keep track of how you are doing. Don't be discouraged if you have a negative net worth. If you follow a plan to get into a positive position, you're doing the right thing.

Know Your Income And Expenses

The next step is to keep track of your income and your expenses for every month. Write down what you and others in your family earn, and then your monthly expenses. Include a category for savings and investing. What are you paying yourself every month? Many people get into the habit of saving and investing by following this advice: always pay yourself or your family first. Many people find it easier to pay themselves first if they allow their bank to automatically remove money from their paycheck and deposit it into a savings or investment account. Likely even better, for tax purposes, is to participate in an employer sponsored retirement plan such as a 401(k), 403(b), or 457(b). These plans will typically not only automatically deduct money from your paycheck, but will immediately reduce the taxes you are paying. Additionally, in many plans the employer matches some or all of your contribution. When your employer does that, it's offering "free money." Any time you have automatic deductions made from your paycheck or bank account, you'll increase the chances of being able to stick to your plan and to realize your goals.

✔ Quick Tip
But I Spend Everything I Make

If you are spending all your income, and never have money to save or invest, you'll need to look for ways to cut back on your expenses. When you watch where you spend your money, you will be surprised how small everyday expenses that you can do without add up over a year.

Source: SEC, October 8, 2004.

Small Savings Add Up To Big Money

How much does a cup of coffee cost you? Would you believe $465.84? Or more?

If you buy a cup of coffee every day for $1.00 (an awfully good price for a decent cup of coffee, nowadays), that adds up to $365.00 a year. If you saved that $365.00 for just one year, and put it into a savings account or investment that earns 5% a year, it would grow to $465.84 by the end of five years, and by the end of 30 years, to $1,577.50.

That's the power of compounding. With compound interest, you earn interest on the money you save and on the interest that money earns. Over time, even a small amount saved can add up to big money.

If you are willing to watch what you spend and look for little ways to save on a regular schedule, you can make money grow. You just did it with one cup of coffee.

If a small cup of coffee can make such a huge difference, start looking at how you could make your money grow if you decided to spend less on other things and save those extra dollars.

If you buy on impulse, make a rule that you'll always wait 24 hours to buy anything. You may lose your desire to buy it after a day. And try emptying your pockets and wallet of spare change at the end of each day. You'll be surprised how quickly those nickels and dimes add up!

Pay Off Credit Card Or Other High Interest Debt

Speaking of things adding up, there is no investment strategy anywhere that pays off as well as, or with less risk than, merely paying off all high interest debt you may have. Many people have wallets filled with credit cards, some of which they've "maxed out" (meaning they've spent up to their credit limit). Credit cards can make it seem easy to buy expensive things when you don't have the cash in your pocket—or in the bank. But credit cards aren't free money.

Most credit cards charge high interest rates—as much as 18 percent or more—if you don't pay off your balance in full each month. If you owe money on your credit cards, the wisest thing you can do is pay off the balance in full as quickly as possible. Virtually no investment will give you the high returns you'll need to keep pace with an 18 percent interest charge. That's why you're better off eliminating all credit card debt before investing savings. Once you've paid off your credit cards, you can budget your money and begin to save and invest. Here are some tips for avoiding credit card debt:

- **Put Away The Plastic:** Don't use a credit card unless your debt is at a manageable level and you know you'll have the money to pay the bill when it arrives.

- **Know What You Owe:** It's easy to forget how much you've charged on your credit card. Every time you use a credit card, write down how much you have spent and figure out how much you'll have to pay that month. If you know you won't be able to pay your balance in full, try to figure out how much you can pay each month and how long it'll take to pay the balance in full.

- **Pay Off The Card With The Highest Rate:** If you've got unpaid balances on several credit cards, you should first pay down the card that charges the highest rate. Pay as much as you can toward that debt each month until your balance is once again zero, while still paying the minimum on your other cards.

The same advice goes for any other high interest debt (about 8% or above) which does not offer the tax advantages of, for example, a mortgage.

Once you have paid off those credit cards and begun to set aside some money to save and invest, you're in the savings habit!

Chapter 9

Investment Choices And Risk Tolerance

Determine Your Risk Tolerance

Savings

Your "savings" are usually put into the safest places or products that allow you access to your money at any time. Examples include savings accounts, checking accounts, and certificates of deposit. At some banks and savings and loan associations your deposits may be insured by the Federal Deposit Insurance Corporation (FDIC). But there's a tradeoff for security and ready availability. Your money is paid a low wage as it works for you.

Most smart investors put enough money in a savings product to cover an emergency, like sudden unemployment. Some make sure they have up to six months of their income in savings so that they know it will absolutely be there for them when they need it.

But how "safe" is a savings account if you leave all your money there for a long time, and the interest it earns doesn't keep up with inflation? Let's say you save a dollar when it can buy a loaf of bread. But years later when you withdraw that dollar plus the interest you earned, it might only be able to

About This Chapter: This chapter includes "Determine Your Risk Tolerance," and "Investment Products: Your Choices," U.S. Securities and Exchange Commission (SEC), October 2004.

♣ It's A Fact!!
Comparing Savings And Investment Plans

Instrument	Maturity	Risk	Yield	Minimum Balance	Taxable?
Savings Account	Immediate	None if insured	Low	$5	Yes
Certificate of Deposit	90 days or more	None if insured	Moderate	Varies	Yes
Bonds					
Corporate	5–30 years	Some	Moderate	$1,000	Yes
Municipal	1–20 years	Some	Moderate	$5,000	No federal, some states
Stocks	Immediate	Low to high	Low to high	Varies	Yes
U.S. Treasury					
Bills	1 year or less	None	Moderate	$1,000	Federal only
Notes	1–10 years	None		$1,000	Federal only
Bonds	10–30 years	None		$1,000	Federal only
Mutual Funds	Varies	Low to high	Moderate	Varies	Usually
Retirement Funds	When buyer is 60 years old	Low	Moderate	Varies	At maturity

Source: From *Practical Money Skills for Life*, a financial literacy program from Visa, http://www.practicalmoneyskills.com. © 2008 Visa. All rights reserved. Reprinted with permission.

buy half a loaf. That is why many people put some of their money in savings, but look to investing so they can earn more over long periods of time, say three years or longer.

Investing

When you invest, you have a greater chance of losing your money than when you save. Unlike FDIC-insured deposits, the money you invest in securities, mutual funds, and other similar investments are not federally insured. You could lose your principal, which is the amount you've invested. That's true even if you purchase your investments through a bank. But when you invest, you also have the opportunity to earn more money than when you save.

But what about risk? All investments involve taking on risk. It's important that you go into any investment in stocks, bonds, or mutual funds with a full understanding that you could lose some or all of your money in any one investment. While over the long term the stock market has historically provided around 10% annual returns (closer to 6% or 7% "real" returns when you subtract for the effects of inflation), the long term does sometimes take a rather long, long time to play out. Those who invested all of their money in the stock market at its peak in 1929 (before the stock market crash) would wait over 20 years to see the stock market return to the same level. However, those that kept adding money to the market throughout that time would have done very well for themselves, as the lower cost of stocks in the 1930s made for some hefty gains for those who bought and held over the course of the next twenty years or more.

Diversification

It is true that the greater the risk, the greater the potential rewards in investing, but taking on unnecessary risk is often avoidable. Investors best protect themselves against risk by spreading their money among various investments, hoping that if one investment loses money, the other investments will more than make up for those losses. This strategy, called diversification, can be neatly summed up as, "Don't put all your eggs in one basket." Investors also protect themselves from the risk of investing all their money at the wrong time (think 1929) by following a consistent pattern of adding new money to their investments over long periods of time.

Once you've saved money for investing, consider carefully all your options and think about what diversification strategy makes sense for you. While the U.S. Securities and Exchange Commission (SEC) cannot recommend any particular investment product, you should know that a vast array of investment products exists—including stocks and stock mutual funds, corporate and municipal bonds, bond mutual funds, certificates of deposit, money market funds, and U.S. Treasury securities. Diversification can't guarantee that your investments won't suffer if the market drops. But it can improve the chances that you won't lose money, or that if you do, it won't be as much as if you weren't diversified.

Investment Products: Your Choices

When you make an investment, you are giving your money to a company or an enterprise, hoping that it will be successful and pay you back with even more money.

Some investments make money, and some don't. You can potentially make money in an investment under these conditions:

> ✔ **Quick Tip**
> What are the best saving and investing products for you? The answer depends on when you will need the money, your goals, and if you will be able to sleep at night if you purchase a risky investment where you could lose your principal.
>
> For instance, if you are saving for retirement, and you have 35 years before you retire, you may want to consider riskier investment products, knowing that if you stick to only the savings products or to less risky investment products, your money will grow too slowly—or given inflation or taxes, you may lose the purchasing power of your money. A frequent mistake people make is putting money they will not need for a very long time in investments that pay a low amount of interest.
>
> On the other hand, if you are saving for a short-term goal, five years or less, you don't want to choose risky investments, because when it's time to sell, you may have to take a loss. Since investments often move up and down in value rapidly, you want to make sure that you can wait and sell at the best possible time.
>
> Source: "Determine Your Risk Tolerance," SEC, October 2004.

- The company performs better than its competitors.

- Other investors recognize it's a good company, so that when it comes time to sell your investment, others want to buy it.

- The company makes profits, meaning they make enough money to pay you interest for your bond, or maybe dividends on your stock.

You can lose money under these conditions:

- The company's competitors are better than it is.

- Consumers don't want to buy the company's products or services.

- The company's officers fail at managing the business well, they spend too much money, and their expenses are larger than their profits.

- Other investors that you would need to sell to think the company's stock is too expensive given its performance and future outlook.

- The people running the company are dishonest. They use your money to buy homes, clothes, and vacations, instead of using your money on the business.

- They lie about any aspect of the business: claim past or future profits that do not exist, claim it has contracts to sell its products when it doesn't, or make up fake numbers on their finances to dupe investors.

- The brokers who sell the company's stock manipulate the price so that it doesn't reflect the true value of the company. After they pump up the price, these brokers dump the stock, the price falls, and investors lose their money.

- For whatever reason, you have to sell your investment when the market is down.

Here are some kinds of investments you may consider making:

Stocks And Bonds

Many companies offer investors the opportunity to buy either stocks or bonds. The following example shows you how stocks and bonds differ.

♣ **It's A Fact!!**
Real Estate

Ways To Invest

- Buy a house, live in it, and sell it later at a profit.

- Buy income property (such as an apartment house or a commercial building) and rent it.

- Buy land and hold it until it rises in value.

Advantages

- Excellent protection against inflation.

Disadvantages

- Can be difficult to convert into cash.

- A specialized type of investment requiring study and knowledge of business.

Source: From *Practical Money Skills for Life*, a financial literacy program from Visa, http://www.practicalmoneyskills.com. © 2008 Visa. All rights reserved. Reprinted with permission.

Let's say you believe that a company that makes automobiles may be a good investment. Everyone you know is buying one of its cars, and your friends report that the company's cars rarely break down and run well for years. You either have an investment professional investigate the company and read as much as possible about it, or you do it yourself.

After your research, you're convinced it's a solid company that will sell many more cars in the years ahead. The automobile company offers both stocks and bonds. With the bonds, the company agrees to pay you back your initial investment in ten years, plus pay you interest twice a year at the rate of 8% a year.

If you buy the stock, you take on the risk of potentially losing a portion or all of your initial investment if the company does poorly or the stock market drops in value. But you also may see the stock increase in value beyond what you could earn from the bonds. If you buy the stock, you become an "owner" of the company.

You wrestle with the decision. If you buy the bonds, you will get your money back plus the 8% interest a year. And you think the company will be able to honor its promise to you on the bonds because it has been in business for many years and doesn't look like it could go bankrupt. The company has a long history of making cars and you know that its stock has gone up in price by an average of 9% a year, plus it has typically paid stockholders a dividend of 3% from its profits each year.

You take your time and make a careful decision. Only time will tell if you made the right choice. You'll keep a close eye on the company and keep the stock as long as the company keeps selling a quality car that consumers want to drive, and it can make an acceptable profit from its sales.

Mutual Funds

Because it is sometimes hard for investors to become experts on various businesses—for example, what are the best steel, automobile, or telephone companies—investors often depend on professionals who are trained to investigate companies and recommend companies that are likely to succeed.

✔ Quick Tip

To easily compare mutual fund costs, you can use the SEC's mutual fund cost calculator, available online at http://www.sec.gov/investor/tools/mfcc/mfcc-int.htm.

Source: "Investment Products: Your Choices," SEC, October 2004.

Since it takes work to pick the stocks or bonds of the companies that have the best chance to do well in the future, many investors choose to invest in mutual funds. A mutual fund is a pool of money run by a professional or group of professionals called the investment adviser. In a managed mutual fund, after investigating the prospects of many companies, the fund's investment adviser will pick the stocks or bonds of companies and put them into a fund. Investors can buy shares of the fund, and their shares rise or fall in value as the values of the stocks and bonds in the fund rise and fall.

Investors may typically pay a fee when they buy or sell their shares in the fund, and those fees in part pay the salaries and expenses of the professionals who manage the fund.

Even small fees can and do add up and eat into a significant chunk of the returns a mutual fund is likely to produce, so you need to look carefully at how much a fund costs and think about how much it will cost you over the amount of time you plan to own its shares. If two funds are similar in every way except that one charges a higher fee than the other, you'll make more money by choosing the fund with the lower annual costs.

Mutual Funds Without Active Management: One way that investors can obtain for themselves nearly the full returns of the market is to invest in an index fund. This is a mutual fund that does not attempt to pick and choose stocks of individual companies based upon the research of the mutual fund managers or to try to time the market's movements. An index fund seeks to equal the returns of a major stock index, such as the Standard & Poor 500, the Wilshire 5000, or the Russell 3000. Through computer programmed

---

✎ What's It Mean?

Capital Gains: Profits from the sale of a capital asset such as stocks, bonds, or real estate. These profits are tax-deferred; you do not have to pay the tax on these profits until the asset is sold. Long-term capital gains occur on investments held more than 12 months. Short-term capital gains occur on investments held less than 12 months.

Source: From *Practical Money Skills for Life*, a financial literacy program from Visa, http://www.practicalmoneyskills.com. © 2008 Visa. All rights reserved. Reprinted with permission.

buying and selling, an index fund tracks the holdings of a chosen index, and so shows the same returns as an index minus, of course, the annual fees involved in running the fund. The fees for index mutual funds generally are much lower than the fees for managed mutual funds.

Historical data shows that index funds have, primarily because of their lower fees, enjoyed higher returns than the average managed mutual fund. But, like any investment, index funds involve risk.

Watch Turnover To Avoid Paying Excess Taxes: To maximize your mutual fund returns, or any investment returns, know the effect that taxes can have on what actually ends up in your pocket. Mutual funds that trade quickly in and out of stocks will have what is known as high turnover. While selling a stock that has moved up in price does lock in a profit for the fund, this is a profit for which taxes have to be paid. Turnover in a fund creates taxable capital gains, which are paid by the mutual fund shareholders.

The SEC requires all mutual funds to show both their before- and after-tax returns. The differences between what a fund is reportedly earning, and what a fund is earning after taxes are paid on the dividends and capital gains, can be quite striking. If you plan to hold mutual funds in a taxable account, be sure to check out these historical returns in the mutual fund prospectus to see what kind of taxes you might be likely to incur.

Chapter 10

Advice For Investing Wisely

This chapter provides basic information to help investors select a brokerage firm and sales representative, make an initial investment decision, monitor an investment, and address an investment problem. It is intended to help you identify questions you should ask and warning signs to look for in order to avoid possible investment problems.

If you need more information about a topic discussed in this chapter, or you think that the securities laws have been violated, you should contact the appropriate securities regulators. The names, addresses, and telephone numbers of these organizations are listed at the end of the chapter.

Selecting Your Broker

Before making a securities investment, you must decide which brokerage firm—also referred to as a broker/dealer—and sales representative—also referred to as a stockbroker, account executive, or registered representative—to use. Before making these decisions you should take the following steps:

• Think through your financial objectives.

About This Chapter: This chapter includes information from "Invest Wisely: Advice from Your Securities Industry Regulators," U.S. Securities and Exchange Commission (SEC), August 1, 2007.

- Talk with potential salespeople at several firms. If possible, meet them face to face at their offices. Ask each sales representative about his or her investment experience, professional background, and education.

- Find out about the disciplinary history of any brokerage firm and sales representative through the Financial Industry Regulatory Authority's BrokerCheck at www.finra.org/Investors/ToolsCalculators/ BrokerCheck. Your state securities regulator also can tell you if a sales representative is licensed to do business in your state.

- Understand how the sales representative is paid; ask for a copy of the firm's commission schedule. Firms generally pay sales staff based on the amount of money invested by a customer and the number of transactions done in a customer's account. More compensation may be paid to a sales representative for selling a firm's own investment products. Ask what "fees" or "charges" you will be required to pay when opening, maintaining, and closing an account.

Remember!!

Part of making the right investment decision is finding the brokerage firm and the sales representative that best meet your personal financial needs. Do not rush. Do the necessary background investigation on both the firm and the sales representative. Resist salespeople who urge you to immediately open an account with them.

Source: SEC, August 1, 2007.

- Determine the level of service you need. Some brokerage firms provide recommendations, investment advice, and research support, while others may not. The charges you pay may differ depending upon what services are provided by the firm.

- Ask if the brokerage firm is a member of the Securities Investor Protection Corporation (SIPC). SIPC provides limited customer protection if a brokerage firm becomes insolvent. Ask if the firm has other insurance that provides coverage beyond the SIPC limits. SIPC does not insure against losses attributable to a decline in the market value of your securities. For further information, contact SIPC at 805 Fifteenth

Street, N.W., Suite 800, Washington, DC 20005-2207; or call 202-
371-8300.

Making An Investment

The New Account Agreement

Generally, a brokerage firm will require a customer to sign a new account
agreement. You should carefully review the information contained in this
document because it may affect your legal rights regarding your account.

Ask to see any account documentation prepared for you by the sales representative. Do not sign the new account agreement unless you thoroughly
understand it and agree with the terms and conditions it imposes on you.
You can not rely on verbal representations from a sales representative that
are not contained in this agreement.

The sales representative will ask for information about your investment
objectives and personal financial situation, including your income, net worth,
and investment experience. Be honest. The sales representative will use this
information in making investment recommendations to you.

Completion of the new account agreement requires that you make three
critical decisions:

1. Who will control decision-making in your account? You will control the
    investment decisions made in your account unless you decide to give
    discretionary authority to your sales representative to make investment
    decisions for you. Discretionary authority allows a sales representative to
    make investment decisions based on what the sales representative be-
    lieves to be best—without consulting you about the price, the type of
    security, the amount, and when to buy or sell. Do not give discretionary
    authority to your sales representative without seriously considering
    whether this arrangement is appropriate for you.

2. How will you pay for your investment? Most investors maintain a cash
    account that requires payment in full for each a security purchase. An
    alternative type of account is a margin account. Buying securities through
    a margin account means that you can borrow money from the brokerage

firm to buy securities and requires that you pay interest on that loan. You will be required to sign a margin agreement disclosing interest terms. If you purchase securities on margin (by borrowing money from the brokerage firm), the firm has authority to immediately sell any security in your account, without notice to you, to cover any shortfall resulting from a decline in the value of your securities. If the value of your account is less than the amount of the outstanding loan—even due to a one day market drop—you are liable for the balance. This may be a substantial amount of money even after your securities are sold. The margin account agreement generally provides that the securities in your margin account may be lent out by the brokerage firm at any time without notice or compensation to you.

3. How much risk should you assume? In a new account agreement, you must specify your overall investment objective in terms of risk. Categories of risk may have labels such as "income," "growth," or "aggressive growth." Be careful you understand the distinctions between these terms, and be certain that the risk level you choose accurately reflects your investment goals. The investment products recommended to you should reflect the category of risk you have selected.

When opening a new account, the brokerage firm may ask you to sign a legally binding contract to arbitrate any future dispute between you and the firm or your sales representative. This may be part of another document, such as a margin agreement. The federal securities laws do not require that you sign such an agreement. You may choose later to arbitrate a dispute for damages even if you do not sign the agreement. Signing such an agreement means that you give up the right to sue your sales representative and firm in court.

You may have your securities registered either in your name or in the name of your brokerage firm. Ask your sales representative about the relative advantages and disadvantages of each arrangement. If you plan to trade securities regularly, you may prefer to have the securities registered in the name of your brokerage firm to facilitate clearance, settlement, and dividend payment.

✔ **Quick Tip**

Comparison shop for financial services. Just as you would do for any major purchase, look at what is being offered by a few competitors, then try to find the best deal to meet your needs.

Source: Excerpted from "For Any Age or Stage: Practical Advice for Everyone on How to Save and Manage Money," *FDIC Consumer News*, Federal Deposit Insurance Corporation, Spring 2008.

The Investment Decision

Never invest in a product that you don't fully understand. Consult information sources such as business and financial publications. Information regarding the fundamentals of investing and basic financial terminology can be found at your local library.

Ask your sales representative for the prospectus, offering circular, or most recent annual report—and the "Options Disclosure Document" if you are investing in options. Read them. If you have questions, talk with your sales representative before investing.

You also may want to check with another brokerage firm, an accountant, or a trusted business adviser to get a second opinion about a particular investment you are considering.

Keep good records of all information you receive, copies of forms you sign, and conversations you have with your sales representative.

Nobody invests to lose money. However, investments always entail some degree of risk. Be aware of these guidelines:

• The higher the expected rate of return, the greater the risk; depending on market developments, you could lose some or all of your initial investment. With some investments, such as options, you can lose more than the amount of your investment. Ask whether the security can be redeemed or if there is a market for it.

- Some investments cannot easily be sold or converted to cash. Check to see if there is any penalty or charge if you must sell an investment quickly or before its maturity date.

- Investments in securities issued by a company with little or no operating history or published information may involve greater risk.

- Securities investments, including mutual funds, are not federally insured against a loss in market value.

- Securities you own may be subject to tender offers, mergers, reorganizations, or third party actions that can affect the value of your ownership interest. Pay careful attention to public announcements and information sent to you about such transactions. They involve complex investment decisions. Be sure you fully understand the terms of any offer to exchange or sell your shares before you act. In some cases, such as partial or two-tier tender offers, failure to act can have detrimental effects on your investment.

- The past success of a particular investment is no guarantee of future performance.

> **Remember!!**
> Remember that investments can lose value. Investment products include stocks, bonds, and mutual funds. Over the long term, investments might produce higher returns than bank deposits. However, investments are not deposits, they are not FDIC-insured—not even the ones sold through FDIC-insured institutions—and they can lose value. Because of the risks associated with any investment, always deal with a reputable, licensed salesperson and research the product before making a purchase.
>
> Source: Excerpted from "For Any Age or Stage: Practical Advice for Everyone on How to Save and Manage Money," *FDIC Consumer News*, Federal Deposit Insurance Corporation, Spring 2008.

Protect Yourself

A high pressure sales pitch can mean trouble. Be suspicious of anyone who tells you, "Invest quickly or you will miss out on a once in a lifetime opportunity."

Remember the following:

- Never send money to purchase an investment based simply on a telephone sales pitch.

- Never make a check out to a sales representative personally.

- Never send checks to an address different from the business address of the brokerage firm or a designated address listed in the prospectus.

If your sales representative asks you to do any of these things, contact the branch manager or compliance officer of the brokerage firm.

Never allow your transaction confirmations and account statements to be delivered or mailed to your sales representative as a substitute for receiving them yourself. These documents are your official record of the date, time, amount, and price of each security purchased or sold. When you receive them you should verify that the information in these statements is correct.

Certain activities may indicate problems in the handling of your account and, possibly, violations of state and federal securities laws. Be alert for the following signs of trouble:

- Recommendations from a sales representative based on "inside" or "confidential information," an "upcoming favorable research report," a "prospective merger or acquisition," or the announcement of a "dynamic new product."

- Representations of spectacular profit, such as, "Your money will double in six months." Remember, if it sounds too good to be true, it probably is!

- "Guarantees" that you will not lose money on a particular securities transaction, or agreements by a sales representative to share in any losses in your account.

- An excessive number of transactions in your account. Such activity generates additional commissions for your sales representative, but may provide no better investment opportunities for you.

- A recommendation from your sales representative that you make a dramatic change in your investment strategy, such as moving from low risk investments to speculative securities, or concentrating your investments exclusively in a single product.

- Switching your investment in a mutual fund to a different fund with the same or similar investment objectives. Unless there is a legitimate investment purpose, a switch recommended by your sales representative may simply be an attempt to generate additional commissions for the sales representative.

- Pressure to trade the account in a manner that is inconsistent with your investment goals and the risk you want or can afford to take.

- Assurances from your sales representative that an error in your account is due solely to computer or clerical error. Insist that the branch manager or compliance officer promptly send you a written explanation. Verify that the problem has been corrected on your next account statement.

If You Have A Problem

If you have a problem with your sales representative or your account, promptly talk to the sales representative's manager or the firm's compliance officer. Confirm your complaint to the firm in writing. Keep written records of all conversations. Ask for written explanations.

If the problem is not resolved to your satisfaction, contact the appropriate regulators listed at the end of this document. Investor complaint information assists these regulators in identifying violations of the securities laws and prosecuting violators. However, none of these organizations is authorized to provide legal representation to individual investors or to get your money back for you.

Obtain information on using arbitration to resolve your dispute by contacting the Financial Industry Regulatory Authority, New York Stock Exchange,

Municipal Securities Rulemaking Board, and Chicago Board Options Exchange. Each of these organizations operates a forum to resolve disputes between brokerage firms and their customers. You may also wish to consult an attorney knowledgeable about securities laws. Your local bar association can assist you in locating a securities attorney.

Securities Regulators And Exchanges

American Stock Exchange, Inc.
86 Trinity Place
Phone: 212-306-1000
Website: http://www.amex.com

Chicago Board Options Exchange, Inc.
400 LaSalle Street
Chicago, IL 60605
Phone: 312-786-7705
Website: http://www.cboe.com

Chicago Stock Exchange, Inc.
400 LaSalle Street
Chicago, IL 60605
Phone: 312-663-2222
Website: http://www.chx.com

Financial Industry Regulatory Authority (FINRA)
1735 K Street
Washington, DC 20006
Phone: 301-590-6500
Website: http://www.finra.org

International Securities Exchange
60 Broad Street
New York, NY 10004
Phone: 212-943-2400
Website: http://www.ise.com

Municipal Securities Rulemaking Board
1818 N Street, N.W.
Washington, DC 20036
Phone: 202-223-9347
Website:
http://www.msrb.org

National Stock Exchange
440 South LaSalle Street
Suite 2600
Chicago, IL 60605
Phone: 312-786-8803
Website: http://www.nsx.com

Nasdaq
One Liberty Plaza
165 Broadway
New York, NY 10006
Phone: 212-401-8700
Website:
http://www.nasdaq.com

New York Stock Exchange, Inc.
11 Wall Street
New York, NY 10005
Phone: 212-656-3000
Website: http://www.nyse.com

U.S. Securities and Exchange Commission
100 F Street, N.E.
Washington, DC 20549-0213
Toll-Free: 800-SEC-0330 (732-0330)
Phone: 202-551-6551
Fax: 202-772-9295
Website: http://www.sec.gov
Complaints: http://www.sec.gov/complaint.shtml

Chapter 11

Beginners Guide To Asset Allocation, Diversification, And Rebalancing

Even if you are new to investing, you may already know some of the most fundamental principles of sound investing. How did you learn them? Through ordinary, real-life experiences that have nothing to do with the stock market.

For example, have you ever noticed that street vendors often sell seemingly unrelated products—such as umbrellas and sunglasses? Initially, that may seem odd. After all, when would a person buy both items at the same time? Probably never—and that's the point. Street vendors know that when it's raining, it's easier to sell umbrellas but harder to sell sunglasses. And when it's sunny, the reverse is true. By selling both items—in other words, by diversifying the product line—the vendor can reduce the risk of losing money on any given day.

If that makes sense, you've got a great start on understanding asset allocation and diversification. This chapter will cover those topics more fully and will also discuss the importance of rebalancing from time to time.

Let's begin by looking at asset allocation.

About This Chapter: Text in this chapter is from "Beginners' Guide to Asset Allocation, Diversification, and Rebalancing," U.S. Securities and Exchange Commission (www.sec.gov), May 24, 2007.

Asset Allocation 101

Asset allocation involves dividing an investment portfolio among different asset categories, such as stocks, bonds, and cash. The process of determining which mix of assets to hold in your portfolio is a very personal one. The asset allocation that works best for you at any given point in your life will depend largely on your time horizon and your ability to tolerate risk.

- **Time Horizon:** Your time horizon is the expected number of months, years, or decades you will be investing to achieve a particular financial goal. An investor with a longer time horizon may feel more comfortable taking on a riskier, or more volatile, investment because he or she can wait out slow economic cycles and the inevitable ups and downs of our markets. By contrast, a teen saving for a college education would likely take on less risk because he or she has a shorter time horizon.

- **Risk Tolerance:** Risk tolerance is your ability and willingness to lose some or all of your original investment in exchange for greater potential returns. An aggressive investor, or one with a high-risk tolerance, is more likely to risk losing money in order to get better results. A conservative investor, or one with a low-risk tolerance, tends to favor investments that will preserve his or her original investment. In the

♣ It's A Fact!!
Risk Versus Reward

When it comes to investing, risk and reward are inextricably entwined. You've probably heard the phrase "no pain, no gain"—those words come close to summing up the relationship between risk and reward. Don't let anyone tell you otherwise: All investments involve some degree of risk. If you intend to purchases securities—such as stocks, bonds, or mutual funds—it's important that you understand before you invest that you could lose some or all of your money.

The reward for taking on risk is the potential for a greater investment return. If you have a financial goal with a long time horizon, you are likely to make more money by carefully investing in asset categories with greater risk, like stocks or bonds, rather than restricting your investments to assets with less risk, like cash equivalents. On the other hand, investing solely in cash investments may be appropriate for short-term financial goals.

words of the famous saying, conservative investors keep a "bird in the hand," while aggressive investors seek "two in the bush."

Investment Choices

While the U.S. Securities and Exchange Commission (SEC) cannot recommend any particular investment product, you should know that a vast array of investment products exists—including stocks and stock mutual funds, corporate and municipal bonds, bond mutual funds, lifecycle funds, exchange-traded funds, money market funds, and U.S. Treasury securities. For many financial goals, investing in a mix of stocks, bonds, and cash can be a good strategy. Let's take a closer look at the characteristics of the three major asset categories.

- **Stocks:** Stocks have historically had the greatest risk and highest returns among the three major asset categories. As an asset category, stocks are a portfolio's "heavy hitter," offering the greatest potential for growth. Stocks hit home runs, but also strike out. The volatility of stocks makes them a very risky investment in the short term. Large company stocks as a group, for example, have lost money on average about one out of every three years. And sometimes the losses have been quite dramatic. But investors that have been willing to ride out the volatile returns of stocks over long periods of time generally have been rewarded with strong positive returns.

- **Bonds:** Bonds are generally less volatile than stocks but offer more modest returns. As a result, an investor approaching a financial goal might increase his or her bond holdings relative to his or her stock holdings because the reduced risk of holding more bonds would be attractive to the investor despite their lower potential for growth. You should keep in mind that certain categories of bonds offer high returns similar to stocks. But these bonds, known as high-yield or junk bonds, also carry higher risk.

- **Cash:** Cash and cash equivalents—such as savings deposits, certificates of deposit, treasury bills, money market deposit accounts, and money market funds—are the safest investments, but offer the lowest return of the three major asset categories. The chances of losing money on an investment in this asset category are generally extremely low. The federal government guarantees many investments in cash equivalents. Investment losses in non-guaranteed cash equivalents do occur, but infrequently. The principal concern for investors investing in cash equivalents is inflation risk. This is the risk that inflation will outpace and erode investment returns over time.

Stocks, bonds, and cash are the most common asset categories. These are the asset categories you would likely choose from when investing in a retirement savings program or a college savings plan. But other asset categories—including real estate, precious metals and other commodities, and private equity—also exist, and some investors may include these asset categories within a portfolio. Investments in these asset categories typically have category-specific risks. Before you make any investment, you should understand the risks of the investment and make sure the risks are appropriate for you.

Why Asset Allocation Is So Important

By including asset categories with investment returns that move up and down under different market conditions within a portfolio, an investor can protect against significant losses. Historically, the returns of the three major asset categories have not moved up and down at the same time. Market conditions that cause one asset category to do well often cause another asset category to have average or poor returns. By investing in more than one asset category, you'll reduce the risk that you'll lose money and your portfolio's overall investment returns will have a smoother ride. If one asset category's investment return falls, you'll be in a position to counteract your losses in that asset category with better investment returns in another asset category.

✎ What's It Mean?

Diversification: The practice of spreading money among different investments to reduce risk is known as diversification. By picking the right group of investments, you may be able to limit your losses and reduce the fluctuations of investment returns without sacrificing too much potential gain.

In addition, asset allocation is important because it has major impact on whether you will meet your financial goal. If you don't include enough risk in your portfolio, your investments may not earn a large enough return to meet your goal. For example, if you are saving for a long-term goal, such as retirement or college, most financial experts agree that you will likely need to include at least some stock or stock mutual funds in your portfolio. On the other hand, if you include too much risk in your portfolio, the money for your goal may not be there when you need it. A portfolio heavily weighted in stock or stock mutual funds, for instance, would be inappropriate for a short-term goal, such as saving for a family's summer vacation.

How To Get Started

Determining the appropriate asset allocation model for a financial goal is a complicated task. Basically, you're trying to pick a mix of assets that has the highest probability of meeting your goal at a level of risk you can live with. As you get closer to meeting your goal, you'll need to be able to adjust the mix of assets.

If you understand your time horizon and risk tolerance—and have some investing experience—you may feel comfortable creating your own asset allocation model. "How to" books on investing often discuss general "rules of thumb," and various online resources can help you with your decision. For example, although the SEC cannot endorse any particular formula or methodology, the Iowa Public Employees Retirement System offers an online asset allocation calculator (http://www.ipers.org/calcs/AssetAllocator.html). In the end, you'll be making a very personal choice. There is no single asset allocation model that is right for every financial goal. You'll need to use the one that is right for you.

Some financial experts believe that determining your asset allocation is the most important decision that you'll make with respect to your investments—that it's even more important than the individual investments you buy. With that in mind, you may want to consider asking a financial professional to help you determine your initial asset allocation and suggest adjustments for the future. But before you hire anyone to help you with these enormously important decisions, be sure to do a thorough check of his or her credentials and disciplinary history.

The Connection Between Asset Allocation And Diversification

Diversification is a strategy that can be neatly summed up by the timeless adage "Don't put all your eggs in one basket." The strategy involves spreading your money among various investments in the hope that if one investment loses money, the other investments will more than make up for those losses.

Many investors use asset allocation as a way to diversify their investments among asset categories. But other investors deliberately do not. For example, investing entirely in stock, in the case of a twenty-five year-old investing for retirement, or investing entirely in cash equivalents, in the case of a family saving for the down payment on a house, might be reasonable asset allocation strategies under certain circumstances. But neither strategy attempts to reduce risk by holding different types of asset categories. So choosing an

♣ **It's A Fact!!**
Options For One-Stop
Shopping—Lifecycle Funds

To accommodate investors who prefer to use one investment to save for a particular investment goal, such as retirement, some mutual fund companies have begun offering a product known as a "lifecycle fund." A lifecycle fund is a diversified mutual fund that automatically shifts towards a more conservative mix of investments as it approaches a particular year in the future, known as its "target date." A lifecycle fund investor picks a fund with the right target date based on his or her particular investment goal. The managers of the fund then make all decisions about asset allocation, diversification, and rebalancing. It's easy to identify a lifecycle fund because its name will likely refer to its target date. For example, you might see lifecycle funds with names like "Portfolio 2015," "Retirement Fund 2030," or "Target 2045."

asset allocation model won't necessarily diversify your portfolio. Whether your portfolio is diversified will depend on how you spread the money in your portfolio among different types of investments.

Diversification 101

A diversified portfolio should be diversified at two levels: between asset categories and within asset categories. So in addition to allocating your investments among stocks, bonds, cash equivalents, and possibly other asset categories, you'll also need to spread out your investments within each asset category. The key is to identify investments in segments of each asset category that may perform differently under different market conditions.

One of way of diversifying your investments within an asset category is to identify and invest in a wide range of companies and industry sectors. But the stock portion of your investment portfolio won't be diversified, for example, if you only invest in only four or five individual stocks. You'll need at least a dozen carefully selected individual stocks to be truly diversified.

Because achieving diversification can be so challenging, some investors may find it easier to diversify within each asset category through the ownership of mutual funds rather than through individual investments from each asset category. A mutual fund is a company that pools money from many investors and invests the money in stocks, bonds, and other financial instruments. Mutual funds make it easy for investors to own a small portion of many investments. A total stock market index fund, for example, owns stock in thousands of companies. That's a lot of diversification for one investment!

Be aware, however, that a mutual fund investment doesn't necessarily provide instant diversification, especially if the fund focuses on only one particular industry sector. If you invest in narrowly focused mutual funds, you may need to invest in more than one mutual fund to get the diversification you seek. Within asset categories, that may mean considering, for instance, large company stock funds as well as some small company and international stock funds. Between asset categories, that may mean considering stock funds, bond funds, and money market funds. Of course, as you add more investments to your portfolio, you'll likely pay additional fees and expenses, which will, in turn, lower your investment returns. So you'll need to consider these costs when deciding the best way to diversify your portfolio.

Changing Your Asset Allocation

The most common reason for changing your asset allocation is a change in your time horizon. In other words, as you get closer to your investment goal, you'll likely need to change your asset allocation. For example, most people investing for retirement hold less stock and more bonds and cash equivalents as they get closer to retirement age. You may also need to change your asset allocation if there is a change in your risk tolerance, financial situation, or the financial goal itself.

But savvy investors typically do not change their asset allocation based on the relative performance of asset categories—for example, increasing the proportion of stocks in one's portfolio when the stock market is hot. Instead, that's when they "rebalance" their portfolios.

Rebalancing 101

Rebalancing is bringing your portfolio back to your original asset allocation mix. This is necessary because over time some of your investments may become out of alignment with your investment goals. You'll find that some of your investments will grow faster than others. By rebalancing, you'll ensure that your portfolio does not overemphasize one or more asset categories, and you'll return your portfolio to a comfortable level of risk.

For example, let's say you determined that stock investments should represent 60% of your portfolio. But after a recent stock market increase, stock investments represent 80% of your portfolio. You'll need to either sell some of your stock investments or purchase investments from an under-weighted asset category in order to reestablish your original asset allocation mix.

When you rebalance, you'll also need to review the investments within each asset allocation category. If any of these investments are out of alignment with your investment goals, you'll need to make changes to bring them back to their original allocation within the asset category.

There are basically three different ways you can rebalance your portfolio:

1. You can sell off investments from over-weighted asset categories and use the proceeds to purchase investments for under-weighted asset categories.

2. You can purchase new investments for under-weighted asset categories.

3. If you are making continuous contributions to the portfolio, you can alter your contributions so that more investments go to under-weighted asset categories until your portfolio is back into balance.

Before you rebalance your portfolio, you should consider whether the method of rebalancing you decide to use will trigger transaction fees or tax consequences. Your financial professional or tax adviser can help you identify ways that you can minimize these potential costs.

✔ Quick Tip
Stick With Your Plan: Buy Low, Sell High

Shifting money away from an asset category when it is doing well in favor an asset category that is doing poorly may not be easy, but it can be a wise move. By cutting back on the current "winners" and adding more of the current so-called "losers," rebalancing forces you to buy low and sell high.

When To Consider Rebalancing

You can rebalance your portfolio based either on the calendar or on your investments. Many financial experts recommend that investors rebalance their portfolios on a regular time interval, such as every six or twelve months. The advantage of this method is that the calendar is a reminder of when you should consider rebalancing.

Others recommend rebalancing only when the relative weight of an asset class increases or decreases more than a certain percentage that you've identified in advance. The advantage of this method is that your investments tell you when to rebalance. In either case, rebalancing tends to work best when done on a relatively infrequent basis.

Where To Find More Information

For more information on investing wisely and avoiding costly mistakes, please visit the Investor Information section of the SEC's website (available online at http://www.sec.gov). You also can learn more about several investment topics, including asset allocation, diversification and rebalancing in the context of saving for retirement by visiting the Financial Industry Regulatory Authority's Smart 401(k) Investing website (http://apps.finra.org/Investor_Information/Smart/401k/000100.asp) as well as the Department of Labor's Employee Benefits Security Administration website (http://www.dol.gov/ebsa).

You can find out more about your risk tolerance by completing free online questionnaires available on numerous websites maintained by investment publications, mutual fund companies, and other financial professionals. Some of the websites will even estimate asset allocations based on responses to the questionnaires. While the suggested asset allocations may be a useful starting point for determining an appropriate allocation for a particular goal, investors should keep in mind that the results may be biased towards financial products or services sold by companies or individuals maintaining the websites.

Once you've started investing, you'll typically have access to online resources that can help you manage your portfolio. The websites of many mutual fund companies, for example, give customers the ability to run a "portfolio analysis" of their investments. The results of a portfolio analysis can help you analyze your asset allocation, determine whether your investments are diversified, and decide whether you need to rebalance your portfolio.

Chapter 12

A Beginner's Guide To Financial Statements

Understanding Financial Statements

The Basics

If you can read a nutrition label or a baseball box score, you can learn to read basic financial statements. If you can follow a recipe or apply for a loan, you can learn basic accounting. The basics aren't difficult and they aren't rocket science. Let's begin by looking at what financial statements do.

"Show me the money!"

We all remember Cuba Gooding, Jr.'s immortal line from the movie *Jerry Maguire*, "Show me the money!" Well, that's what financial statements do. They show you the money. They show you where a company's money came from, where it went, and where it is now.

Balance Sheets: A balance sheet provides detailed information about a company's assets, liabilities and shareholders' equity.

Assets are things that a company owns that have value. This typically means they can either be sold or used by the company to make products or

---

About This Chapter: This chapter begins with information from "Beginners' Guide to Financial Statements," U.S. Securities and Exchange Commission (SEC), February 5, 2007. Additional text is from "Corporate Reports, How to Get," SEC, August 28, 2006.

provide services that can be sold. Assets include physical property, such as plants, trucks, equipment and inventory. It also includes things that can't be touched but nevertheless exist and have value, such as trademarks and patents. And cash itself is an asset. So are investments a company makes.

Liabilities are amounts of money that a company owes to others. This can include all kinds of obligations, like money borrowed from a bank to launch a new product, rent for use of a building, money owed to suppliers for materials, payroll a company owes to its employees, environmental cleanup costs, or taxes owed to the government. Liabilities also include obligations to provide goods or services to customers in the future.

What's It Mean?

There are four main financial statements:

Balance Sheets: Balance sheets show what a company owns and what it owes at a fixed point in time.

Income Statements: Income statements show how much money a company made and spent over a period of time.

Cash Flow Statements: Cash flow statements show the exchange of money between a company and the outside world also over a period of time.

Statements Of Shareholders' Equity: The fourth financial statement, called a "statement of shareholders' equity," shows changes in the interests of the company's shareholders over time.

Source: SEC, February 5, 2007.

Shareholders' equity is sometimes called capital or net worth. It's the money that would be left if a company sold all of its assets and paid off all of its liabilities. This leftover money belongs to the shareholders, or the owners, of the company.

The following formula summarizes what a balance sheet shows:

Assets = Liabilities + Shareholders' Equity

A company's assets have to equal, or "balance," the sum of its liabilities and shareholders' equity.

A company's balance sheet is set up like the basic accounting equation shown above. On the left side of the balance sheet, companies list their assets.

On the right side, they list their liabilities and shareholders' equity. Sometimes balance sheets show assets at the top, followed by liabilities, with shareholders' equity at the bottom.

Assets are generally listed based on how quickly they will be converted into cash. Current assets are things a company expects to convert to cash within one year. A good example is inventory. Most companies expect to sell their inventory for cash within one year. Noncurrent assets are things a company does not expect to convert to cash within one year or that would take longer than one year to sell. Noncurrent assets include fixed assets. Fixed assets are those assets used to operate the business but that are not available for sale, such as trucks, office furniture and other property.

Liabilities are generally listed based on their due dates. Liabilities are said to be either current or long-term. Current liabilities are obligations a company expects to pay off within the year. Long-term liabilities are obligations due more than one year away.

Remember!!

A balance sheet shows a snapshot of a company's assets, liabilities, and shareholders' equity at the end of the reporting period. It does not show the flows into and out of the accounts during the period.

Source: SEC, February 5, 2007.

Shareholders' equity is the amount owners invested in the company's stock plus or minus the company's earnings or losses since inception. Sometimes companies distribute earnings, instead of retaining them. These distributions are called dividends.

Income Statements: An income statement is a report that shows how much revenue a company earned over a specific time period (usually for a year or some portion of a year). An income statement also shows the costs and expenses associated with earning that revenue. The literal "bottom line" of the statement usually shows the company's net earnings or losses. This tells you how much the company earned or lost over the period.

Income statements also report earnings per share (or "EPS"). This calculation tells you how much money shareholders would receive if the company decided to distribute all of the net earnings for the period. (Companies almost never distribute all of their earnings. Usually they reinvest them in the business.)

To understand how income statements are set up, think of them as a set of stairs. You start at the top with the total amount of sales made during the accounting period. Then you go down, one step at a time. At each step, you make a deduction for certain costs or other operating expenses associated with earning the revenue. At the bottom of the stairs, after deducting all of the expenses, you learn how much the company actually earned or lost during the accounting period. People often call this "the bottom line."

At the top of the income statement is the total amount of money brought in from sales of products or services. This top line is often referred to as gross revenues or sales. It's called "gross" because expenses have not been deducted from it yet. So the number is "gross" or unrefined.

The next line is money the company doesn't expect to collect on certain sales. This could be due, for example, to sales discounts or merchandise returns.

When you subtract the returns and allowances from the gross revenues, you arrive at the company's net revenues. It's called "net" because, if you can imagine a net, these revenues are left in the net after the deductions for returns and allowances have come out.

Moving down the stairs from the net revenue line, there are several lines that represent various kinds of operating expenses. Although these lines can be reported in various orders, the next line after net revenues typically shows the costs of the sales. This number tells you the amount of money the company spent to produce the goods or services it sold during the accounting period.

The next line subtracts the costs of sales from the net revenues to arrive at a subtotal called "gross profit" or sometimes "gross margin." It's considered "gross" because there are certain expenses that haven't been deducted from it yet.

The next section deals with operating expenses. These are expenses that go toward supporting a company's operations for a given period—for example, salaries of administrative personnel and costs of researching new products. Marketing expenses are another example. Operating expenses are different from "costs of sales," which were deducted above, because operating expenses cannot be linked directly to the production of the products or services being sold.

Depreciation is also deducted from gross profit. Depreciation takes into account the wear and tear on some assets, such as machinery, tools and furniture, which are used over the long term. Companies spread the cost of these assets over the periods they are used. This process of spreading these costs is called depreciation or amortization. The "charge" for using these assets during the period is a fraction of the original cost of the assets.

After all operating expenses are deducted from gross profit, you arrive at operating profit before interest and income tax expenses. This is often called "income from operations."

Next companies must account for interest income and interest expense. Interest income is the money companies make from keeping their cash in interest-bearing savings accounts, money market funds, and the like. On the other hand, interest expense is the money companies paid in interest for money they borrow. Some income statements show interest income and interest expense separately. Some income statements combine the two numbers. The

♣ It's A Fact!!
Earnings Per Share Or EPS

Most income statements include a calculation of earnings per share or EPS. This calculation tells you how much money shareholders would receive for each share of stock they own if the company distributed all of its net income for the period.

To calculate EPS, you take the total net income and divide it by the number of outstanding shares of the company.

Source: SEC, February 5, 2007.

interest income and expense are then added or subtracted from the operating profits to arrive at operating profit before income tax.

Finally, income tax is deducted and you arrive at the bottom line: net profit or net losses. (Net profit is also called net income or net earnings.) This tells you how much the company actually earned or lost during the accounting period. Did the company make a profit or did it lose money?

Cash Flow Statements: Cash flow statements report a company's inflows and outflows of cash. This is important because a company needs to have enough cash on hand to pay its expenses and purchase assets. While an income statement can tell you whether a company made a profit, a cash flow statement can tell you whether the company generated cash.

✔ **Quick Tip**

Read The Footnotes

A horse called "Read The Footnotes" ran in the 2004 Kentucky Derby. He finished seventh, but if he had won, it would have been a victory for financial literacy proponents everywhere. It's so important to read the footnotes. The footnotes to financial statements are packed with information. Here are some of the highlights:

- **Significant Accounting Policies And Practices:** Companies are required to disclose the accounting policies that are most important to the portrayal of the company's financial condition and results. These often require management's most difficult, subjective or complex judgments.

- **Income Taxes:** The footnotes provide detailed information about the company's current and deferred income taxes. The information is broken down by level—federal, state, local and/or foreign, and the main items that affect the company's effective tax rate are described.

- **Pension Plans And Other Retirement Programs:** The footnotes discuss the company's pension plans and other retirement or post-employment benefit programs. The notes contain specific information about the assets and costs of these programs, and indicate whether and by how much the plans are over- or under-funded.

A cash flow statement shows changes over time rather than absolute dollar amounts at a point in time. It uses and reorders the information from a company's balance sheet and income statement.

The bottom line of the cash flow statement shows the net increase or decrease in cash for the period. Generally, cash flow statements are divided into three main parts. Each part reviews the cash flow from one of three types of activities: (1) operating activities; (2) investing activities; and (3) financing activities.

- *Operating Activities:* The first part of a cash flow statement analyzes a company's cash flow from net income or losses. For most companies, this section of the cash flow statement reconciles the net income (as

---

- **Stock Options:** The notes also contain information about stock options granted to officers and employees, including the method of accounting for stock-based compensation and the effect of the method on reported results.

Read The MD&A

You can find a narrative explanation of a company's financial performance in a section of the quarterly or annual report titled, "Management's Discussion and Analysis of Financial Condition and Results of Operations." MD&A is management's opportunity to provide investors with its view of the financial performance and condition of the company. It's management's opportunity to tell investors what the financial statements show and do not show, as well as important trends and risks that have shaped the past or are reasonably likely to shape the company's future.

The U.S. Securities and Exchange Commission (SEC)'s rules governing MD&A require disclosure about trends, events, or uncertainties known to management that would have a material impact on reported financial information. The purpose of MD&A is to provide investors with information that the company's management believes to be necessary to an understanding of its financial condition, changes in financial condition and results of operations. It is intended to help investors to see the company through the eyes of management. It is also intended to provide context for the financial statements and information about the company's earnings and cash flows.

Source: SEC, February 5, 2007.

shown on the income statement) to the actual cash the company received from or used in its operating activities. To do this, it adjusts net income for any non-cash items (such as adding back depreciation expenses) and adjusts for any cash that was used or provided by other operating assets and liabilities.

- *Investing Activities:* The second part of a cash flow statement shows the cash flow from all investing activities, which generally include purchases or sales of long-term assets, such as property, plant and equipment, as well as investment securities. If a company buys a piece of machinery, the cash flow statement would reflect this activity as a cash outflow from investing activities because it used cash. If the company decided to sell off some investments from an investment portfolio, the proceeds from the sales would show up as a cash inflow from investing activities because it provided cash.

- *Financing Activities:* The third part of a cash flow statement shows the cash flow from all financing activities. Typical sources of cash flow include cash raised by selling stocks and bonds or borrowing from banks. Likewise, paying back a bank loan would show up as a use of cash flow.

Financial Statement Ratios And Calculations

You've probably heard people banter around phrases like "P/E ratio," "current ratio," and "operating margin." But what do these terms mean and why don't they show up on financial statements? Listed below are just some of the many ratios that investors calculate from information on financial statements and then use to evaluate a company. As a general rule, desirable ratios vary by industry.

Debt-To-Equity Ratio: This ratio compares a company's total debt to shareholders' equity. Both of these numbers can be found on a company's balance sheet. To calculate debt-to-equity ratio, you divide a company's total liabilities by its shareholder equity:

Debt-to-Equity Ratio = Total Liabilities / Shareholders' Equity

If a company has a debt-to-equity ratio of two to one, it means that the company has two dollars of debt to every one dollar shareholders invest in the company. In other words, the company is taking on debt at twice the rate that its owners are investing in the company.

Inventory Turnover Ratio: This compares a company's cost of sales on its income statement with its average inventory balance for the period. To calculate the average inventory balance for the period, look at the inventory numbers listed on the balance sheet. Take the balance listed for the period of the report and add it to the balance listed for the previous comparable period, and then divide by two. (Remember that balance sheets are snapshots in time. So the inventory balance for the previous period is the beginning balance for the current period, and the inventory balance for the current period is the ending balance.) To calculate the inventory turnover ratio, you divide a company's cost of sales (just below the net revenues on the income statement) by the average inventory for the period:

Inventory Turnover Ratio =
Cost of Sales / Average Inventory for the Period

If a company has an inventory turnover ratio of two to one, it means that the company's inventory turned over twice in the reporting period.

Operating Margin: This compares a company's operating income to net revenues. Both of these numbers can be found on a company's income statement. To calculate operating margin, you divide a company's income from operations (before interest and income tax expenses) by its net revenues:

Operating Margin = Income from Operations / Net Revenues

Operating margin is usually expressed as a percentage. It shows, for each dollar of sales, what percentage was profit.

P/E Ratio: This ratio compares a company's common stock price with its earnings per share. To calculate a company's P/E ratio, you divide a company's stock price by its earnings per share:

P/E Ratio = Price per share / Earnings per share

If a company's stock is selling at $20 per share and the company is earning $2 per share, then the company's P/E Ratio is ten to one. The company's stock is selling at ten times its earnings.

Working Capital: This is the money leftover if a company paid its current liabilities (that is, its debts due within one-year of the date of the balance sheet) from its current assets.

Working Capital = Current Assets − Current Liabilities

♣ **It's A Fact!!**
Bringing It All Together
Although this chapter discusses each financial statement separately, keep in mind that they are all related. The changes in assets and liabilities that you see on the balance sheet are also reflected in the revenues and expenses that you see on the income statement, which result in the company's gains or losses. Cash flows provide more information about cash assets listed on a balance sheet and are related, but not equivalent, to net income shown on the income statement. And so on. No one financial statement tells the complete story. But combined, they provide very powerful information for investors. And information is the investor's best tool when it comes to investing wisely.

Source: SEC, February 5, 2007.

How To Get Corporate Reports

You can get information about companies from a variety of sources.

Corporate Reports

Corporate reports are a treasure trove of information for investors: they tell you whether a company is making money or losing money and why. You'll find this information in the company's quarterly reports on Form 10-Q, annual reports (with audited financial statements) on Form 10-K, and periodic reports of significant events on Form 8-K.

It's usually easy to find information about large companies from the companies themselves, newspapers, brokerage firms, and the SEC. By contrast, it can be extremely difficult to find information about small companies. Generally, smaller companies only have to file reports with the SEC if they have $10 million or more in assets and 500 or more shareholders, or list their securities on an exchange or Nasdaq.

You can get corporate reports from the following sources:

The SEC: You can find out whether a company files by using the SEC's database known as EDGAR (which stands for Electronic Data Gathering, Analysis, and Retrieval). EDGAR is available online at http://www.sec.gov/edgar.shtml. For companies that do not file on EDGAR, you can contact the SEC at:

Office of Public Reference
100 F Street, N.E., Room 1580
Washington, DC 20549-0102
Phone: 202-551-8090
Fax: 202-777-1027
E-mail: publicinfo@sec.gov

Please note that you may have to pay a photocopying charge of $0.26 per page, plus postage, for any filing you order.

The Company: Ask the company if it is registered with the SEC and files reports. That information may be listed on the SEC website (available online at http://www.sec.gov). Check out new or smaller companies thoroughly because many frauds involve these types of companies.

👉 Remember!!

To invest wisely and avoid investment scams, research each investment opportunity thoroughly and ask questions.

Source: SEC, August 28, 2006.

Other Government Regulators: Banks do not have to file reports with the SEC, but file with banking regulators. Visit their websites: Federal Reserve System's National Information Center of Banking Information (http://www.ffiec.gov/nicpubweb/nicweb/nichome.aspx?sfgdata=4), the Office of the Comptroller of the Currency (http://www.occ.treas.gov), or the Federal Deposit Insurance Corporation (http://www.fdic.gov).

Other Types Of Information

To find out whether a company has been cleared to sell its securities in a particular state and whether it is in good standing, you can contact the following:

- **Your State Securities Regulator:** Contact the North American Securities Administrators Association (http://www.nasaa.org) to get the name and phone number of your state securities regulator to see if the company has been cleared to sell securities in your state and to find out about the people behind the company.

- **The Secretary Of State Where The Company Is Incorporated:** You can find out whether the company is a corporation in good standing and has filed annual reports with the state through the secretary of state where the company is incorporated. Check the National Association of Secretaries of State's website (http://www.nass.org) for a list of most secretaries of state.

You can find general financial information about companies from the following reference books and commercial databases. The SEC cannot recommend or endorse any particular research firm, its personnel, or its products. But there are a number of resources you may consult:

- *Bloomberg News Service* and *Lexis/Nexis* provide news stories about a company. *Dun & Bradstreet, Moody's, Hoover's Profiles*, and *Standard & Poor's Corporate Profiles* provide financial data about companies. These and other sources are available in many public libraries or law and business school libraries.

Chapter 13

Working With Financial Professionals

Financial Planners

A financial planner typically prepares financial plans for his or her clients. The kinds of services financial planners offer can vary widely. Some financial planners assess every aspect of your financial life—including saving, investments, insurance, taxes, retirement, and estate planning—and help you develop a detailed strategy or financial plan for meeting all your financial goals. Other professionals call themselves financial planners, but they may only be able to recommend that you invest in a narrow range of products and sometimes products that aren't securities.

When hiring a financial planner, you should know exactly what services you need, what services the planner can deliver, and any limitations on what he or she can recommend. In addition, you should understand what services you're paying for, how much those services cost, and how the planner gets paid. Financial planners charge for their services in different ways: some charge either a fixed fee or an hourly fee for the time it takes to develop a financial plan, but don't sell investment products; some are paid by commissions on the products they sell; and others use a combination of fees and commissions.

About This Chapter: This chapter includes excerpts from the following documents produced by the U.S. Securities and Exchange Commission (SEC): "Financial Planners," March 28, 2008, "Investment Advisers: What You Need to Know before Choosing One," August 1, 2007, "How to Pick a Financial Professional," February 1, 2007, and "How to Avoid Problems," January 27, 2006.

Financial planners may come from many different educational and professional backgrounds. If you're considering using a financial planner, be sure to ask about their background. If they have a credential, ask them what it means and what they had to do to earn it.

Some financial planners have credentials like Certified Financial Planner® (CFP) or CFA (Chartered Financial Analyst). Find out what organization issued the credential, and then contact the organization to verify whether the professional you're considering did, in fact, earn the credential and whether the professional remains in good standing with the organization. For a helpful list of various financial industry credentials (including the name of the issuing organization and any education or experience required to attain the credential), please consult the Financial Industry Regulatory Authority (FINRA)'s "Understanding Professional Designations" website (available online at http://apps.finra.org/DataDirectory/1/prodesignations.aspx).

> ✔ **Quick Tip**
>
> If the professional you're considering claims to have a CFP® certification, visit the website of the Certified Financial Planner Board of Standards (http://www.cfp.net). The Board is an independent regulatory organization that licenses financial planners as CFP® professionals. Check to see if the professional is certified as a CFP® professional and whether his or her certification has been suspended or revoked by the Board. You can also call the Board at 800-487-1497 to obtain additional disciplinary information about the professional.
>
> Source: SEC, March 28, 2008.

Questions And Answers About Choosing Investment Advisers

What is an investment adviser?

Investment advisers are in the business of giving advice about securities to clients. For instance, individuals who receive compensation for giving advice on investing in stocks, bonds, or mutual funds, are investment advisers. Some investment advisers manage portfolios of securities.

What is the difference between an investment adviser and a financial planner?

Most financial planners are investment advisers, but not all investment advisers are financial planners. Some financial planners assess every aspect of your financial life—including saving, investments, insurance, taxes, retirement, and estate planning—and help you develop a detailed strategy or financial plan for meeting all your financial goals.

How do investment advisers get paid?

Before you hire any financial professional—whether it's a stockbroker, a financial planner, or an investment adviser—you should always find out and make sure you understand how that person gets paid. Investment advisers generally are paid in any of the following ways:

• A percentage of the value of the assets they manage for you

• An hourly fee for the time they spend working for you

• A fixed fee

• A commission on the securities they sell

• Some combination of the above

Each compensation method has potential benefits and possible drawbacks, depending on your individual needs. Ask the investment advisers you interview to explain the differences to you before you do business with them, and get several opinions before making your decision. Also ask if the fee is negotiable.

How do I find out whether an investment adviser ever had problems with a government regulator or has a disciplinary history?

Most investment advisers must fill out a form called "Form ADV." They must file their Form ADVs with either the SEC or the state securities agency in the state where they have their principal place of business, depending on the amount of assets they manage.

Form ADV consists of two parts. Part 1 contains information about the adviser's education, business, and whether they've had problems with regulators or clients. Part 2 outlines the adviser's services, fees, and strategies. Before you hire someone to be your investment adviser, always ask for, and carefully read, both parts of Form ADV.

You can get copies of Form ADV from the investment adviser, your state securities regulator, or the SEC, depending on the size of the adviser. You can find out how to get in touch with your state securities regulator through the North American Securities Administrators Association, Inc.'s website (http://www.nasaa.org/QuickLinks/ContactYourRegulator.cfm) or by calling 202-737-0900. Ask your state securities regulator whether they've had any complaints about the adviser.

If the SEC registers the investment adviser, you can get the Form ADV by sending an e-mail to the SEC's Office of Investor Education and Advocacy at publicinfo@sec.gov. You also can make a request by sending a fax to 202-777-1027. Please note that you will have to pay a photocopying charge of $0.24 per page, plus tax and postage. In addition, at the SEC's headquarters, you can visit our Public Reference Room from 10:00 a.m. to 3:00 p.m. to obtain copies of SEC records and documents.

How To Pick A Financial Professional

Are you the type of person who will read as much as possible about potential investments and ask questions about them? If so, maybe you don't need investment advice. But if you're busy with other responsibilities or feel you don't know enough about investing on your own, then you may need professional investment advice.

You can get investment advice from most financial institutions that sell investments, including brokerages, banks, mutual funds, and insurance companies. You can also hire a broker, an investment adviser, an accountant, a financial planner, or other professional to help you make investment decisions.

> **✔ Quick Tip**
> Investment professionals offer a variety of services at a variety of prices. It pays to comparison shop.
>
> Source: SEC, February 1, 2007.

Federal or state securities laws require brokers, investment advisers, and their firms to be licensed or registered, and to make important information public. But it's up to you to find that information and use it to protect your investment dollars. The good news is that this information is easy to get, and one phone call or web search may save you from sending your money to a con artist, a bad financial professional, or disreputable firm.

> ✔ **Quick Tip**
> Remember, there is no such thing as a free lunch. Professional financial advisers do not perform their services as an act of charity. If they are working for you, they are getting paid for their efforts. Some of their fees are easier to see immediately than are others. But, in all cases, you should always feel free to ask questions about how and how much your adviser is being paid. And if the fee is quoted to you as a percentage, make sure that you understand what that translates to in dollars.
>
> Source: SEC, February 1, 2007.

Before you invest or pay for any investment advice, make sure your brokers, investment advisers, and investment adviser representatives have not had run-ins with regulators or other investors. You also should check to see whether they are registered or licensed.

This is very important, because if you do business with an unregistered securities broker or a firm that later goes out of business, there may be no way for you to recover your money—even if an arbitrator or court rules in your favor.

Brokers

Brokers make recommendations about specific investments like stocks, bonds, or mutual funds. While taking into account your overall financial goals, brokers generally do not give you a detailed financial plan. Brokers are generally paid commissions when you buy or sell securities through them. If they sell you mutual funds make sure to ask questions about what fees are included in the mutual fund purchase. Brokerages vary widely in the quantity and quality of the services they provide for customers. Some have large research staffs, large national operations, and are prepared to service almost any kind of financial transaction you may need. Others are small and may specialize in promoting investments in unproven and very risky companies. And there's everything else in between.

A discount brokerage charges lower fees and commissions for its services than what you'd pay at a full-service brokerage. But generally you have to research and choose investments by yourself.

A full-service brokerage costs more, but the higher fees and commissions pay for a broker's investment advice based on that firm's research. The best way to choose an investment professional is to start by asking your friends and colleagues who they recommend. Try to get several recommendations, and then meet with potential advisers face-to-face. Make sure you get along. Make sure you understand each other. After all, it's your money. [For more information about selecting a broker and opening a brokerage account, see Chapter 10—Advice For Investing Wisely.]

Ask Questions!

You can never ask a dumb question about your investments and the people

---

✔ Quick Tip

Be aware of the risks involved with buying stocks on margin. Beginning investors generally should not get started with a margin account. Make sure you understand how a margin account works, and what happens in the worst case scenario before you agree to buy on margin.

Unlike other loans, like for a car or a home, that allow you to pay back a fixed amount every month, when you buy stocks on margin you can be faced with paying back the entire margin loan all at once if the price of the stock drops suddenly and dramatically. The firm has the authority to immediately sell any security in your account, without notice to you, to cover any shortfall resulting from a decline in the value of your securities. You may owe a substantial amount of money even after your securities are sold. The margin account agreement generally provides that the securities in your margin account may be lent out by the brokerage firm at any time without notice or compensation to you.

Source: SEC, February 1, 2007.

who help you choose them, especially when it comes to how much you will be paying for any investment, both in upfront costs and ongoing management fees.

To get you started, here are some of the most important questions you should ask when choosing an investment professional or someone to help you:

- What training and experience do you have? How long have you been in business?

- What is your investment philosophy? Do you take a lot of risks or are you more concerned about the safety of my money?

- Describe your typical client. Can you provide me with references, the names of people who have invested with you for a long time?

- How do you get paid? By commission? Based on a percentage of assets you manage? Another method? Do you get paid more for selling your own firm's products?

- How much will it cost me in total to do business with you?

- What experience do you have, especially with people in my circumstances?

- Where did you go to school? What is your recent employment history?

- What licenses do you hold? Are you registered with the SEC, a state, or FINRA?

- Are the firm, the clearing firm, and any other related companies that will do business with me members of the Securities Investor Protection Corporation (SIPC)?

- What products and services do you offer?

- Can you only recommend a limited number of products or services to me? If so, why?

- Have you ever been disciplined by any government regulator for unethical or improper conduct or been sued by a client who was not happy with the work you did?

- For registered investment advisers, will you send me a copy of both parts of your Form ADV?

♣ **It's A Fact!!**

Once you've checked out the registration and record of your financial professional or firm, there's more to do. For example, if you plan to do business with a brokerage firm, you should find out whether the brokerage firm and its clearing firm are members of the Securities Investor Protection Corporation (SIPC). SIPC provides limited customer protection if a brokerage firm becomes insolvent—although it does not insure against losses attributable to a decline in the market value of your securities. If you've placed your cash or securities in the hands of a non-SIPC member, you may not be eligible for SIPC coverage if the firm goes out of business.

Source: SEC, December 6, 2007.

Your investment professional should understand your investment goals and your tolerance for risk. An investment professional has a duty to make sure that he or she only recommends investments that are suitable for you. That is, that the investment makes sense for you based on your other securities holdings, your financial situation, your means, and any other information that your investment professional thinks is important.

The best investment professional is one who fully understands your objectives and matches investment recommendations to your goals. You'll want someone you can understand, because your investment professional should teach you about investing and the investment products.

How Should I Monitor My Investments?

Investing makes it possible for your money to work for you. In a sense, your money has become your employee, and that makes you the boss. You'll want to keep a close watch on how your employee, your money, is doing.

Some people like to look at the stock quotations every day to see how their investments have done. That's probably too often. You may get too caught up in the ups and downs of the "trading" value of your investment, and sell when its value goes down temporarily—even though the performance of the company is still stellar. Remember, you're in for the long haul.

Some people prefer to see how they're doing once a year. That's probably not often enough. What's best for you will most likely be somewhere in between, based on your goals and your investments.

But it's not enough to simply check an investment's performance. You should compare that performance against an index of similar investments over the same period of time to see if you are getting the proper returns for the amount of risk that you are assuming. You should also compare the fees and commissions that you're paying to what other investment professionals charge.

While you should monitor performance regularly, you should pay close attention every time you send your money somewhere else to work.

Every time you buy or sell an investment you will receive a confirmation slip from your broker. Make sure each trade was completed according to your instructions. Make sure the buying or selling price was what your broker quoted. And make sure the commissions or fees are what your broker said they would be.

✔ Quick Tip

Watch out for unauthorized trades in your account. If you get a confirmation slip for a transaction that you didn't approve beforehand, call your broker. It may have been a mistake. If your broker refuses to correct it, put your complaint in writing and send it to the firm's compliance officer. Serious complaints should always be made in writing.

Source: SEC, February 1, 2007.

Remember, too, that if you rely on your investment professional for advice, he or she has an obligation to recommend investments that match your investment goals and tolerance for risk. Your investment professional should not be recommending trades simply to generate commissions. That's called "churning," and it's illegal.

How To Avoid Problems

While most investment professionals are honest and hardworking, you must watch out for those few unscrupulous individuals. They can make your life's savings disappear in an instant.

☞ Remember!!

Brokers And Brokerage Firms

The Central Registration Depository (or CRD) is a computerized database that contains information about most brokers, their representatives, and the firms they work for. You can ask either your state securities regulator (get in touch with your state securities regulator through the North American Securities Administrators Association, Inc.'s website (http://www.nasaa.org/QuickLinks/ContactYourRegulator.cfm) or the Financial Industry Regulatory Authority (http://www.finra.org/Investors/ToolsCalculators/BrokerCheck) to provide you with information from the CRD.

Investment Advisers

People or firms that get paid to give advice about investing in securities generally must register with either the SEC or the state securities agency where they have their principal place of business.

To find out about investment advisers and whether they are properly registered, read their registration forms, called the "Form ADV." The Form ADV has two parts. Part 1 has information about the adviser's business and whether they've had problems with regulators or clients. Part 2 outlines the adviser's services, fees and investment strategies. Before you hire an investment adviser, always ask for and carefully read both parts of the ADV.

Because some investment advisers and their representatives are also brokers, you may want to check both the CRD and Form ADV.

Source: Excerpted from "Protect Your Money: Check Out Brokers and Investment Advisors," SEC, December 6, 2007,

---

Make sure the investment professional and firm are registered with the SEC and licensed to do business in your state. And find out from your state's securities regulator whether the investment professional or her firm have ever been disciplined, or whether they have any complaints against them. You'll find contact information for securities regulators in the U.S. by visiting the website of the North American Securities Administrators Association (NASAA) (http://www.nasaa.org) or by calling 202-737-0900.

You should also find out as much as you can about any investments that your investment professional recommends. First, make sure the investments are registered. Keep in mind, however, the mere fact that a company has registered and files reports with the SEC doesn't guarantee that the company will be a good investment.

Likewise, the fact that a company hasn't registered and doesn't file reports with the SEC doesn't mean the company is a fraud. Still, you may be asking for serious losses if, for instance, you invest in a small, thinly traded company that isn't widely known solely on the basis of what you may have read online. One simple phone call to your state regulator could prevent you from squandering your money on a scam.

What If I Have A Problem?

Sometimes all it takes is a simple phone call to your investment professional to resolve a problem. Maybe there was an honest mistake that can be corrected. If talking to the investment professional doesn't resolve the problem, talk to the firm's manager, and write a letter to confirm your conversation. If that doesn't lead to a resolution, you may have to initiate private legal action. You may need to take action quickly because legal time limits for doing so vary. Your local bar association can provide referrals for attorneys who specialize in securities law. At the same time, call or write to the SEC and let then know what the problem was. Investor complaints are very important to the SEC. You may think you're the only one experiencing a problem, but typically, you're not alone. Sometimes it takes only one investor's complaint to trigger an investigation that exposes a bad broker or an illegal scheme. You can use the SEC's online complaint form to send a complaint electronically. If you do not want to communicate electronically, either print and fill out a form or write then a letter. Their address is: SEC Complaint Center, 100 F Street NE, Washington, DC 20549-0213. You can also send a fax to 202-772-9295.

> ✔ **Quick Tip**
>
> Be wary of promises of quick prof-its, offers to share "inside information," and pressure to invest before you have an opportunity to investigate. These are all warn-ing signs of fraud.
>
> Source: SEC, January 27, 2006.

Chapter 14

Understanding Securities Analyst Recommendations

Introduction

As stock market participation has expanded from Wall Street to Main Street, investment information has exploded as well. TV financial news, business magazines, newspapers, internet websites and chat rooms, corporate filings and news releases, stock analyst reports—there is a din of data for investors to sift through today. Unfortunately, quantity is no guarantee of quality: It has never been harder for small investors to assess which information they should rely upon in making decisions. As a result, some investors have depended too heavily on the one-word recommendations of just a few analysts—not understanding the particular context in which such recommendations often are generated, and the particular ways in which they often must be read.

Strengthening that understanding is the purpose of this information. Analysts play a useful role in our capital markets, but investors should understand that role. For example, by doing in-depth research for their large institutional clients and employers, analysts can help substantial sums of capital be directed

About This Chapter: "FINRA Guide to Understanding Securities Analyst Recommendations," © 2008 Financial Industry Regulatory Authority, Inc. (FINRA). Reprinted with permission from FINRA.

to more productive uses in our economy. This chapter explains what analysts do and places it in perspective, so investors can learn what other information they need for managing their portfolios.

♣ It's A Fact!!

This chapter covers two basic types of issues. The first stems from the fact that analysts' ratings today do not have clear, standardized meanings. The second relates to the potential conflicts of interest that you, as an investor, should be aware of in assessing the usefulness to you of any particular analyst recommendation.

Same Word, Different Meanings

Analysts usually summarize their research reports with a brief recommendation. Every firm uses its own rating system. Table 14.1 shows examples from three firms.

As you can see, comparing these ratings scales is not easy. The same term might mean one thing for one firm and something else for another firm. For example, as you can see in the Table, Firm A rates its most positive recommendations as "Buy," but Firm B does not. When Firm B uses a "Buy," it means that Firm B likes the stock, but not as much as the stocks that it rates "Strong Buy." Likewise, one firm's "Underperform" might mean that it expects a stock to appreciate 10% slower than the overall market over an 18-month period. For another firm, the same term "Underperform" might mean that it expects the stock to drop 5% within a 12-month period. Clear "Sell" ratings have grown rare. Some firms no longer even use "Sell" or any word obviously like it. Frequently, a "Hold" rating in effect means "Sell."

Even providers of so-called "consensus" ratings, such as I/B/E/S [Institutional Broker's Estimate System] and First Call, use their own rating scales. These organizations apply numerical formulas to map several analysts' different ratings scales to their own rating conventions. They then average their standardized recommendations to create a "consensus" rating for a particular security.

For all these reasons, be careful about what you assume whenever you invest or even consider changes in your portfolio. Keep in mind:

- Is it right for YOU? A "Buy" rating does not mean that every investor should acquire the stock; nor does a "Sell" rating mean that every investor should immediately sell it. Your own financial situation and investment needs are what matter. If you consider any individual rating, do not view it in absolute or abstract terms, but in the context of your own unique financial situation.

- Never rely on a rating alone. Do your investment homework. When considering an analyst recommendation, look at the full research report, not just the one-word rating. The full report will often provide information that is essential to explain risk factors or to put the recommendation into its proper perspective.

- Analysts differ in quality. As in any other field, not every analyst can be the best. To learn about different analysts' track records, you can either follow their recommendations over time, or refer to rankings that are found in certain investor-oriented magazines, newsletters, and internet websites. (One written source of analyst rankings is found in *Institutional Investor* magazine, while two web-based sources of such

Table 14.1. Analyst Meanings

Firm A	Firm B	Firm C
Buy	Strong Buy	Recommended List
Outperform	Buy	Trading Buy
Neutral	Hold	Market Outperformer
Underperform	Sell	Market Perform
Avoid		Market Underperformer

rankings may be found at www.zacks.com and www.validea.com. The Financial Industry Regulatory Authority [FINRA] does not endorse these or any other specific sources of analyst rankings.)

Conflicts Of Interest

Research analysts study companies and draw on a wealth of industry, economic, and business trend information to help their clients make better investment decisions. Retail investors may believe that most analysts work for them—that their primary obligation is to the investing public. But in fact, the full story is much more complicated.

Some analysts are unaffiliated: they sell their independent research to financial or investing institutions, banks, insurance companies, or private investors on a project or subscription basis. But a large number of analysts are employed by institutions whose financial stake in their recommendations may go well beyond their accuracy.

> **✔ Quick Tip**
>
> If you have questions or would like additional information regarding analyst recommendations, please call, e-mail, or write the Financial Industry Regulatory Authority (FINRA) at:
>
> 1735 K Street
> Washington, DC 20006
> Phone: 301-590-6500
> Website: http://www.finra.org

For example, many analysts work for large financial firms that underwrite securities. An underwriter acts as an intermediary between the company publicly offering securities and investors buying the new stock. Even after the initial public offering, or IPO, it may have an ongoing relationship with the company or own a significant amount of the company's stock. And it will often stand to benefit from analyst recommendations that would tend to support the price of or encourage trading in that security.

Other analysts work for institutional money managers, such as mutual funds, hedge funds, or investment advisers. They may provide research and advice for institutional clients whose investment decisions can differ significantly from those faced by ordinary investors. A mutual fund that relied on its analyst's earlier positive recommendation in acquiring the stock of a company might be harmed by any revised recommendation that would tend to lower the market value of the security.

Just by thinking about these kinds of employment arrangements, you can begin to imagine the kinds of conflicts that analysts may face as they develop and offer their opinions in research reports. For example:

- **Investment Banking Relationships:** Providing investment banking services, such as underwriting an IPO or advising on a merger or acquisition, can be a lucrative source of revenue for an analyst's firm. Thus, the analyst may feel an incentive not to say or write things that could jeopardize existing or potential client relationships for their investment banking colleagues. On the other hand, the analyst may also be more knowledgeable or diligent in his research because his firm did the underwriting.

- **Analyst Compensation:** Brokerage firms' compensation arrangements can put pressure on analysts to issue positive research reports and recommendations. For example, many analysts are paid at least partly and indirectly on the basis of their firms' underwriting profits. So they may be reluctant to make recommendations that could reduce such profits, and hence their own compensation.

- **Brokerage Commissions:** An analyst's report can help firms make money indirectly by generating more buying and selling of covered securities—which, in turn, result in additional commissions for the firm.

- **Buy-Side Pressures:** A mutual fund with large holdings in a stock has little desire to see an analyst put out a "Sell" recommendation on that security and possibly contribute to a sharp decline in its price. Hence the proliferation of euphemistic ratings—such as "Hold," "Retain," and "Market Perform"—which small investors may take at face value, but which professional and institutional investors know are often tantamount to "Sell." As a result, ratings inflation became as widespread and unhealthy in our markets as grade inflation in our schools.

- **Ownership Interests In The Company:** An analyst, other employees, and the firm itself may own significant positions in the companies or market sectors on which the analyst conducts research and makes recommendations. The analyst may own such shares directly, or through employee stock-purchase pools.

These economic realities certainly do not mean that analysts are corrupt or even biased. But because analysts are called upon to make so many judgments that are not black and white, any of the above factors can put pressure on their objectivity—no matter how honest or competent they may be. So you should bear these realities in mind before making an investment decision.

Making Your Investment Decision

The fact that analysts or their firms may have conflicts of interest does not mean that their recommendations are without value. Often research reports will contain quantifiable measures—such as earnings predictions or comparisons to other companies in an industry sector—that you may decide provide useful insight even if you do not take the analyst's rating at face value. In any case, you should take all potential conflicts into consideration in assessing how much weight you should give the recommendation.

The important thing to remember is that you should never rely solely on an analyst recommendation when making an investment decision. There are many other important sources of information and factors you may wish to consider. For example:

- Research the company's reports yourself, using the SEC's EDGAR (Electronic Data Gathering, Analysis, and Retrieval) database at www.sec.gov/edgar.shtml. If you do not have access to the internet, call the company for copies. If you can't analyze them on your own, ask your broker or another trusted financial professional for help.

- Speak with your broker or financial adviser and ask questions about the company and its prospects. When doing so, ask your broker about the relationship of his own firm, if any, to the company whose stock you are considering.

- Learn about the company by consulting independent news reports, commercial databases, and other references.

- Find out whether the analyst's firm underwrote one of the company's recent stock offerings—especially its initial public offering (IPO).

- Find out more about analyst recommendations by consulting your broker or some of the other sources discussed in this chapter.

In short, whatever a given analyst recommendation may say, always consider whether a particular investment is right for you in light of your own financial circumstances. Remember, you are the boss, it's your money, and your situation and goals that matter.

Remember!!

In considering how to assess analyst recommendations, it may help to consider that truly good, free investment advice is about as easy to get as a truly good, free lunch. If it's free to you, it was probably designed with someone else's interests in mind. If you want it tailored to fit your situation and interests, chances are, you'll have to pay for it.

One handy way to summarize much of the advice in this chapter is to remember, "Before you invest, investigate" (Securities Industry Association, Best Practices for Research). This may seem like just a slogan, but in fact, it is sound advice. Because there is no substitute for investors who know how to look behind analyst recommendations—as well as brokers who will work to help them do so.

Chapter 15

How To Avoid The Most Common Investment Scams

How To Avoid Fraud

Scam artists don't care whether you worked hard all your life to earn your money or whether you hit the lottery the first time you played. It is your money they want. The only thing that may stand between a fraudster and your money is your preparedness when you are approached.

Fraudsters rely on the sad truth that many people simply don't bother to investigate before they invest. It's not enough to ask a promoter for more information or for references—fraudsters have no incentive to set you straight. Savvy investors take the time to do their own independent research.

Research Before Investing: You'll want to fully understand the company's business and its products or services before investing. Before buying any stock,

About This Chapter: This chapter includes excerpts from the following documents produced by the U.S. Securities and Exchange Commission (SEC): "How to Avoid Fraud," April 11, 2005; "Oil and Gas Scams: Common Red Flags and Steps You Can Take to Protect Yourself," August 1, 2007; and "Pump&Dump.con: Tips for Avoiding Stock Scams on the Internet," January 11, 2005. Excerpts from the following documents produced by the Federal Trade Commission (FTC) are also included: "Hang up on Cross-Border Phone Fraud," May 2002; and "Putting Telephone Scams ... on Hold," November 2007. Additional information under the heading "Advance Fee Fraud (4-1-9 Fraud)" is excerpted from "Frequently Asked Questions," U.S. Secret Service, 2008.

check out the company's financial statements (see Chapter 12 for more information). All but the smallest public companies have to file financial statements with the U.S. Securities and Exchange Commission (SEC). If the company doesn't file with the SEC, you'll have to do a great deal of work on your own to make sure the company is legitimate and the investment appropriate for you. That's because the lack of reliable, readily available information

---

♣ It's A Fact!!

Here are some red flags warnings of fraud:

- If it sounds too good to be true, it is. Compare promised yields with current returns on well-known stock indexes. Any investment opportunity that claims you'll get substantially more could be highly risky. And that means you might lose money.

- "Guaranteed returns" aren't. Every investment carries some degree of risk, and the level of risk typically correlates with the return you can expect to receive. Low risk generally means low yields, and high yields typically involve high risk. If your money is perfectly safe, you'll most likely get a low return. High returns represent potential rewards for folks who are willing and financially able to take big risks. Most fraudsters spend a lot of time trying to convince investors that extremely high returns are "guaranteed" or "can't miss." Don't believe it.

- Beauty isn't everything. Don't be fooled by a pretty website—they are remarkably easy to create.

- Pressure to send money RIGHT NOW. Scam artists often tell their victims that this is a once-in-a-lifetime offer, and it will be gone tomorrow. But resist the pressure to invest quickly, and take the time you need to investigate before sending money. If it is that good an opportunity, it will wait.

- Con artists are experts at gaining your confidence. So be certain to treat all unsolicited investment opportunities with extreme caution. Whether you hear about the opportunity through an e-mail, phone call, or a fax, be certain to check out both the person and firm making the offer and the investment they are pushing.

Source: SEC, April 2005.

about company finances can open the door to fraud. Remember that unsolicited e-mails, message board postings, and company news releases should
never be used as the sole basis for your investment decisions.

Know The Salesperson: Spend some time checking out the person touting
the investment before you invest—even if you already know the person so-
cially. Always find out whether the securities salespeople who contact you
are licensed to sell securities in your state and whether they or their firms
have had run-ins with regulators or other investors [see Chapter 13—Working
With Financial Professionals for more information].

Be Wary Of Unsolicited Offers: Be especially careful if you receive an
unsolicited fax or e-mail about a company—or see it praised on an internet
bulletin board—but can find no current financial information about the company from other independent sources. Many fraudsters use e-mail, faxes, and
internet postings to tout thinly traded stocks, in the hopes of creating a buying frenzy that will push the share price up so that they can sell their shares.
Once they dump their stock and quit promoting the company, the share
price quickly falls. And be extra wary if someone you don't know and trust
recommends foreign or "off-shore" investments. When you send your money
abroad, and something goes wrong, it's more difficult to find out what hap-
pened and to locate your money.

Oil And Gas Scams

If you think you've found the right oil or gas investment to strike it rich,
consider this: it may be a scam. While some oil and gas investment opportunities are legitimate, many oil and gas ventures are frauds. Many of these
schemes start in so-called boiler rooms, where skilled telemarketers use high
pressure sales tactics to convince you to hand over your hard-earned money.

Once they have your money, scam artists pay themselves first, often using
funds to pay personal expenses. In the end, only some of your money may be
invested in an actual oil or natural gas well, or none at all.

Here are some steps you can take to avoid being scammed:

• Ask questions and check out the answers. Savvy investors take the
  time to do their own independent research.

- Contact state oil and gas regulatory agencies. You may be able to verify information provided in offering materials by contacting the oil and gas regulatory agency in which the wells are allegedly being drilled. For example, these agencies generally have information about a company's drilling history that could confirm claims of prior success.

- Research the company before you invest. Remember that unsolicited materials should never be used as the sole basis for an investment decision.

Pump And Dump Schemes

One of the most common internet frauds involves the classic "pump and dump" scheme. Here's how it works: A company's website may feature a glowing press release about its financial health or some new product or innovation. Newsletters that purport to offer unbiased recommendations may suddenly tout the company as the latest hot stock. Messages in chat rooms and bulletin board postings may urge you to buy the stock quickly or to sell before the price goes down. Or you may even hear the company mentioned by a radio or TV analyst.

Unwitting investors then purchase the stock in droves, creating high demand and pumping up the price. But when the fraudsters behind the scheme sell their shares at the peak and stop hyping the stock, the price plummets, and investors lose their money.

✔ Quick Tip
When you see an offer on the internet, assume it is a scam, until you can prove through your own research that it is legitimate. And remember that the people touting the stock may well be insiders of the company or paid promoters who stand to profit handsomely if you trade.

Source: SEC, January 11, 2005.

Fraudsters frequently use this ploy with small, thinly traded companies because it's easier to manipulate a stock when there's little or no information available about the company. To steer clear of potential scams, always investigate before you invest.

> ### 🖝 Remember!!
>
> Investor enthusiasm for the internet has created tremendous financial op-
> portunities in recent years—for stock market fraudsters! That's because they
> often use the internet to lure innocent investors into their scams. But you can
> survive stock market fraud and avoid becoming a victim if you follow these
> steps before you invest:
>
> * Be skeptical
>
> * Consider the source
>
> * Independently verify claims
>
> * Beware of high pressure pitches
>
> * Research the company
>
> * Confirm registration with the SEC's EDGAR database or your state
>   securities regulator
>
> Source: From "Investor Alert: Stock Market Fraud 'Survivor' Checklist," U.S.
> Securities and Exchange Commission (SEC), March 1, 2001.

Cross-Border Phone Fraud

Cross-border telemarketing fraud is a serious problem—and it appears to
be growing. U.S. and Canadian consumers lose billions of dollars a year to
telemarketers who pitch bogus products, services, and investments.

Phony Prize Promotions And Sweepstakes Schemes

Often telemarketers, including those operating across national borders,
"guarantee" that you've won valuable prizes, such as vacations, automobiles,
or large sums of cash, but want you to pay fees for shipping, taxes, customs,
or other non-existent expenses. Beware of anyone who asks you to pay to
claim a prize or free gift. You may not receive anything at all, or you may get
a cheap gift that is worth far less than the fees that you have paid.

Some sweepstakes scams draw you in by claiming that you're a winner.
Then they tell you that your chance of getting better prizes will grow if you

✔ **Quick Tip**

If you receive an unsolicited call
telling you that "You're a winner," remember:

• Don't pay for a free prize or gift. Free is free.

• Don't share your credit card and bank account numbers. Scam artists often ask for them during an unsolicited sales pitch, and then use them to commit other frauds against you.

• If you are approached to pay money to recover funds that you are owed, independently contact the appropriate government agency to check out those claims.

Source: FTC, 2002.

first pay entitlement fees to qualify for larger winnings. You may even receive a small item as an inducement to get you to send even more money.

Some rip-off artists target consumers who have previously lost money to illegal foreign sweepstakes schemes. They tell the victims that the government has won a lawsuit against the company that originally scammed them. The victims are told that they need to first pay legal fees or taxes to the government in order to regain their money.

International Lottery Scams

"Congratulations! You may receive a certified check for up to $400,000 U.S. CASH! One Lump sum! Tax free! Your odds to WIN are 1-6."

Hang onto your wallet. It's a fraud. Scam operators are using the telephone and direct mail to entice consumers to buy chances in high-stakes foreign lotteries from as far away as Australia and Europe.

Most promotions for foreign lotteries are likely to be phony. Many scam operators don't even buy the promised lottery tickets. Others buy some tickets but keep the "winnings" for themselves. In addition, lottery hustlers use victims' bank account numbers to make unauthorized withdrawals or their credit card numbers to run up additional charges.

U.S. federal law enforcement authorities are intercepting and destroying millions of foreign lottery offers before they reach consumers.

Ignore all mail and phone solicitations for foreign lottery promotions. If you get what looks like lottery material from a foreign country, turn it over to your local postmaster in the U.S. or to the Competition Bureau in Canada.

By responding to just one foreign lottery offer, you've opened the door to many more bogus offers for lottery or investment "opportunities." Your name will be added to "sucker lists" that fraudulent telemarketers buy and sell.

In both the U.S. and Canada, it's illegal to play a foreign lottery—through the mail or on the telephone or internet. Don't add insult to injury by inviting federal charges.

Putting Telephone Scams... On Hold

Telemarketing fraud is a multi-billion dollar business in the United States. Every year, thousands of consumers lose as little as a few dollars to as much as their life savings to telephone con artists.

That's why the Federal Trade Commission (FTC) encourages you to be skeptical when you hear a phone solicitation and to be aware of the

♣ It's A Fact!!

People lose millions of dollars each year to "get rich quick" schemes that promise high returns with little or no risk. These can include movies or cable television production deals, internet gambling, rare coins, art, or other "investment opportunities." The schemes vary, but one thing is consistent: Unscrupulous promoters of investment fraud rely on the fact that investing may be complicated, and many people don't research the investment process.

Source: FTC, 2007.

♣ **It's A Fact!!**

Chain Letters

Everybody's received them—chain letters or e-mail messages that promise a big return on a small investment. The promises include unprecedented good luck, mountains of recipes, or worse, huge financial rewards for sending as little as $5 to someone on a list or making a telephone call.

Whether you receive a chain letter by regular mail or e-mail—especially one that involves money—the Federal Trade Commission (FTC) reminds you that:

- Chain letters that involve money or valuable items and promise big returns are illegal. If you start one or send one on, you are breaking the law.

- Chances are you will receive little or no money back on your "investment." Despite the claims, a chain letter will never make you rich.

- Some chain letters try to win your confidence by claiming that they're legal, and even that they're endorsed by the government. Nothing is further from the truth.

- If you've been a target of a chain e-mail scam, contact your internet service provider and forward the e-mail to the FTC at spam@uce.gov.

- The U.S. Postal Inspection Service offers information about chain letters at www.usps.gov/websites/depart/inspect . Or you can call the Postal Inspection Service toll-free, 888-877-7644

Source: From "The Lowdown on Chain Letters," Federal Trade Commission (FTC), February 2008.

Telemarketing Sales Rule, a law that can help you protect yourself from abusive and deceptive telemarketers.

Unlike most other crimes, telemarketing fraud requires one essential element: victim participation. We're all potential targets, because fraud isn't limited by race, ethnic background, gender, age, education or income. The best way to protect yourself is to know the differences between legitimate offers and fraudulent ones.

Often it's hard to know whether a sales call is legitimate. Telephone con artists are skilled at sounding believable—even when they're really telling lies. Sometimes telephone con artists reach you when you're feeling lonely. They may call day after day—until you think a friend, not a stranger, is trying to sell you something. Some telephone salespeople have an answer for everything. You may find it hard to get them off the phone—even if they're selling something you're not interested in—because you don't want to be rude.

You may be promised free gifts, prizes, or vacations—or the "investment of a lifetime"—but only if you act "right away." It may sound like a really good deal. In fact, telephone con artists are only after your money. Don't give it to them.

Advance Fee Fraud (4-1-9 Fraud)

The perpetrators of advance fee fraud, known internationally as "4-1-9 fraud" (after the section of the Nigerian penal code which addresses these schemes), are often very creative and innovative. A large number of victims are enticed into believing they have been singled out from the masses to share in multi-million dollar windfall profits for no apparent reason.

If you ever receive an e-mail or fax from someone you do not know requesting your assistance in a financial transaction, such as the transfer of a large sum of money into an account, or claiming you are the next of kin to an

✔ **Quick Tip**

If you have suffered a significant financial loss related to advance fee fraud, please contact your local Secret Service field office. Telephone numbers are available in the Field Office Directory on this website or may also be found on the inside cover of your local telephone directory. Any investigation regarding this type of fraud will be conducted on a case by case basis at the discretion of the local Secret Service and U.S. Attorney's Office.

Source: U.S. Secret Service, 2008.

✔ Quick Tip
How can I protect myself against telemarketing fraud?

- Don't allow yourself to be pushed into a hurried decision.

- Always request written information, by mail, about the product, service, investment or charity and about the organization that's offering it.

- Don't make any investment or purchase you don't fully understand.

- Ask with what state or federal agencies the firm is registered.

- Check out the company or organization.

- If an investment or major purchase is involved, request that information also be sent to your accountant, financial adviser, banker, or attorney for evaluation and an opinion.

- Ask what recourse you would have if you make a purchase and aren't satisfied.

- Beware of testimonials that you may have no way of verifying.

- Never provide personal financial information over the phone unless you are absolutely certain the caller has a bona fide need to know.

- If necessary, hang up the phone.

Source: Excerpted from "Frequently Asked Questions," U.S. Secret Service, 2008.

wealthy person who has died, or the winner of some obscure lottery, DO NOT respond. These requests are typically sent through public servers via a generic (spammed) e-mail message. Usually, the sender does not yet know your personal e-mail address and is depending on you to respond. Once you reply, whether you intend to string them along or tell them you are not interested, they will often continue to e-mail you in an attempt to harass or intimidate you. If you receive an unsolicited e-mail of this nature, the best course is to simply delete the message.

Chapter 16

Beware Of Online Perils And Internet Fraud

Get The Facts About Online Investing

Faster internet connections along with the ubiquity of personal computers allow an increasing number of investors to manage their finances online, at virtually any hour of the day or night. While online trading can be a "hands-on" learning experience for investors, it may not be appropriate for everyone. Whether you manage your investments on your own via the internet or by working in person with a broker or investment adviser, it is essential that you know what types of securities you are purchasing, how they meet your investment goals, and the risks associated with each investment.

Tips For Online Investors

The following tips were developed by the North American Securities Administrators Association, Inc. to educate investors and to help them think carefully about online investing.

About This Chapter: This chapter begins with "Get the Facts about Online Investing," © 2008 North American Securities Administrators Association (www.nasaa.org). Reprinted with permission. Additional information is excerpted from the following documents produced by the U.S. Securities and Exchange Commission: "Tips for Online Investing," August 1, 2007; "Online Brokerage Accounts: What You Can Do to Safeguard Your Money and Your Personal Information," November 3, 2005; and "Internet Fraud: How to Avoid Internet Investment Scams," August 6, 2007.

Before beginning an online investment program, be sure to:

- Understand that most likely you are not linked directly to the market through your home computer, and that the click of your mouse does not instantly execute trades or cancel orders.

- Determine if the stock quotes and account updates you receive are real-time or delayed.

- Check the online broker's ability to get the best price for investors. Most brokerage firms provide this information on their website.

- Receive information from the firm to substantiate any advertised claims concerning the ease and speed of online trading.

- Obtain information about entering and canceling orders (market, limit, and stop loss), and the details and risks of margin accounts (borrowing to buy stocks).

- Get information from the firm about significant website outages, delays, and other interruptions that may affect your ability to execute trades. Make sure that the firm has an alternative way to execute trades.

- Review the firm's privacy and security policies. Determine if your name will be used for mailing lists or other promotional activities by the firm or any other party.

♣ It's A Fact!!
Online Trading And The Long-Term Investor

Investors can trade securities online as part of a long-term investment plan. Some investors research securities and then place trades without any professional guidance. Other investors use the internet to self-manage a few of their investments and then consult a broker or investment adviser for help in managing the rest of their portfolio.

Online Trading And The Short-Term Trader

Some investors use the internet to trade frequently with the hope of profiting from a rapidly changing market. Although the possibility of quick profits may be alluring, this strategy is risky. Market volatility, inaccurate information about anticipated changes in stock prices, and delays in the execution of online trades may lead to financial losses.

Source: © 2008 North American Securities Administrators Association.

- Receive clear information about sales commissions, transaction fees, and conditions that apply to any advertised discount on commissions.

- Know how to contact a customer service representative if problems occur. Request prompt attention and fair consideration. Be sure to keep good records to substantiate any problems that may occur.

- Contact your local securities division (http://www.nasaa.org/ QuickLinks/ContactYourRegulator.cfm) to verify the registration status and disciplinary history (if any) of the online brokerage firm, or to file a complaint, if appropriate.

Tips For Online Investing: What You Need To Know About Trading In Fast-Moving Markets

The price of some stocks can soar and drop suddenly. In these fast markets when many investors want to trade at the same time and prices change quickly, delays can develop across the board. Executions and confirmations slow down, while reports of prices lag behind actual prices. In these markets, investors can suffer unexpected losses very quickly.

Investors trading over the internet or online, who are used to instant access to their accounts and near instantaneous executions of their trades, especially need to understand how they can protect themselves in fast-moving markets.

You can limit your losses in fast-moving markets if you know what you are buying and the risks of your investment, and know how trading changes during fast markets and take additional steps to guard against the typical problems investors face in these markets.

Online trading is quick and easy; online investing takes time. Although online trading saves investors time and money, it does not take the homework out of making investment decisions. You may be able to make a trade in a nanosecond, but making wise investment decisions takes time. Before you trade, know why you are buying or selling, and the risk of your investment.

Set your price limits on fast-moving stock. To avoid buying or selling a stock at a price higher or lower than you wanted, you need to place a limit order rather than a market order. A limit order is an order to buy or sell a security at a specific price. A buy limit order can only be executed at the limit price or lower, and a sell limit order can only be executed at the limit price or higher. When you place a market order, you can't control the price at which your order will be filled.

Online trading is not always instantaneous. Investors may find that technological choke points can slow or prevent their orders from reaching an online firm causing a delay or failure in an investor's attempt to access an online firm's automated trading system.

If you place an order, don't assume it didn't go through. And, if you cancel an order, make sure the cancellation worked before placing another trade. Talk with your firm about how you should handle a situation where you are unsure if your original order was executed. When you cancel an online trade, it is important to make sure that your original transaction was not executed. Although you may receive an electronic receipt for the cancellation, don't assume that that means the trade was canceled. Or-

> **✔ Quick Tip**
> **Know Your Options**
> **For Placing A Trade**
>
> Most online trading firms offer alternatives for placing trades. These alternatives may include touch-tone telephone trades, faxing your order, or doing it the low-tech way—talking to a broker over the phone. Make sure you know whether using these different options may increase your costs. And remember, if you experience delays getting online, you may experience similar delays when you turn to one of these alternatives.
>
> Source: SEC, August 1, 2007.

ders can only be canceled if they have not been executed. Ask your firm about how you should check to see if a cancellation order actually worked.

If you purchase a security in a cash account, you must pay for it before you can sell it. If you buy and sell a stock before paying for it, you are freeriding, which violates the credit extension provisions of the Federal Reserve Board.

If you trade on margin, your broker can sell your securities without giving you a margin call. Now is the time to reread your margin agreement and pay attention to the fine print. If your account has fallen below the firm's maintenance margin requirement, your broker has the legal right to sell your securities at any time without consulting you first. Some investors have been rudely surprised that "margin calls" are a courtesy, not a requirement. Brokers are not required to make margin calls to their customers.

No regulations require a trade to be executed within a certain time. But if firms advertise their speed of execution, SEC regulations state that they must not exaggerate or fail to tell investors about the possibility of significant delays.

Online Brokerage Accounts: What You Can Do To Safeguard Your Money And Your Personal Information

Like many investors, you may enjoy some of the conveniences of an online brokerage account, like checking your brokerage account information at any time of day or night, buying and selling securities, or even transferring money between your brokerage account and another account. But if you don't take steps to protect your personal information when you go online, you could be telling your own story of identity theft.

How Online Identity Theft Can Happen

Many identity thieves use malicious software programs to attack vulnerable computers of online users. These software programs can monitor your computer activity and send information back to the thief's computer. Sometimes, these programs will log your key strokes, which allows identity thieves to easily obtain username and password information for any of your online accounts, including your brokerage account.

Other identity thieves "phish" for your personal information. "Phishing" involves the use of fraudulent e-mails and copy-cat websites to trick you into revealing valuable personal information—such as your account number, your social security number, and the username and password information you use when accessing your account. Sometimes fraudsters will use phishing scams

♣ It's A Fact!!

What To Do If You Have A Complaint

Act promptly. By law, you only have a limited time to take legal action. Follow these steps to solve your problem:

1. Talk to your broker or online firm and ask for an explanation. Take notes of the answers you receive.

2. If you are dissatisfied with the response and believe that you have been treated unfairly, ask to talk with the broker's branch manager. In the case of an online firm, go directly to step number three.

3. If you are still dissatisfied, write to the compliance department at the firm's main office. Explain your problem clearly, and tell the firm how you want it resolved. Ask the compliance office to respond to you in writing within 30 days.

4. If you're still dissatisfied, then send a letter of complaint to the National Association of Securities Dealers, your state securities administrator, or to the Office of Investor Education and Advocacy at the Securities and Exchange Commission (SEC) along with copies of the letters you've sent already to the firm.

Source: SEC, August 1, 2007.

to try to get you to download keystroke logging or other malicious software programs unsuspectingly.

But not all identity thieves have gone "high tech." Many still use less sophisticated ways of stealing your personal information, such as looking over your shoulder when you're typing sensitive information or searching through your trash for confidential account information.

How To Protect Yourself Online

You'll need to protect yourself against identity thieves, whether hackers, phishers, or snoops, when you use your online brokerage account. Here are a few suggestions on ways to keep your personal information and money more secure when you go online:

- **Beef Up Your Security:** Personal firewalls and security software packages (with anti-virus, anti-spam, and spyware detection features) are a must-have for those who engage in online financial transactions. Make sure your computer has the latest security patches, and make sure that you access your online brokerage account only on a secure web page using encryption. The website address of a secure website connection starts with "https" instead of just "http" and has a key or closed padlock in the status bar (which typically appears in the lower right-hand corner of your screen).

- **Use A Security Token** (if available): Using a security token can make it even harder for an identity thief to access your online brokerage account. That's because these small number-generating devices offer a second layer of security—a one-time pass-code that typically changes every 30 or 60 seconds. These unpredictable pass-codes can frustrate identity thieves. While fraudsters can use keystroke logging programs to obtain regular username and password information, they can't use these programs to obtain the security token pass-code. Ask your brokerage firm if you can protect your online account with a security token or similar security device.

- **Be Careful What You Download:** When you download a program or file from an unknown source, you risk loading malicious software programs on your computer. Fraudsters often hide these programs within seemingly benign applications. Think twice before you click on a pop-up advertisement or download a "free" game or gadget.

✔ Quick Tip

Security Tip: Even if a web page starts with "https" and contains a key or closed padlock, it's still possible that it may not be secure. Some phishers, for example, make spoofed websites which appear to have padlocks. To double-check, click on the padlock icon on the status bar to see the security certificate for the site. Following the "Issued to" in the pop-up window you should see the name matching the site you think you're on. If the name differs, you are probably on a spoofed site.

Source: SEC, November 3, 2005.

• **Use Your Own Computer:** It's generally safer to access your online brokerage account from your own computer than from other computers. If you use a computer other than your own, for example, you won't know if it contains viruses or spyware. If you do use another computer, be sure to delete all of the your "Temporary Internet Files" and clear all of your "History" after you log off your account.

> ✔ **Quick Tip**
>
> **Security Tip:** Even though a web address in an e-mail may look legitimate, fraudsters can mask the true destination. Rather than merely clicking on a link provided in an e-mail, type the web address into your browser yourself (or use a bookmark you previously created).
>
> Source: SEC, November 3, 2005.

• **Don't Respond To E-Mails Requesting Personal Information:** Legitimate entities will not ask you to provide or verify sensitive information through a non-secure means, such as e-mail. If you have reason to believe that your financial institution actually does need personal information from you, pick up the phone and call the company yourself—using the number in your rolodex, not the one the e-mail provides!

• **Be Smart About Your Password:** The best passwords are ones that are difficult to guess. Try using a password that consists of a combination of numbers, letters (both upper case and lower case), punctuation, and special characters. You should change your password regularly and use a different password for each of your accounts. Don't share your password with others and never reply to "phishing" e-mails with your password or other sensitive information. You also shouldn't store your password on your computer. If you need to write down your password, store it in a secure, private place.

• **Use Extra Caution With Wireless Connections:** Wireless networks may not provide as much security as wired internet connections. In fact, many "hotspots"—wireless networks in public areas like airports, hotels and restaurants—reduce their security so it's easier for individuals to access and use these wireless networks. Unless you use a security token, you may decide that accessing your online brokerage account through a wireless connection isn't worth the security risk. You can learn more about security issues relating to wireless networks on the website of the Wi-Fi Alliance (http://www.wi-fi.org).

- **Log Out Completely:** Closing or minimizing your browser or typing in a new web address when you're done using your online account may not be enough to prevent others from gaining access to your account information. Instead, click on the "log out" button to terminate your online session. In addition, you shouldn't permit your browser to "remember"

✔ Quick Tip
Protect Your Passwords

Keep your passwords in a secure place, out of plain view, and avoid storing them on your computer. Don't share your passwords on the internet, over e-mail, or on the phone. Your internet service provider (ISP) should never ask for your password. And if you access your accounts in a public place, be sure to position yourself so that no one can see your hands or your screen as you type your PIN or password.

In addition, hackers may try to figure out your passwords to gain access to your computer. You can make it tougher for them by doing the following:

- Using passwords that have at least eight characters and include numbers or symbols. The longer your password is, the tougher it is for a hacker to discover it.

- Avoiding common words: some hackers use programs that can try every word in the dictionary.

- Not using your personal information, your login name, or adjacent keys on the keyboard as passwords.

- Changing your passwords regularly (at a minimum, every 90 days).

- Not using the same password for each online account you access.

Source: Excerpted from "Investing Wisely Online," OnGuard Online (http://onguardonline.gov), September 2006.

your username and password information. If this browser feature is active, anyone using your computer will have access to your brokerage account information.

How To Know If Your Identity Has Been Stolen

Sometimes, it can be extraordinarily difficult to determine whether someone has stolen your identity. If you take the steps below, you may be able to find out whether you've been victim of identity theft and protect yourself from further harm:

- **Read Your Statements:** Read them thoroughly as soon as they arrive to make sure that all transactions shown are ones that you actually made, and check to see whether all of the transactions that you thought you made appear as well. If you see a mistake on your statement or don't receive a statement, contact your brokerage firm immediately.

- **Monitor Your Credit Report:** You can obtain a free credit report every 12 months from three different credit bureaus by contacting the Annual Credit Report Request Service (available online at https://www.annualcreditreport.com).

What To Do If You Run Into Trouble

Always act quickly when you come face to face with a potential fraud, especially if you've lost money or believe your identity has been stolen.

- **Identity Theft:** If you think that your personal information has been stolen, visit the Federal Trade Commission's Identity Theft Resource Center at www.consumer.gov/idtheft/index.html for information on how to file a complaint and control the damage.

- **Securities Scams:** Before you do business with any investment-related firm or individual, do your own independent research to check out their background and confirm whether they are legitimate. Report investment-related scams to the SEC using our online Complaint Center (available online at http://www.sec.gov/complaint.shtml).

- **Phishy E-Mails:** If a phishing scam rolls into your e-mail box, be sure to tell the company right away. You can also report the scam to the

FBI's Internet Fraud Complaint Center at http://www.ifccfbi.gov. If the e-mail purports to come from a brokerage firm or mutual fund company, be sure to pass along that tip to the SEC's Enforcement Division by forwarding the e-mail to enforcement@sec.gov.

✔ Quick Tip

Investor Tip: Read your brokerage account agreement carefully because many firms take the position that you are responsible for the security of your account information, such as your username, password, and account number. In addition, your brokerage account agreement may provide information about what specific steps you should take if you notice any unauthorized account activity.

Source: SEC, November 3, 2005.

Internet Fraud: How To Avoid Internet Investment Scams

The internet serves as an excellent tool for investors, allowing them to easily and inexpensively research investment opportunities. But the internet is also an excellent tool for fraudsters. That's why you should always think twice before you invest your money in any opportunity you learn about through the internet.

Navigating The Frontier: Where The Frauds Are

The internet allows individuals or companies to communicate with a large audience without spending a lot of time, effort, or money. Anyone can reach tens of thousands of people by building an internet website, posting a message on an online bulletin board, entering a discussion in a live "chat" room, or sending mass e-mails. It's easy for fraudsters to make their messages look real and credible. But it's nearly impossible for investors to tell the difference between fact and fiction.

Online Investment Newsletters: Hundreds of online investment newsletters have appeared on the internet in recent years. Many offer investors seemingly unbiased information free of charge about featured companies or recommending "stock picks of the month." While legitimate online newsletters can help investors gather valuable information, some online newsletters are tools for fraud.

Some companies pay the people who write online newsletters cash or securities to "tout" or recommend their stocks. While this isn't illegal, the federal securities laws require the newsletters to disclose who paid them, the amount, and the type of payment. But many fraudsters fail to do so. Instead, they'll lie about the payments they received, their independence, their so-called research, and their track records. Their newsletters masquerade as sources of unbiased information, when in fact they stand to profit handsomely if they convince investors to buy or sell particular stocks.

Some online newsletters falsely claim to independently research the stocks they profile. Others spread false information or promote worthless stocks. The most notorious sometimes "scalp" the stocks they hype, driving up the price of the stock with their baseless recommendations and then selling their own holdings at high prices and high profits.

Bulletin Boards: Online bulletin boards—whether newsgroups, usenet, or web-based bulletin boards—have become an increasingly popular forum for investors to share information. Bulletin boards typically feature "threads" made up of numerous messages on various investment opportunities.

While some messages may be true, many turn out to be bogus—or even scams. Fraudsters often pump up a company or pretend to reveal "inside" information about upcoming announcements, new products, or lucrative contracts.

Also, you never know for certain who you're dealing with—or whether they're credible—because many bulletin boards allow users to hide their identity behind multiple aliases. People claiming to be unbiased observers who've carefully researched the company may actually be company insiders, large shareholders, or paid promoters. A single person can easily create the illusion of widespread interest in a small, thinly-traded stock by posting a series of messages under various aliases.

E-Mail Spams: Because "spam"—junk e-mail—is so cheap and easy to create, fraudsters increasingly use it to find investors for bogus investment schemes or to spread false information about a company. Spam allows the unscrupulous to target many more potential investors than cold calling or mass mailing. Using a bulk e-mail program, spammers can send personalized messages to thousands and even millions of internet users at a time.

☞ Remember!!

If you want to invest wisely and steer clear of frauds, you must get the facts. Never, ever, make an investment based solely on what you read in an online newsletter or bulletin board posting, especially if the investment involves a small, thinly-traded company that isn't well known.

Source: SEC, August 6, 2007.

Part Three
Banks And Bonds

Chapter 17

Basic Facts About Banks And Banking

Banks And Our Economy

"Bank" is a term people use broadly to refer to many different types of financial institutions. What you think of as your "bank" may be a bank and trust company, a savings bank, a savings and loan association, or other depository institution.

What Is A Bank?

Banks are privately owned institutions that, generally, accept deposits and make loans. Deposits are money people leave in an institution with the understanding that they can get it back at any time or at an agreed-upon future time. A loan is money let out to a borrower to be generally paid back with interest. This action of taking deposits and making loans is called financial intermediation. A bank's business, however, does not end there.

Most people and businesses pay their bills with bank checking accounts, placing banks at the center of our payments system. Banks are the major

About This Chapter: This chapter includes "ABC's of Banking: Lesson One - Banks and Our Economy," "Lesson Two - Banks, Thrifts and Credit Unions - What's the Difference?" and "Lesson Three - Banks and Their Regulators," provided by the State of Connecticut, Department of Banking, based on information from the Conference of State Bank Supervisors (CSBS). © 2001 State of Connecticut. Reprinted with permission. Despite the older date of these documents, the information provided about the different types, functions, and operations of banks and other financial institutions is still pertinent.

source of consumer loans—loans for cars, houses, education—as well as main lenders to businesses, especially small businesses.

Banks are often described as our economy's engine, in part because of these functions, but also because of the major role banks play as instruments of the government's monetary policy.

How Banks Create Money

Banks can't lend out all the deposits they collect, or they wouldn't have funds to pay out to depositors. Therefore, they keep primary and secondary reserves. Primary reserves are cash, deposits due from other banks, and the reserves required by the Federal Reserve System. Secondary reserves are securities banks purchase, which may be sold to meet short-term cash needs. These securities are usually government bonds. Federal law sets requirements for the percentage of deposits a bank must keep on reserve, either at the local Federal Reserve Bank or in its own vault. Any money a bank has on hand after it meets its reserve requirement is its excess reserves.

It's the excess reserves that create money. This is how it works (using a theoretical 20% reserve requirement): You deposit $500 in YourBank. YourBank keeps $100 of it to meet its reserve requirement, but lends $400 to Ms. Smith. She uses the money to buy a car. The Sav-U-Mor Car Dealership deposits $400 in its account at TheirBank. TheirBank keeps $80 of it on reserve, but can lend out the other $320 as its own excess reserves. When that money is lent out, it becomes a deposit in a third institution, and the cycle continues. Thus, in this example, your original $500 becomes $1,220 on deposit in three different institutions. This phenomenon is called the multiplier effect. The size of the multiplier depends on the amount of money banks must keep on reserve.

The Federal Reserve can contract or expand the money supply by raising or lowering banks' reserve requirements. Banks themselves can contract the money supply by increasing their own reserves to guard against loan losses or to meet sudden cash demands. A sharp increase in bank reserves, for any reason, can create a "credit crunch" by reducing the amount of money a bank has to lend.

How Banks Make Money

While public policy makers have long recognized the importance of banking to economic development, banks are privately owned, for-profit institutions. Banks are generally owned by stockholders; the stockholders' stake in the bank forms most of its equity capital, a bank's ultimate buffer against losses. At the end of the year, a bank pays some or all of its profits to its shareholders in the form of dividends. The bank may retain some of its profits to add to its capital. Stockholders may also choose to reinvest their dividends in the bank.

Banks earn money in three ways:

• They make money from what they call the spread, or the difference between the interest rate they pay for deposits and the interest rate they receive on the loans they make.

• They earn interest on the securities they hold.

• They earn fees for customer services, such as checking accounts, financial counseling, loan servicing and the sales of other financial products (for example, insurance and mutual funds).

Banks earn an average of just over 1% of their assets (loans and securities) every year. This figure is commonly referred to as a bank's "return on assets," or ROA.

Banks And Public Policy

Our government's earliest leaders struggled over the shape of our banking system. They knew that banks have considerable financial power. Should this power be concentrated in a few institutions, they asked, or shared by many? Alexander Hamilton argued strongly for one central bank; that idea troubled Thomas Jefferson, who believed that local control was the only way to restrain banks from becoming financial monsters.

We've tried both ways, and our current system seems to be a compromise. It allows for a multitude of banks, both large and small. Both the federal and state governments issue bank charters for "public need and convenience," and regulate banks to ensure that they meet those needs. The Federal Reserve controls the money supply at a national level; the nation's individual banks facilitate the flow of money in their respective communities.

Since banks hold government-issued charters and generally belong to the federal Bank Insurance Fund, state and federal governments have considered banks as instruments of broad financial policy beyond money supply. Governments encourage or require different types of lending; for instance, they enforce nondiscrimination policies by requiring equal opportunity lending. They promote economic development by requiring lending or investment in banks' local communities, and by deciding where to issue new bank charters. Using banks to accomplish economic policy goals requires a constant balancing of banks' needs against the needs of the community. Banks must be profitable to stay in business, and a failed bank doesn't meet anyone's needs.

Banks, Thrifts, And Credit Unions—What's The Difference?

There are three major types of depository institutions in the United States. They are commercial banks, thrifts (which include savings and loan associations and savings banks), and credit unions.

These three types of institutions have become more like each other in recent decades, and their unique identities have become less distinct. They still differ, however, in specialization and emphasis, and in their regulatory and supervisory structures.

Commercial banks are the traditional "department stores" of the financial services world. Thrift institutions and credit unions are more like specialty shops that, over time, have expanded their lines of business to better compete for market share.

Commercial Banks

Commercial banks are generally stock corporations whose principal obligation is to make a profit for their shareholders. Basically, banks receive deposits, and hold them in a variety of different accounts, extend credit through loans and other instruments, and facilitate the movement of funds. While commercial banks mostly specialize in short-term business credit, they also make consumer loans and mortgages, and have a broad range of financial powers. Their corporate charters and the powers granted to them under state and federal law determine the range of their activities.

States and the federal government each issue bank charters. State-chartered banks operate under state supervision and, if they fail, are closed under provisions of state as well as federal law. National banks are chartered and regulated by the Office of the Comptroller of the Currency (OCC), a division of the Treasury Department. Banks can choose between a state or a federal charter when starting their business, and can also convert from one charter to another after having been in business. Commercial banks receive deposit insurance from the Federal Deposit Insurance Corporation (FDIC) through the Bank Insurance Fund (BIF). All national banks, and some state-chartered banks, are members of the Federal Reserve System.

Savings And Loans/Savings Banks

Savings and loan associations and savings banks specialize in real estate lending, particularly loans for single-family homes and other residential properties. They can be owned by shareholders ("stock" ownership) or by their depositors and borrowers ("mutual" ownership). These institutions are referred to as "thrifts," because they originally offered only savings accounts, or time deposits. Over the past two decades, however, they have acquired a wide range of financial powers, and now offer checking accounts (demand deposits) and make business and consumer loans as well as mortgages.

Both savings and loan associations and savings banks may be chartered by either the federal Office of Thrift Supervision (OTS) or by a state government regulator. Generally, savings and loan associations are insured by the Savings Association Insurance Fund (SAIF), and savings banks are insured by the Bank Insurance Fund (BIF).

Savings institutions must hold a certain percentage of their loan portfolio in housing-related assets to retain their charter, as well as their membership in the Federal Home Loan Bank System. This is called the "qualified thrift lender" (QTL) test. Savings institutions must maintain 65% of their portfolio in housing-related or other qualified assets to maintain their status. Recent liberalization of the QTL test has allowed thrifts to use some non-housing assets to meet this requirement.

The number of thrifts declined dramatically in the late 1980s and early 1990s. The savings and loan crisis of the 1980s forced many institutions to close or merge with others, at an extraordinary cost to the federal government. However, there has been a resurgence of interest in the thrift charter

♣ It's A Fact!!

Credit unions were first chartered in the U.S. in 1909, at the state level. The federal government began to charter credit unions in 1934 under the Farm Credit Association, and created the National Credit Union Administration (NCUA) in 1970. States and the federal government continue to charter credit unions; almost all credit unions are insured by the National Credit Union Share Insurance Fund, which is controlled by the NCUA.

Source: © 2007 State of Connecticut.
Reprinted with permission.

in recent years. The recapitalization of the thrift fund, a revitalized industry and legislative changes have made the charter—once thought doomed to extinction—an appealing route to financial modernization for some. Due to liberalization of the qualified thrift lender test, many insurance companies and securities firms, as well as commercial firms, are now able to qualify as unitary thrift holding companies and to own depository institutions, by-passing prohibitions in the Glass Steagall Act and the Bank Holding Company Act. Critics of a revitalized thrift charter have said that it has advantaged a certain class of financial institutions, highlighting the need for broader financial modernization through federal legislation.

Credit Unions

Credit unions are cooperative financial institutions, formed by groups of people with a "common bond." These groups of people pool their funds to form the institution's deposit base; the group owns and controls the institution together. Membership in a credit union is not open to the general public, but is restricted to people who share the common bond of the group that created the credit union. Examples of this common bond are working for the same employer, belonging to the same church or social group, or living in the same community. Credit unions are nonprofit institutions that seek to encourage savings and make excess funds within a community available at low cost to their members.

Credit unions accept deposits in a variety of accounts. All credit unions offer savings accounts, or time deposits; the larger institutions also offer checking and money market accounts. Credit unions' financial powers have expanded to include almost anything a bank or savings association can do, including making home loans, issuing credit cards, and even making some commercial loans. Credit unions are exempt from federal taxation and sometimes receive subsidies, in the form of free space or supplies, from their sponsoring organizations.

Banks And Their Regulators

Bank regulation, or supervision, involves four federal agencies and fifty state agencies. At first glance this regulatory scheme seems hopelessly complicated, but it's not that hard to understand once you know what each agency does.

State And Federal Charters

You may have seen or heard the term "dual banking system." This refers to the fact that both states and the federal government issue bank charters for the need and convenience of their citizens. The Office of the Comptroller of the Currency (OCC) charters national banks; the state banking departments charter state banks. In addition, the Office of Thrift Supervision (OTS) charters federal savings banks and savings associations. The words

♣ **It's A Fact!!**

How did we get so many regulators?

Many people have said that we would never design our current regulatory system as it is if we were starting from scratch. But our current system has evolved with the country and has changed with the country's needs.

The states were the first to charter banks in the United States. The Federal government chartered the First and Second Banks of the United States in the early 19th century. These were the first national banks, and they performed functions similar to today's Federal Reserve System. From 1837, when the Second Bank's charter expired, to 1863 there were no national banks and no federal regulators.

The National Bank Act of 1863 created the Office of the Comptroller of the Currency, and authorized it to charter national banks. The original purpose of both the OCC and national banks was to circulate a universal currency, thus making tax collection easier and helping to finance the Civil War. The dual banking system took shape in the late 19th century as states reformed their chartering policies and regulatory systems in response to the National Bank Act.

A series of money shortages early in the 20th century made it clear that the country needed some central authority to monitor and control the money supply. The Federal Reserve Act of 1913 established this authority through a network of twelve Federal Reserve Banks, overseen by a Board of Governors. The Federal Reserve System had regulatory authority over all its member banks; this was the first time a federal agency had direct authority over state-chartered banks, although state bank membership in the Federal Reserve was voluntary.

"national," "federal" or "state" in a institution's name have nothing to do with where it operates; rather they refer to the type of charter the bank holds.

Chartering agencies ensure that new banks have the necessary capital and management expertise to meet the public's financial needs. The charterer is an institution's primary regulator, with front-line duty to protect the public from unsafe and unsound banking practices. Chartering agencies conduct on-site examinations to assess banks' condition and monitor compliance with

The FDIC was created by the Banking Act of 1933 in response to the avalanche of bank failures that followed the stock market crash of 1929. The FDIC originally insured deposits up to $5,000. The 1933 Banking Act required all state-chartered banks to join the Federal Reserve within a certain period of time or lose their deposit insurance, but this requirement was eventually repealed. The FDIC established its own standards for state nonmember bank acceptance into the fund.

Bank holding companies were new corporate entities that began appearing in the 1940s. The banks were all regulated, but no one regulated the holding company subsidiaries that weren't banks, and no one watched the flow of resources among affiliates within the holding company. The Bank Holding Company Act of 1956 gave the Federal Reserve regulatory responsibility for these companies, while leaving the supervision of banks within holding companies in the hands of their traditional regulators.

In 1989, the Financial Institutions Reform, Recovery, and Enforcement Act (FIRREA) expanded the FDIC's supervisory and enforcement authority, and extended its responsibilities to include the thrift deposit insurance role held by the former Federal Savings and Loan Insurance Corporation (FSLIC).

Most recently, 1991's FDICIA also expanded the authority of federal regulators to intervene in troubled institutions. FDICIA also mandated specific enforcement actions for unhealthy institutions—the first time prescribed "early intervention" provisions had been included in federal statutes.

Source: © 2007 State of Connecticut. Reprinted with permission.

banking laws. They issue regulations, take enforcement actions, and close banks if they fail.

The Deposit Insurer

The Federal Deposit Insurance Corporation (FDIC) insures the deposits of banks up to a maximum of $100,000 per account holder. [Note: In late 2008, the maximum insured amount was temporarily increased to $250,000 and scheduled to return to $100,000 on January 1, 2010.] All states require newly chartered state banks to join the FDIC before they can accept deposits from the public. Under the 1991 Federal Deposit Insurance Corporation Improvement Act (FDICIA), both state-chartered and national banks must apply to the FDIC for deposit insurance; previously, national banks had received insurance automatically with their new charters.

> ✔ **Quick Tip**
> You can find more deposit insurance information at the Federal Deposit Insurance Corporation (FDIC) website, http://www.fdic.gov.
>
> Source: © 2007 State of Connecticut. Reprinted with permission.

The FDIC is the federal regulator of the approximately 5,000 state-chartered banks that do not belong to the Federal Reserve System. It cooperates with state banking departments to supervise and examine these banks, and has considerable authority to intervene to prevent unsafe and unsound banking practices. The FDIC also has backup examination and regulatory authority over national and Fed-member banks.

The FDIC deals with failed institutions by either liquidating them or selling the institutions to redeem insured deposits.

The Central Bank

The Federal Reserve System ("the Fed") controls the flow of money in and out of banks by raising or lowering its requirements for bank reserves and by buying and selling federal securities. It lends money to banks at low interest rates (the "discount rate") to help banks meet their short-term liquidity needs, and is known as the "lender of last resort" for banks experiencing liquidity crises. Together, the FDIC and the Federal Reserve form the federal safety net that protects depositors when banks fail.

Membership in the Federal Reserve System is required for national banks and is optional for state banks. While many large state banks have become Fed members, most state banks have chosen not to join. The Federal Reserve is the federal regulator of about 1,000 state-chartered member banks and cooperates with state bank regulators to supervise these institutions.

The Federal Reserve also regulates all bank holding companies. Its regulatory focus is not so much on the banks within a holding company as on the umbrella structure of the holding company itself. Holding companies must apply to the Federal Reserve to acquire new subsidiaries or to engage in new activities. The Fed monitors the capital condition and general financial health of holding companies, and may take enforcement actions against them. The Federal Reserve is also responsible for federal oversight of foreign banks operating in the United States.

Chapter 18

Internet And High-Tech Banking Options

What You Should Know About Internet Banking

There is a lot you should know about internet banking. It can save you time, money and effort, but it's important to protect yourself from potential pitfalls. Below is information on banking options, different types of online banking, services and advantages, protecting your privacy, "cookies" and privacy, security, regulations that protect consumers, and filing a complaint against a financial institution.

Banking Consumers' Options

- You can go to a traditional "brick and mortar" institution that has a building and personal service representatives, but doesn't offer internet banking services.

- Or you can bank at a "brick and click" financial institution that has a physical structure, and also offers internet banking services.

- Or you can choose a "virtual" bank or financial institution that has no public building and exists only online.

About This Chapter: This chapter begins with "What You Should Know about Internet Banking," reprinted with permission from the Federal Reserve Bank of Chicago, www.chicagofed.org, © 2008. Additional information includes excerpts from "Safe Internet Banking," Federal Deposit Insurance Corporation (FDIC), July 11, 2007, and "Speed Paying and Banking," *FDIC Consumer News*, Spring 2007.

Internet banking, and other types of online banking, offer advantages such as speed and convenience. But since the internet is a public network, it presents some privacy and security issues. Knowing the "Do's and Don'ts" of internet banking can help make your online banking experience more productive, safe. and enjoyable.

Two Different Types Of Online Banking

Internet banking is usually conducted through a personal computer (PC) that connects to a banking website via the internet. For example, a consumer at home accesses a financial institution's website via a modem and phone line or other telecommunications connection, and an internet service provider such as America Online, Microsoft's MSN Network, Earthlink, Juno, or AT&T WorldNet.

> ## ✎ What's It Mean?
>
> <u>Automatic Teller Machines:</u> Allow customers to obtain cash and conduct banking transactions; some ATMs sell bus passes, postage stamps, gift certificates, and mutual funds.
>
> <u>Online Banking:</u> Banking through online services. Bank websites allow customers to check balances, pay bills, transfer funds, compare savings plans, and apply for loans on the internet.
>
> Source: From *Practical Money Skills for Life*, a financial literacy program from Visa, http://www.practicalmoneyskills.com. © 2008 Visa. All rights reserved. Reprinted with permission.

Internet banking also can be conducted via wireless technology through both personal digital assistants (PDAs) or cellular phones.

Electronic banking is conducted by using automatic teller machines (ATMs), telephones (not via the internet), or debit cards. Debit cards look like a credit card. But unlike a credit card, using a debit card removes funds from your bank account immediately.

What Internet Banking Offers—Services And Advantages

As a consumer, you can use internet banking to:

- Access account information, review bills, pay bills, transfer funds, apply for credit or trade securities.

- You can find out if a check has cleared or when a bill is due.

- You can apply for mortgages, shop for the best loan rates and compare insurance policies and prices.

- And you can do all of these things anytime you want to—day or night.

Some people like to tie banking functions into personal financial software such as Intuit's Quicken or Microsoft's Money. This can make record-keeping and tax preparation quicker and easier. Many consumers also like the idea of not waiting in line to do their banking, and paying their bills without shuffling papers and buying stamps.

Protecting Your Privacy

You need to be concerned about privacy and security. Consider this: When you bank via the internet, your personal and financial information may be shared with others without your knowledge.

A financial institution may want to share information about you to help market products specific to your needs and interests. For example, it might share information about your average checking account balance with an affiliate selling life insurance or securities.

Financial institutions have policies about what information they collect, how they use this information and with whom they will share it. Financial institutions are required to provide customers with a copy of their privacy policy. Reviewing this policy can tell you what information your financial institution keeps about you, and what information, if any, it shares with its affiliates or others.

You have the right to tell your financial institution not to share your personal information with others without your consent. You should be given a choice to "opt out," allowing you to limit sharing of your personal information.

- Do check for an "opt out" option.

How "Cookies" Could Affect Your Privacy

Internet technology allows financial institutions and other websites to track your browsing habits while at their site. This may be done using a small file stored on your PC called a "cookie." Tracking your browsing gives financial institutions information about your apparent interests and preferences. It helps them to potentially market goods and services to you based on these interests and preferences.

- Do check your financial institution's website privacy statement. Determine if the website uses cookies or otherwise tracks your browsing habits. If this tracking practice concerns you, your PC's web browser may offer useful options.

A web browser is a program on your PC that enables you to browse websites over the internet (Internet Explorer and Netscape are two examples of browsers). Check the Preferences or Tools areas of your browser to look for cookies. Your browser may offer the option to notify you before a cookie is created, identifying who is attempting to place the cookie and giving you the option to accept or reject it. Your browser also may offer you the option to reject all cookies, or to accept all cookies.

Just be aware that some websites are designed to function properly only when their cookies are accepted. Blocking cookies may prevent normal access to certain websites or to some of their online options. If this happens, you can easily begin accepting cookies again.

- Do check your browser's options for accepting or rejecting cookies.

Security Tips—How To Protect Your Personal Information

Since the internet is a public network, it's important to safeguard your banking information, credit card numbers, Social Security number, and other personal information.

Some consumers have had credit card numbers and Social Security numbers stolen and used fraudulently. Of course, this can happen even if you don't bank online. By taking reasonable steps to protect your personal information, you can reduce the chances that it may be stolen.

- Do ask your financial institution about its security practices. How does it safeguard your information during transmission and on their website?

Websites use uniform resource locators (URL) as a kind of internet street address. You can tell your browser which website you want to go to with the URL. When a URL begins with http plus an "s", it identifies the site as "secure," meaning that it encrypts or scrambles transmitted information. This prevents others from seeing your information when it travels over the internet.

Also, most browsers and web pages display a small icon of a locked padlock or a key to show that the site is encrypting your information during transmission. Your browser may also notify you when you are entering a "secure" website.

- Do make sure your transmissions are encrypted before doing any online transactions or sending personal information.

Is E-Mail Safe?

E-mail is usually not secure. It's not a good idea to send personal information such as your Social Security number, personal identification number (PIN) or account numbers via e-mail, unless you know it is encrypted.

- Don't send personal information by ordinary e-mail.

- Do change any passwords or PINs you receive via e-mail that are not encrypted.

Consumer Regulations That Protect You

There are federal regulations that protect consumers against unauthorized transactions, including internet bank transactions as well as those conducted via an automated teller machine (ATM) or using a debit card.

The Electronic Funds Transfer Act, or Regulation E, says a consumer's liability for an unauthorized transaction is determined by how soon the financial institution is notified. A consumer could be liable for the entire amount unless the unauthorized transaction is reported within 60 days of receipt of the financial institution's statement detailing the unauthorized transaction. The sooner the unauthorized transaction is reported, the less the level of liability; therefore, it's important to report unauthorized transactions immediately to limit loss. It's also important to remember that it might take time while the unauthorized transaction is being investigated for money deducted from your account to be credited back to it.

♣ It's A Fact!!

Security Tips: Dos

- Do make sure you are on the right website. Impostors have created websites with similar names to trick unsuspecting consumers into revealing personal information.

- Do make sure that the financial institution is properly insured. It should be insured by the Federal Deposit Insurance Corporation (FDIC). FDIC coverage only applies to deposit products such as savings accounts, checking accounts, and Certificates of Deposit (CDs). The coverage does not apply to transactions involving mutual funds, stocks, bonds, and annuities.

- Do be "password smart." When possible, use a mix of letters and numbers for added safety. Change your password regularly. Keep your password or PIN to yourself. Avoid easy-to-guess passwords like first names, birthdays, anniversaries or Social Security numbers.

- Do check bank, debit, and credit card statements thoroughly every month. Keep good records. Save information about banking transactions. Check this information for agreement with account statements, debit card bills, and credit card bills. Look for any errors or discrepancies.

- Do report errors, problems, or complaints promptly.

- Do keep virus protection software up-to-date. Back-up key files regularly.

- Do exit the banking site immediately after completing your banking.

Security Tips: Don'ts

- Don't have other browser windows open at the same time you are banking online.

- Don't disclose personal information such as credit card and Social Security numbers unless you know whom you are dealing with, why they want this information and how they plan to use it.

- Don't download files sent by strangers or click on hyperlinks from people or sites you don't know. Sometimes doing this can infect your computer with viruses that can damage hardware or software.

Source: © 2008 Federal Reserve Bank of Chicago.

The Truth-in-Lending Act, or Regulation Z, governs illegal credit card use. While bank transactions conducted over the internet are governed by Regulation E, credit card purchases over the internet are governed by Regulation Z. When making purchases via the internet, it's smart to use a credit card. That's because if a credit card is stolen or used by an unauthorized party, liability should be no more than $50 if proper notice is given to the credit card vendor. The vendor can be telephoned, but it's best to follow up the call with a letter stating that the transaction was made by an unauthorized user, and detailing the account number and the dollar amount of the unauthorized transaction. Consumers do not have to pay the disputed amount during investigation.

All financial institutions are also subject to Regulation P covering privacy and the Interagency Guidelines for Safeguarding Consumer Information.

All federally insured financial institutions are subject to federal regulations concerning the distribution of personal information. These institutions must comply with established guidelines for safeguarding this information. They are also subject to onsite examinations to ensure compliance with consumer laws and regulations.

How To File A Complaint

It's best to contact a customer service representative or senior manager at your financial institution and discuss the problem first. The problem may simply be a misunderstanding.

But if you are still not satisfied, you can file a written complaint containing the following information:

- Your name, address, and daytime telephone number, and the name and address of the financial institution involved in your complaint or inquiry.

- Your account number, type of account, the names of the people you talked to, and a description of the problem.

- Describe exactly what happened and the dates involved. Include copies of any letters or other documents that may help to investigate the complaint; however, don't send originals. Sign and date your letter.

You may write directly to the financial institution with which you experienced the problem, or to the authority that regulates that institution. If you don't know the right regulatory authority, call the institution and ask. Or contact one or more of the following:

The Federal Reserve System
Regulates state-chartered banks that are members of the Federal Reserve System
Phone: 202-452-3693
Website: http://www.federalreserve.gov

The Federal Deposit Insurance Corporation (FDIC)
Regulates state-chartered, non-member banks
Phone: 800-934-3342
Website: http://www.fdic.gov

The Office of Thrift Supervision
Regulates savings & loans, as well as savings banks
Phone: 800-842-6929
Website: http://www.ots.treas.gov

The Office of Comptroller of the Currency (OCC)
Regulates national banks
Phone: 800-613-6743
Website: http://www.occ.treas.gov

The National Credit Union Administration
Regulates credit unions
Phone: 703-518-6330
Website: http://www.ncua.gov

If your financial institution is regulated by the Federal Reserve Bank of Chicago, please direct your complaint to:

Federal Reserve Bank of Chicago
Consumer Complaints Department
230 South LaSalle Street
Chicago, IL 60604-1413
Phone: 800-372-4211
Website: http://www.chicagofed.org

Safe Internet Banking

Confirm that an online bank is legitimate and that your deposits are insured. Read key information about the bank posted on its website: Most bank websites have an "About Us" section or something similar that describes the institution. You may find a brief history of the bank, the official name and address of the bank's headquarters, and information about its insurance coverage from the FDIC.

Protect yourself from fraudulent websites: For example, watch out for copycat websites that deliberately use a name or web address very similar to, but not the same as, that of a real financial institution. The intent is to lure you into

---

✔ **Quick Tip**

Verify The Bank's Insurance Status

To verify a bank's insurance status, look for the familiar FDIC logo or the words "Member FDIC" or "FDIC Insured" on the website.

Also, you should check the FDIC's online database of FDIC-insured institutions. You can search for an institution by going to Bank Find, which is available online at http://www4.fdic.gov/IDASP/main_bankfind.asp. Search by name, city, state, or zip code of the bank, and click the "Find" button. A positive match will display the official name of the bank, the date it became insured, its insurance certificate number, the main office location for the bank (and branches), its primary government regulator, and other links to detailed information about the bank. If your bank does not appear on this list, contact the FDIC.

Some bank websites provide links directly to the FDIC's website to assist you in identifying or verifying the FDIC insurance protection of their deposits.

Also remember that not all banks operating on the internet are insured by the FDIC. Many banks that are not FDIC-insured are chartered overseas. If you choose to use a bank chartered overseas, it is important for you to know that the FDIC may not insure your deposits. Check with your bank or the FDIC if you are not certain.

Source: Federal Deposit Insurance Corporation, July 11, 2007.

clicking onto their website and giving your personal information, such as your account number and password. Always check to see that you have typed the correct website address for your bank before conducting a transaction.

For insurance purposes, be aware that a bank may use different names for its online and traditional services; this does not mean you are dealing with separate banks: This means, for example, that to determine your maximum FDIC insurance coverage, your deposits at the parent bank will be added together with those at the separately named bank website and will be insured for up to the maximum amount covered for one bank. Talk to your banker if you have questions.

Speed Paying And Banking

New technologies are constantly adding speed, convenience, and flexibility to practically everything we do—including how we bank and pay for goods and services. If you think banking over the internet is the latest trend, you may be in for some surprises…and for some revolutionary new ways to conduct your daily financial transactions using pre-paid cards, credit and debit cards, and cell phones.

But while the new services can provide benefits, they also can present questions and concerns about security. "There is always the possibility that a customer could lose a cell phone or bank card, so it is crucial to safeguard passwords, monitor your bank accounts, and quickly report and deactivate a lost device so it can't be used to access an account or transfer funds," explains Donald Saxinger, an FDIC electronic banking specialist.

Cards With A Pre-Loaded Value: These cards come in several varieties that serve different purposes but generally enable a cardholder to pay for goods or services. With each purchase, as the card is swiped through a card reader, the value goes down. It also may be possible to add value onto some pre-paid cards. Sometimes fees may be associated with these cards, so be sure to ask about the potential costs. Examples of the increasingly common and popular pre-paid cards include gift cards, pre-paid debit cards issued by financial institutions for use at a variety of businesses and ATMs, payroll cards, and debit cards for health savings accounts.

♣ It's A Fact!!

If a pre-paid card is lost or stolen: A consumer's liability for a lost card may vary depending on the type of card and who is issuing it. For example, a pre-loaded card issued by a bank or a major card network may provide more consumer protections than one issued by a retailer, "but to be sure you need to shop around, read the card's terms and conditions, and find out what to do if you lose your card," says David Nelson, a fraud specialist at the FDIC.

Source: *FDIC Consumer News*, Spring 2007.

Contactless Credit And Debit Cards: You're probably used to swiping your credit or debit card's magnetic stripe through a sales terminal. But with the new generation of what are being called "contactless" cards, you can wave your card in front of the sales terminal (or quickly tap it on a screen) at participating retailers. A special reader at the sales counter will use a radio signal to gather the payment information from an electronic chip embedded in your credit or debit card. Another possibility (first introduced for use at gas pumps) is a small piece of plastic— perhaps a tag you can keep on your key chain or attached to your car's windshield—with a computer chip inside that can send information about which credit or debit card to charge. After getting a signal that your transaction has been recorded, you'll probably have the option to get a printed receipt. The transaction also will appear on your statement.

♣ It's A Fact!!

If a contactless card is lost or stolen: You will have the same security protections and limits on loss under federal laws and financial industry policies as you would for any unauthorized use of your "regular" credit or debit card issued by a financial institution. That would include any zero-liability against losses that a financial institution may provide for a card. For details, contact your card issuer.

Source: *FDIC Consumer News*, Spring 2007.

Banking By Cell Phone

Most cell phones today enable you to do much more than simply make a call. New cell phones allow you to send text messages, take still pictures and videos, browse the internet, watch TV, and, increasingly, conduct some of your banking business. Depending on the services offered by your financial institution (such as your bank or credit card issuer) and your cell phone service provider, the options may include the following:

• Text messaging with your financial institution

• Accessing your online bank account from your cell phone

• Instantly paying for purchases using your cell phone

Given how easy it is to lose a mobile phone, a consumer considering banking by cell phone should take some precautions. "First," says FDIC electronic banking specialist Donald Saxinger, "make sure your bank requires a password or PIN to use a cell phone for banking. Also confirm with your bank that account numbers, passwords and other sensitive information are not stored on the phone, where they can be retrieved by a thief."

Saxinger also says that if you lose a cell phone that you used to do

---

✔ Quick Tip
Questions To Ask Your Banker Before Trying A High-Tech Service

• How will this service make my banking simpler or more convenient?

• Will mistakes or unauthorized transactions be simple to detect and correct?

• What is my liability under federal law if a criminal obtains my account numbers and other personal information and commits fraud or steals money from my account? Does the bank or other company involved offer additional limits on liability beyond what's in the law?

• What security procedures do you recommend for consumers?

• What does the bank do to protect my privacy, such as information about my account balance and how I spend my money?

• How much will it cost to use the service, including any equipment or cards I must purchase or any monthly or per-transaction fees?

Source: *FDIC Consumer News,* Spring 2007.

banking, you can take additional steps to protect against unauthorized access to your bank account. "Immediately contact your cell phone provider, which may be able to deactivate the phone or have sensitive information erased," he says. "Also consider calling your bank to find out about any additional precautions it may be able to take or what more you can do."

And what if a thief is able to obtain your password and then tap into your bank or credit card account? You'd have the same security protections and limits on liability as for other unauthorized electronic uses of your account. Contact your bank for more information.

Final Thoughts

Considering the way technology is changing, these and other sophisticated new banking services are sure to get more user friendly. "What may seem to be futuristic, space-age banking services today may become very common in only a few years," says Janet Kincaid, FDIC Senior Consumer Affairs Officer. "Soon you could be one of the many people using a cell phone to buy a soda."

No matter what, David Nelson, a fraud specialist at FDIC, adds, "it's also nice to know that you'll still have options to bank at a branch, at home, or wherever or however you're most comfortable."

Chapter 19
Pros And Cons Of Different Savings Options

You have money, you need a place to put it for a while and the financial institutions are lining up at the door. You may be tempted to fall for whatever suitor makes a good first impression, but remember: This choice is all about you.

The best short-term savings account is the one that best matches your needs in the following areas:

1. **Access:** How often will you need to dip into the account, and what's your preferred method of access—ATM, check-writing, online, and the like?

2. **Interest:** How much will the institution pay you for babysitting your money, and does the amount you need to park in the account qualify for the best rates?

3. **Service:** Might you require bells and whistles, such as in-person customer service, or are you more of a DIY, low-maintenance customer?

4. **Penalties:** Should your plans change—you need to get to your moola sooner than planned, for example—how harsh of a punishment will you need to endure?

Now, let's review the major aspirants:

Checking Accounts

Checking accounts are meant for transactions, not savings. That's why many don't pay much, if any, interest. However, some banks do combine the conveniences of checking with the return of a money market account. Also, as "asset management" accounts at brokerages become more feature-rich—offering unlimited check writing, ATM access, and money market rates—more folks are shunning the banks in favor of brokers.

Pros

• Your money is only a check or an ATM machine away.

• A bank branch is usually not far, often in your grocery store, if you're so old-fashioned as to want to deal with a human being.

• As with all bank deposits, checking accounts are insured by the Federal Deposit Insurance Corporation.

Cons

• Depending on the bank, you may not earn much, if anything, on the money in your account.

• Many checking accounts require a minimum balance or charge fees, or both, which are a pox upon your pecuniary patience.

✎ What's It Mean?

Commercial Bank: A bank that offers a broad range of deposit accounts, including checking, savings, and time deposits, and extends loans to individuals and businesses—in contrast to investment banking firms such as brokerage firms, which generally are involved in arranging for the sale of corporate or municipal securities.

Panic: A series of unexpected cash withdrawals from a bank caused by a sudden decline in depositor confidence or fear that the bank will be closed by the chartering agency; many depositors withdraw cash almost simultaneously. Since the cash reserve a bank keeps on hand is only a small fraction of its deposits, a large number of withdrawals in a short period of time can deplete available cash and force the bank to close and possibly go out of business.

Source: Excerpted from "An Outline of the U.S. Economy, Glossary of Economic Terms," by Christopher Conte and Albert R. Karr, U.S. Department of State, 2001.

Savings Accounts

In the old days, savings accounts—or passbook accounts, as they're sometimes known—were the most popular rest area for short-term savings. Fortunately, folks are getting smarter and parking their pelf in higher-yielding investments. The pittance you earn in most savings accounts isn't enough to even keep up with inflation.

Pros

- The money in a savings account is insured by the Federal Deposit Insurance Corporation (FDIC).

- Account minimums are often low.

Cons

- The return on savings accounts is so low, some mattresses pay more in interest.

High-Yield Bank Accounts

Nowadays, you can find high-yield savings and checking accounts. They're an ideal place to park money for your monthly bills. They offer flexibility (you can add or withdraw funds at any time) and liquidity (your dough isn't locked in for a specific time period). Some even boast interest rates on par with more restrictive investments like certificates of deposit (CDs). The best rates by far are offered by online-only banks that keep costs low by cutting back on frills.

Pros

- Better rates than many standard bank accounts.
- Same FDIC insurance applies to high-yield accounts.

Cons

- Bare-bones banks with no ATM/debit access or check-writing privileges can be a big hassle if you need your cash fast.

- Customers must coordinate their cash flow by transferring money back and forth from the online bank to a linked checking/savings or brokerage account. That means delays—two to five days—before everything's reconciled.

- Watch out for limited-time teaser rates by researching the product's six-month interest rate history.

Money Market Deposit Accounts

Money market deposit accounts are offered by banks, usually require a minimum balance, and permit a limited number of transactions per month (six transfers, three of which can be checks written on the account).

Pros

- Money market deposit accounts are very liquid. Most allow for easy access through checks, transfers, and even ATMs.

- Because they are offered by banks, money market accounts are insured by the FDIC.

Cons

- Unfortunately, you may pay for the liquidity by receiving less in return than from certificates of deposit.

- If your account falls below the minimum required balance, or you exceed the limited number of transactions, you might pay a penalty.

Money Market Funds

Money market funds are offered by brokerages and mutual fund families. These funds invest in highly liquid, safe securities such as certificates of deposit, government securities, and commercial paper (that is, short-term obligations issued by corporations).

Pros

- With a money market fund, you can have the money in your hot little hands very quickly. Often, you can write checks or use an ATM card.

- The returns on money market funds are typically higher than the return on money market accounts.

- Issuers go to great lengths to keep the net asset value (NAV) (the price of each share of the fund) at $1, so your principal is relatively safe [Editor's note: In 2008, after the NAV of one fund fell below $1, the U.S. Treasury Department established a temporary guaranty program to help stabilize investor confidence. The program established protection of money market fund shares held as of September 19, 2008 for money market mutual funds meeting specific criteria. The guarantee program was set up initially for a period of three months with a provision for possible renewal through September 18, 2009. See http://www.ustreas.gov/press/releases/hp1163.htm for more details.]

✎ What's It Mean?

Asset: A possession of value, usually measured in terms of money.

Bond: A certificate reflecting a firm's promise to pay the holder a periodic interest payment until the date of maturity and a fixed sum of money on the designated maturing date.

Source: Excerpted from "An Outline of the U.S. Economy, Glossary of Economic Terms," by Christopher Conte and Albert R. Karr, U.S. Department of State, 2001.

Cons

- Money market funds are not FDIC insured.

- There is no guarantee that the NAV will remain at $1.

Certificates Of Deposit (CDs)

CDs are debt instruments with a specific maturity, which can be anywhere from three months to 60 months (that is, five years). Most CDs are issued by banks, but they can be bought through brokerages.

Pros

- CDs are very safe because most are offered by banks, so they are FDIC insured.

- Depending on how long it is to maturity, CDs may pay more than money markets.

Cons

- Your money is off-limits until the CD matures. If you must, you can redeem the CD early, but you'll pay a penalty.

U.S. Government Bills Or Notes

"Treasuries" are backed by the full faith and credit of the U.S. government. Treasury bills mature in less than a year; Treasury notes mature between two and 10 years.

Pros

- Treasuries are considered the safest investments in the world.
- They can be bought directly, commission-free, at TreasuryDirect (www.treasurydirect.gov).
- They are exempt from state and local taxes.

Cons

- If you shop around, you might get a better return from money markets, CDs, and corporate bonds.
- If you need your money before the security matures, you may not get back all of your original investment.

I Bonds

No, they have nothing to do with the internet. I Bonds are inflation-indexed savings bonds issued by the U.S. government. The amount an I Bond pays is adjusted semiannually to keep up with inflation and protect the purchasing power of your money.

Pros

- I Bonds are backed by the full faith and credit of the U.S. government.
- The "I" in I Bond protects your investment against inflation risk.
- They are sold in manageable denominations, ranging from $50 to $10,000.

• They can be bought from most financial institutions, including TreasuryDirect.

• The earnings are exempt from state and local taxes, and can be tax-free if used for post-secondary education expenses.

• Taxes on earnings can be deferred for up to 30 years.

Cons

• You must hold an I Bond for at least 12 months, and you will pay a penalty of three months' earnings if you redeem the bond before owning it for five years.

Municipal Bonds

Municipal bonds (or "munis," as the big talkers refer to them) are issued by state and local governments in order to build schools, highways, and other projects for the public good. Municipal bonds are most attractive to high-income investors looking for tax-friendly income.

Pros

• Munis are just a step down from U.S. securities in terms of safety.

• Income is exempt from federal taxes, and might be exempt from state and local taxes if you live in the municipality that issued the bond (check on the tax implications beforehand).

Cons

• Interest from munis is relatively low. Unless you're in a high tax bracket, you'll usually get a better return from other investments.

• You may have to pay a commission to buy municipal bonds.

• If you need your money before the bond matures, you may not get back all of your original investment.

Corporate Bonds

Corporate bonds represent debt issued by companies, from the blue chips to the "cow chips," if you know what we mean. The more creditworthy the company, the less it'll pay in interest. Moody's and Standard & Poor's rate companies as to their ability to meet their debt obligations. Only short-term bonds are appropriate for short-term savings.

Pros

- Corporate bonds usually pay more than government securities, money markets, and CDs.

Cons

- The company that issued the bond could suspend interest payments, or even go belly up.

- You may have to pay a commission to buy bonds.

- If you need your money before the bond matures, you may not get back all of your original investment.

Bond Funds

Bond funds are mutual funds that pool the money of investors to buy bonds of all stripes.

Pros

- They are an efficient way to buy bonds in small increments and get the diversification that minimizes the risk that you picked a bond from a deadbeat company.

Cons

- The NAV (that is, the share price) of a bond mutual fund fluctuates, because of interest rate movements and the bonds bought and sold inside the fund. Therefore, you're not sure exactly how much of your original investment will be around when it's time to take your dough. Likewise, the yield on a mutual fund fluctuates.

- You will pay an ongoing expense to own the fund, called the "expense ratio," and you may have to pay a commission, called a "load."

Chapter 20

Account Choices To Consider For Saving Money

Choosing A Savings Account

Factors that determine the dollar yield on an account:

- All money earned comes from the interest rate (also called rate of return, or annual yield).

The following factors reduce money earned and can even turn it into a loss:

- Fees, charges, and penalties are usually based on minimum balance requirements or transaction fees.

- Some accounts require a certain balance before paying any interest. On money-market accounts, most banks will pay different interest rates for different size balances. (Higher balance earns a higher rate.)

- Most calculate the balance daily for purposes of paying interest. Some use average of all daily balances.

About This Chapter: This chapter includes "Choosing a Savings Account," "Money Market Accounts," and "CDs," from *Practical Money Skills for Life*, a financial literacy program from Visa, http:// www.practicalmoneyskills.com. © 2008 Visa. All rights reserved. Reprinted with permission.

♣ It's A Fact!!
Types Of Savings Accounts

Passbook Account

- Depositor receives a booklet in which deposits, withdrawals, and interest are recorded.

- Average interest rate is lower at banks and savings and loans than at credit unions.

- Funds are easily accessible.

Statement Account

- Basically the same as a passbook account, except depositor receives monthly statements instead of a passbook.

- Accounts are usually accessible through 24-hour automated teller machines (ATMs).

- Interest rates are the same as passbook account.

- Funds are easily accessible.

Interest-Earning Checking Account

- Combines benefits of checking and savings.

- Depositor earns interest on any unused money in his/her account.

Source: From *Practical Money Skills for Life*, a financial literacy program from Visa, http:// www.practicalmoneyskills.com. © 2008 Visa. All rights reserved. Reprinted with permission.

Money Market Accounts: What They Are And How They Work

- Checking/savings account.

- Interest rate paid built on a complex structure that varies with size of balance and current level of market interest rates.

- Can access your money from an ATM, a teller, or by writing up to three checks a month.

Benefits

- Immediate access to your money.

Trade-Offs

- Usually requires a minimum balance of $1,000 to $2,500.

- Limited number of checks can be written each month.

- Average yield (rate of return) higher than regular savings accounts.

CDs: What They Are And How They Work

- Bank pays a fixed amount of interest for a fixed amount of money during a fixed amount of time.

Benefits

- No risk

- Simple

- No fees

- Offers higher interest rates than savings accounts

Trade-Offs

- Restricted access to your money

- Withdrawal penalty if cashed before expiration date (penalty might be higher than the interest earned)

Types Of Certificates Of Deposit

- Rising-rate CDs with higher rates at various intervals, such as every six months.

- Stock-indexed CDs with earnings based on the stock market.

- Callable CDs with higher rates and long-term maturities, as high as 10–15 years. However, the bank may "call" the account after a stipulated period, such as one or two years, if interest rates drop.

- Global CDs combine higher interest with a hedge on future changes in the dollar compared to other currencies.

- Promotional CDs attempt to attract savers with gifts or special rates.

Chapter 21

A Guide To Deposit Insurance Coverage

The FDIC—short for the Federal Deposit Insurance Corporation—is an independent agency of the United States government. The FDIC protects depositors against the loss of their insured deposits if an FDIC-insured bank or savings association fails. FDIC insurance is backed by the full faith and credit of the United States government.

If a depositor's accounts at one FDIC-insured bank or savings association total $100,000 or less, the deposits are fully insured. [Editor's Note: See "Temporary Increase in FDIC Coverage" on the next two pages for information about changes made in 2008 that increased insurance coverage limits to $250,000 until January 1, 2010.] A depositor can have more than $100,000 [or $250,000 until January 1, 2010] at one insured bank or savings association and still be fully insured provided the accounts meet certain requirements. In addition, federal law provides for insurance coverage of up to $250,000 for certain retirement accounts.

FDIC Insurance Basics

The FDIC insures deposits in most banks and savings associations located in the United States. For simplicity, the term "insured bank" is used to

About This Chapter: Excerpted from "Your Insured Deposits: FDIC's Guide to Deposit Insurance Coverage," Federal Deposit Insurance Corporation (FDIC), January 2007. For additional information and for facts about account types not described in this chapter and current insurance limits, please contact the FDIC. The address, phone numbers, and internet information are given at the end of the chapter.

mean any bank or savings association that has FDIC insurance. To check whether a bank or savings association is insured by the FDIC, call toll-free at: 877-275-3342, use "BankFind" at: http://www2.fdic.gov/idasp/main_bankfind.asp, or look for the FDIC official teller sign where deposits are received.

What does FDIC deposit insurance cover?

FDIC insurance covers all types of deposits received at an insured bank, including deposits in checking accounts, negotiable order of withdrawal (NOW) accounts, and savings accounts, money market deposit accounts

---

♣ It's A Fact!!
Temporary Increase In FDIC Coverage

FDIC insurance covers funds in deposit accounts, including checking and savings accounts, money market deposit accounts, and certificates of deposit (CDs). FDIC insurance does not, however, cover other financial products and services that insured banks may offer, such as stocks, bonds, mutual fund shares, life insurance policies, annuities or municipal securities. There is no need for depositors to apply for FDIC insurance or even to request it. Coverage is automatic.

To ensure funds are fully protected, depositors should understand their coverage limits. The FDIC provides separate coverage for deposits held in different account ownership categories. The coverage limits shown in the chart below refer to the total of all deposits that an account holder has in the same ownership categories at each FDIC-insured bank. The chart shows only the most common ownership categories that apply to individual and family deposits, and it assumes that all FDIC requirements are met.

FDIC Deposit Insurance Coverage Limits

These coverage limits were announced in October 2008. On January 1, 2010, the standard coverage limit will return to $100,000 for all deposit categories except IRAs and Certain Retirement Accounts, which will continue to be insured up to $250,000 per owner:

• Single Accounts (owned by one person): $250,000 per owner

A Guide To Deposit Insurance Coverage 217

[Editor's note: Money market funds are not covered], and time deposits such as certificates of deposit (CDs).

FDIC deposit insurance covers the balance of each depositor's account, dollar-for-dollar, up to the insurance limit, including principal and any accrued interest through the date of the insured bank's closing.

The FDIC does not insure money invested in stocks, bonds, mutual funds, life insurance policies, annuities, or municipal securities, even if these investments were bought from an insured bank.

- Joint Accounts (two or more persons): $250,000 per co-owner

- IRAs and certain other retirement accounts: $250,000 per owner

- Trust Accounts: $250,000 per owner per beneficiary subject to specific limitations and requirements

- Corporation, Partnership and Unincorporated Association Accounts: $250,000 per corporation, partnership or unincorporated association

- Employee Benefit Plan Accounts: $250,000 for the non-contingent, ascertainable interest of each participant

- Government Accounts: $250,000 per official custodian

- Non-Interest Bearing Transaction Accounts: Unlimited coverage, only at participating FDIC-insured banks and savings associations. Unlimited deposit insurance coverage is available through December 31, 2009, for non-interest bearing transaction accounts at institutions participating in FDIC's Temporary Liquidity Guarantee Program.

If you have questions about FDIC coverage limits and requirements, visit www.myFDICinsurance.gov, call toll-free 877-ASK-FDIC, or ask a representative at your bank.

Source: "Financial Institution Letters: FDIC Deposit Insurance Coverage," Federal Deposit Insurance Corporation (FDIC), October 23, 2008.

♣ It's A Fact!!

The National Credit Union Administration (NCUA) is the federal agency that administers the National Credit Union Share Insurance Fund (NCUSIF). The NCUSIF, like the FDIC's Deposit Insurance Fund, is a federal insurance fund backed by the full faith and credit of the U.S. Government.

The NCUSIF insures member savings in federally insured credit unions, which account for approximately 98 percent of all credit unions. All federal credit unions and the vast majority of state-chartered credit unions are covered by NCUSIF insurance protection.

Credit unions that are insured by NCUSIF must prominently display the official NCUA insurance sign. No credit union may terminate its federal insurance without first notifying its members.

Here are some important facts to remember about your share insurance provided by the NCUSIF:

- Not one penny of insured savings has ever been lost by a member of a federally insured credit union.

- As a member of a federally insured credit union, you do not pay directly for your share insurance protection. Your credit union places a deposit into the NCUSIF and pays an insurance assessment based on the total amount of insured shares and deposits in the credit union. Federally insured credit unions are required to deposit and maintain one percent of their insured shares and deposits in the NCUSIF.

- Share accounts in federally insured credit unions are insured up to the Standard Maximum Share Insurance Amount (SMSIA), $250,000 as of October 3, 2008. The Emergency Economic Stabilization Act of 2008 increased the insurance coverage on all accounts up to $250,000 until December 31, 2009.

For additional information about multiple accounts and other special situations, visit the National Credit Union Administration website at http://www.ncua.gov.

Source: Excerpted from "Is My Credit Union Federally Insured?" National Credit Union Administration (www.nuca.gov), 2008.

The FDIC does not insure U.S. Treasury bills, bonds, or notes. These are backed by the full faith and credit of the United States government.

How much insurance coverage does the FDIC provide?

The basic insurance amount is $100,000 [or $250,000 until January 1, 2010] per depositor, per insured bank.

The $100,000 [or $250,000 until January 1, 2010] amount applies to all depositors of an insured bank except for owners of certain retirement accounts, which are insured up to $250,000 per owner, per insured bank.

Deposits in separate branches of an insured bank are not separately insured. Deposits in one insured bank are insured separately from deposits in another insured bank.

Deposits maintained in different categories of legal ownership at the same bank can be separately insured. Therefore, it is possible to have deposits of more than $100,000 [or $250,000 until January 1, 2010] at one insured bank and still be fully insured.

Ownership Categories

Single Accounts

A single account is a deposit owned by one person. The following deposit account types are included in this ownership category:

- Accounts held in one person's name alone

- Accounts established for one person by an agent, nominee, guardian, custodian, or conservator, including Uniform Transfers to Minors Act accounts, escrow accounts, and brokered deposit accounts

- Accounts held in the name of a business that is a sole proprietorship (for example, a "DBA account")

- Accounts established for a decedent's estate

- Any account that fails to qualify for coverage under another ownership category.

All single accounts owned by the same person at the same insured bank are added together and the total is insured up to $100,000 [or $250,000 until January 1, 2010].

If an individual has a deposit account titled in his or her name alone but gives another person the right to withdraw deposits from the account, the account will be insured as a single account only if the insured bank's deposit account records indicate that the other signer is authorized to make withdrawals pursuant to a Power of Attorney, or the account is owned by one person and the other person is authorized to withdraw deposits on the owner's behalf (for example, a convenience account).

If the insured bank's account records do not indicate that such a relationship exists, the deposit would be insured as a joint account.

Joint Accounts

A joint account is a deposit owned by two or more people. To qualify for insurance under this ownership category, all of the following requirements must be met:

- All co-owners must be people. Legal entities such as corporations, trusts, estates, or partnerships are not eligible for joint account coverage.

- All co-owners must have equal rights to withdraw funds from the account. For example, if one co-owner can withdraw funds on his or her signature alone but the other co-owner can withdraw deposits only with the signature of both co-owners, the co-owners do not have equal withdrawal rights.

- All co-owners must sign the deposit account signature card unless the account is a CD or is established by an agent, nominee, guardian, custodian, executor, or conservator.

If all of these requirements are met, each co-owner's share of every account that is jointly held at the same insured bank is added together with the co-owner's other shares, and the total is insured up to $100,000 [or $250,000 until January 1, 2010].

✤ It's A Fact!!

Insurance coverage of joint accounts is not increased by rearranging the owners' names or by changing the styling of their names. Alternating the use of "or," "and" or "and/or" to separate the names of co-owners in a joint account title also does not affect the amount of insurance coverage provided.

In addition, using different Social Security numbers on multiple accounts held by the same co-owners will not increase insurance coverage.

Source: FDIC, January 2007.

The FDIC assumes that all co-owners' shares are equal unless the deposit account records state otherwise.

For example, a husband and wife could have up to $200,000 [or $500,000 until January 1, 2010] in one or more joint accounts at the same insured bank and the deposits would be fully insured. The husband's ownership share is insured up to $100,000 [or $250,000 until January 1, 2010] and the wife's ownership share is insured up to $100,000 [or $250,000 until January 1, 2010].

Frequently Asked Questions (FAQ) About FDIC Insurance

Whose deposits does the FDIC insure?

Any person or entity can have FDIC deposit insurance in an insured bank located in the United States. A person does not have to be a U.S. citizen or resident to have deposits insured by the FDIC.

Does FDIC insurance protect creditors and shareholders?

FDIC insurance only protects depositors, although some depositors may also be creditors or shareholders of an insured bank.

How long does the FDIC take to pay insurance on deposits after an insured bank fails?

Federal law requires the FDIC to make payment as soon as possible. Historically, the FDIC pays insurance within a few days after a bank closing either by establishing an account at another insured bank or by providing a check. Deposits purchased through a broker may take longer to be paid because the FDIC may need to obtain the broker's records to determine insurance coverage.

Customers with uninsured deposits receive the insured portion of their account as described above. They will wait longer to receive payment for some or all of their uninsured deposits. The amount of uninsured deposits they may receive, if any, is based on the sale of the failed bank's assets. Depending on the quality and value of these assets, it may take several years to sell the assets. As assets are sold, uninsured depositors receive periodic payment on their uninsured deposit claim.

Does the FDIC insure an unpaid cashier's check, interest check, money order, or expense check issued by an insured bank?

If a depositor holds one or more of these items from an insured bank, and the insured bank fails before the item is cashed elsewhere, the FDIC will add the item to any other deposits held in the same ownership category at the same insured bank. For example, an outstanding interest check payable to a depositor will be added to their other single ownership accounts, if any, and the total insured up to $100,000 [or $250,000 until January 1, 2010].

Does the FDIC insure safe deposit boxes if a bank fails?

The FDIC does not insure safe deposit boxes or their contents. In the event of a bank failure, the FDIC in most cases arranges for an acquiring bank to take over the failed bank's offices, including locations with safe deposit boxes. If no acquirer is found, box holders would be sent instructions for removing the contents of their boxes.

How does the FDIC determine ownership of deposits?

The FDIC presumes that deposits are owned as shown on the deposit account records of the insured bank. The deposit account records of an insured bank include account ledgers, signature cards, certificates of deposit, passbooks, and certain computer records. Account statements, deposit slips, and canceled checks are not considered deposit account records for purposes of determining deposit insurance coverage.

✔ Quick Tip

Can I increase my insurance coverage by depositing funds with different insured banks?

Deposits with each FDIC-insured bank are insured separately from any deposits at another insured bank. If an insured bank has branch offices, the main office and all branch offices are considered one insured bank— a depositor cannot increase insurance coverage by placing deposits at different branches of the same insured bank. Similarly, deposits held with the internet division of an insured bank are considered the same as deposits with the "brick and mortar" part of the bank, even if the internet division uses a different name. If two banks are affiliated, such as having a common holding company, but are separately chartered (indicated by having two different FDIC Certificate numbers), deposits in each bank would be separately insured.

Source: FDIC, January 2007.

Can I increase my insurance coverage by dividing my deposits into several different accounts at the same insured bank?

Deposit insurance coverage can be increased only if the accounts are held in different categories of ownership. These categories include single accounts, retirement accounts, joint accounts, and revocable trust accounts.

What happens to deposit insurance coverage after an account owner dies?

The FDIC insures a deceased person's accounts as if the person were still alive for another six months. During this grace period, the insurance coverage

What are fiduciary accounts?

These are deposit accounts owned by one party but held in a fiduciary capacity by another party. Fiduciary relationships may include, but are not limited to, an agent, nominee, guardian, executor, or custodian. Common fiduciary accounts include Uniform Transfers to Minors accounts, escrow accounts, Interest On Lawyer Trust Accounts (IOLTA), and deposit accounts obtained through a broker.

What are the FDIC disclosure requirements for fiduciary accounts?

The fiduciary nature of the account must be disclosed in the bank's deposit account records (for example, "Jane Doe as Custodian for Susie Doe" or "First Real Estate Title Company, Client Escrow Account"). The name and ownership interest of each owner must be ascertainable from the deposit account records of the insured bank or from records maintained by the agent (or by some person or entity that has agreed to maintain records for the agent). Special disclosure rules apply to multi-tiered fiduciary relationships. If an agent pools the deposits of several owners into one account and the disclosure rules are satisfied, the deposits of each owner will be insured as that owner's deposits.

How does the FDIC insure funds deposited by a fiduciary?

Funds deposited by a fiduciary on behalf of one or more persons or entities (the owner) are insured as the deposits of the owner if the fiduciary meets the disclosure requirements for fiduciary accounts.

Would funds deposited by a fiduciary be insured separately from the owners' other accounts at the same bank?

Funds deposited by a fiduciary on behalf of one or more persons or entities (the owners) would be added to any other deposits of the owners at the same insured bank and the total would be subject to the insurance limit for the applicable ownership category.

For example: A broker purchases a CD for $100,000 on a customer's behalf at ABC Bank in the customer's name alone and the customer already has a checking account in his or her name alone at that same bank for $15,000. The two accounts would be added together and insured up to a total of $100,000 [or $250,000 until January 1, 2010] in the single ownership account category, with $15,000 uninsured [under the standard coverage limit amount].

Source: FDIC, January 2007.

of the owner's accounts will not change unless the accounts are restructured by those authorized to do so. Also, the FDIC will not apply this grace period if it would result in less coverage.

What happens to my coverage if I have deposits at two insured banks that merge?

When two or more insured banks merge, the deposits from the assumed bank continue to be insured separately for at least six months after the merger. This grace period gives a depositor the opportunity to restructure his or her accounts, if necessary.

CDs from the assumed bank are separately insured until the earliest maturity date after the end of the six-month grace period. CDs that mature during the six-month period and are renewed for the same term and in the same dollar amount (either with or without accrued interest) continue to be separately insured until the first maturity date after the six-month period. If a CD matures during the six-month grace period and is renewed on any other basis, it would be separately insured only until the end of the six-month grace period.

For More Information From The FDIC

Federal Deposit Insurance Corporation (FDIC)

Division of Supervision and Consumer Protection
550 17th Street, N.W.
Washington, DC 20429
Phone: 703-562-2222
Website: http://www.fdic.gov

Phone Resources

- You can call toll-free at 877-ASK-FDIC (877-275-3342) from 8 a.m. until 8 p.m. (Eastern Time) Monday through Friday.

- TTY users can call toll-free at 800-925-4618

Online Resources

- Calculate insurance coverage using the FDIC's online Electronic Deposit Insurance Estimator at www2.fdic.gov/edie. The estimator can also be accessed through www.myfdicinsurance.gov.

- Read more about FDIC insurance online at: www.fdic.gov/deposit/deposits

- Order FDIC deposit insurance products online at: www2.fdic.gov/depositinsuranceregister

- Send questions by e-mail using the FDIC's online Customer Assistance Form at www2.fdic.gov/starsmail

Chapter 22

What You Should Know About Certificates Of Deposit (CDs)

Investors searching for relatively low-risk investments that can easily be converted into cash often turn to certificates of deposit (CDs). A CD is a special type of deposit account with a bank or thrift institution that typically offers a higher rate of interest than a regular savings account. Unlike other investments, CDs feature federal deposit insurance up to $100,000. [Editor's Note: In 2008, basic insurance coverage from the Federal Deposit Insurance Corporation (FDIC) was temporarily increased to $250,000. Coverage limits are scheduled to return to $100,000 on January 1, 2010. For current information, visit the FDIC website at www.fdic.gov.]

Here's how CDs work: When you purchase a CD, you invest a fixed sum of money for fixed period of time—six months, one year, five years, or more—and, in exchange, the issuing bank pays you interest, typically at regular intervals. When you cash in or redeem your CD, you receive the money you originally invested plus any accrued interest. But if you redeem your CD before it matures, you may have to pay an "early withdrawal" penalty or forfeit a portion of the interest you earned.

Although most investors have traditionally purchased CDs through local banks, many brokerage firms and independent salespeople now offer CDs.

About This Chapter: From "Certificates of Deposit: Tips for Investors," U.S. Securities and Exchange Commission (www.sec.gov), August 1, 2007.

These individuals and entities—known as "deposit brokers"—can sometimes negotiate a higher rate of interest for a CD by promising to bring a certain amount of deposits to the institution. The deposit broker can then offer these "brokered CDs" to their customers.

At one time, most CDs paid a fixed interest rate until they reached maturity. But, like many other products in today's markets, CDs have become

---

✔ Quick Tip

Don't be embarrassed if you invested in a long-term, brokered CD in the mistaken belief that it was a shorter-term instrument—you are not alone. Instead, you should complain promptly to the broker who sold you the CD. By complaining early you may improve your chances of getting your money back. Here are the steps you should take:

1. Talk to the broker who sold you the CD, and explain the problem fully, especially if you misunderstood any of the CD's terms. Tell your broker how you want the problem resolved.

2. If your broker can't resolve your problem, then talk to his or her branch manager.

3. If that doesn't work, then write a letter to the compliance department at the firm's main office. The branch manager should be able to provide with contact information for that department. Explain your problem clearly, and tell the firm how you want it resolved. Ask the compliance office to respond to you in writing within 30 days.

4. If you're still not satisfied, then send the U.S. Securities and Exchange Commission (SEC) your complaint using their online complaint form. Be sure to attach copies of any letters you've sent already to the firm. If you don't have access to the internet, please write to them at the address below:

    Office of Investor Education and Advocacy
    U.S. Securities and Exchange Commission
    100 F Street, N.E.
    Washington, DC 20549-0213

The SEC will forward your complaint to the firm's compliance department and ask that they look into the problem and respond to you in writing.

more complicated. Investors may now choose among variable rate CDs, long-term CDs, and CDs with other special features.

Some long-term, high-yield CDs have "call" features, meaning that the issuing bank may choose to terminate—or call—the CD after only one year or some other fixed period of time. Only the issuing bank may call a CD, not the investor. For example, a bank might decide to call its high-yield CDs if

Please note that sometimes a complaint can be successfully resolved. But in many cases, the firm denies wrongdoing, and it comes down to one person's word against another's. In that case, the SEC cannot do anything more to help resolve the complaint. They cannot act as a judge or an arbitrator to establish wrongdoing and force the firm to satisfy your claim. And they cannot act as your lawyer.

You should also contact the banking regulator that oversees the bank that issued the CD:

- The Board of Governors of the Federal Reserve System (available online at http://www.federalreserve.gov/pubs/complaints) oversees state-chartered banks and trust companies that belong to the Federal Reserve System.

- The Federal Deposit Insurance Corporation (http://www.fdic.gov/consumers/questions/index.html) regulates state-chartered banks that do not belong to the Federal Reserve System.

- The Office of the Controller of the Currency (http://www.occ.treas.gov/customer.htm) regulates banks that have the word "National" in or the letters "N.A." after their names.

- The National Credit Union Administration (http://www.ncua.gov/ConsumerInformation/fraudhotline.html) regulates federally charted credit unions.

- The Office of Thrift Supervision (http://www.ots.treas.gov/docs/4/48780.html) oversees federal savings and loans and federal savings banks.

Source: SEC, August 1, 2007.

interest rates fall. But if you've invested in a long-term CD and interest rates subsequently rise, you'll be locked in at the lower rate.

Before you consider purchasing a CD from your bank or brokerage firm, make sure you fully understand all of its terms. Carefully read the disclosure statements, including any fine print. And don't be dazzled by high yields. Ask questions—and demand answers—before you invest. These tips can help you assess what features make sense for you:

- **Find Out When The CD Matures:** As simple as this sounds, many investors fail to confirm the maturity dates for their CDs and are later shocked to learn that they've tied up their money for five, ten, or even twenty years. Before you purchase a CD, ask to see the maturity date in writing.

- **Investigate Any Call Features:** Callable CDs give the issuing bank the right to terminate—or "call"—the CD after a set period of time. But they do not give you that same right. If interest rates fall, the issuing bank might call the CD. In that case, you should receive the full amount of your original deposit plus any unpaid accrued interest. But you'll have to shop for a new one with a lower rate of return. Unlike the bank, you can never "call" the CD and get your principal back. So if interest rates rise, you'll be stuck in a long-term CD paying below-market rates. In that case, if you want to cash out, you will lose some of your principal. That's because your broker will have to sell your CD at a discount to attract a buyer. Few buyers would be willing to pay full price for a CD with a below-market interest rate.

- **Understand The Difference Between Call Features And Maturity:** Don't assume that a "federally insured one-year non-callable" CD matures in one year. It doesn't. These words mean the bank cannot redeem the CD during the first year, but they have nothing to do with the CD's maturity date. A "one-year non-callable" CD may still have a maturity date 15 or 20 years in the future. If you have any doubt, ask the sales representative at your bank or brokerage firm to explain the CD's call features and to confirm when it matures.

- **For Brokered CDs, Identify The Issuer:** Because federal deposit insurance is limited to a total aggregate amount for each depositor in each bank or thrift institution, it is very important that you know which

☞ Remember!!

If you have a complaint about a CD you purchased through a bank, try to resolve your complaint directly with an officer of the bank before involving an outside agency. Financial institutions value their customers and most will be helpful.

Source: Excerpted from "Certificates of Deposit: Tips for Savers," Federal Deposit Insurance Corporation (www.fdic.gov), November 23, 2007.

bank or thrift issued your CD. Your broker may plan to put your money in a bank or thrift where you already have other CDs or deposits. You risk not being fully insured if the brokered CD would push your total deposits at the institution over the insurance limit. (If you think that might happen, contact the institution to explore potential options for remaining fully insured, or contact the FDIC.) For more information about federal deposit insurance, visit the Federal Deposit Insurance Corporation (FDIC)'s website or call the FDIC's Consumer Information Center at 877-275-3342. The phone numbers for the hearing impaired are 800-925-4618 or (202) 942-3147.

- **Find Out How The CD Is Held:** Unlike traditional bank CDs, brokered CDs are sometimes held by a group of unrelated investors. Instead of owning the entire CD, each investor owns a piece. Confirm with your broker how your CD is held, and be sure to ask for a copy of the exact title of the CD. If several investors own the CD, the deposit broker will probably not list each person's name in the title. But you should make sure that the account records reflect that the broker is merely acting as an agent for you and the other owners (for example, "XYZ Brokerage as Custodian for Customers"). This will ensure that your portion of the CD qualifies for FDIC coverage.

- **Research Any Penalties For Early Withdrawal:** Deposit brokers often tout the fact that their CDs have no penalty for early withdrawal. While technically true, these claims can be misleading. Be sure to find out how much you'll have to pay if you cash in your CD before maturity and whether you risk losing any portion of your principal. If you are the sole owner of a brokered CD, you may be able to pay an early withdrawal penalty to the bank that issued the CD to get your money back. But if you share the CD with other customers, your broker will have to find a buyer for your portion. If interest rates have fallen since you purchased your CD and the bank hasn't called it, your broker may be able to sell your portion for a profit. But if interest rates have risen, there may be less demand for your lower-yielding CD. That means you would have to sell the CD at a discount and lose some of your original deposit—despite no "penalty" for early withdrawal.

- **Thoroughly Check Out The Broker:** Deposit brokers do not have to go through any licensing or certification procedures, and no state or federal agency licenses, examines, or approves them. Since anyone can claim to be a deposit broker, you should always check whether your broker or the company he or she works for has a history of complaints or fraud. You can do this by calling your state securities regulator or by checking with the Financial Industry Regulatory Authority (FINRA), at http://www.finra.org/Investors/ToolsCalculators/BrokerCheck.

- **Confirm The Interest Rate You'll Receive And How You'll Be Paid:** You should receive a disclosure document that tells you the interest rate on your CD and whether the rate is fixed or variable. Be sure to ask how often the bank pays interest—for example, monthly or semi-annually. And confirm how you'll be paid—for example, by check or by an electronic transfer of funds.

- **Ask Whether The Interest Rate Ever Changes:** If you're considering investing in a variable-rate CD, make sure you understand when and how the rate can change. Some variable-rate CDs feature a "multi-step" or "bonus rate" structure in which interest rates increase or decrease over time according to a pre-set schedule. Other variable-rate CDs pay interest rates that track the performance of a specified market index, such as the S&P 500 or the Dow Jones Industrial Average.

The bottom-line question you should always ask yourself is: Does this investment make sense for me? A high-yield, long-term CD with a maturity date of 15 to 20 years may make sense for many younger investors who want to diversify their financial holdings. But it might not make sense for elderly investors.

Chapter 23

What Are Bonds?

Have you ever borrowed money? Of course you have! Whether we hit our parents up for a few bucks to buy candy as children or asked the bank for a mortgage, most of us have borrowed money at some point in our lives.

Just as people need money, so do companies and governments. A company needs funds to expand into new markets, while governments need money for everything from infrastructure to social programs. The problem large organizations run into is that they typically need far more money than the average bank can provide. The solution is to raise money by issuing bonds (or other debt instruments) to a public market. Thousands of investors then each lend a portion of the capital needed. Really, a bond is nothing more than a loan for which you are the lender. The organization that sells a bond is known as the issuer. You can think of a bond as an IOU given by a borrower (the issuer) to a lender (the investor).

Of course, nobody would loan his or her hard-earned money for nothing. The issuer of a bond must pay the investor something extra for the privilege of using his or her money. This "extra" comes in the form of interest payments, which are made at a predetermined rate and schedule. The interest rate is often referred to as the coupon. The date on which the issuer has to

About This Chapter: Text in this chapter is excerpted "Bond Basics." Reprinted with permission from Investopedia, ULC. © 2008 Investopedia.com.

❧ What's It Mean?

Bonds: What They Are

- A bond is an "IOU," certifying that you loaned money to a government or corporation and outlining the terms of repayment.

How They Work

- Buyer may purchase bond at a discount. The bond has a fixed interest rate for a fixed period of time. When the time is up, the bond is said to have "matured" and the buyer may redeem the bond for the full face value.

Types

- Corporate

    - Sold by private companies to raise money.

    - If company goes bankrupt, bondholders have first claim to the assets, before stockholders.

- Municipal

    - Issued by any non-federal government.

    - Interest paid comes from taxes or from revenues from special projects. Earned interest is exempt from federal income tax.

- Federal Government

    - The safest investment you can make. Even if U.S. government goes bankrupt, it is obligated to repay bonds.

repay the amount borrowed (known as face value) is called the maturity date. Bonds are known as fixed-income securities because you know the exact amount of cash you'll get back if you hold the security until maturity.

For example, say you buy a bond with a face value of $1,000, a coupon of 8%, and a maturity of 10 years. This means you'll receive a total of $80 ($1,000 times 8%) of interest per year for the next 10 years. Actually, because most bonds pay interest semi-annually, you'll receive two payments of $40 a year for 10 years. When the bond matures after a decade, you'll get your $1,000 back.

Why Bother With Bonds?

It's an investing axiom that stocks return more than bonds. In the past, this has generally been true for time periods of at least 10 years or more. However, this doesn't mean you shouldn't invest in bonds. Bonds are appropriate any time you cannot tolerate the short-term volatility of the stock market. Take two situations where this may be true:

- **Retirement:** The easiest example to think of is an individual living off a fixed income. A retiree simply cannot afford to lose his/her principal as income for it is required to pay the bills.

- **Shorter Time Horizons:** Say a young executive is planning to go back for an MBA in three years. It's true that the stock market provides the opportunity for higher growth, which is why his/her retirement fund is mostly in stocks, but the executive cannot afford to take the chance of losing the money going towards his/her education. Because money is needed for a specific purpose in the relatively near future, fixed-income securities are likely the best investment.

These two examples are clear cut, and they don't represent all investors. Most personal financial advisors advocate maintaining a diversified portfolio and changing the weightings of asset classes throughout your life. For example, in your 20s and 30s a majority of wealth should be in equities. In your 40s and 50s the percentages shift out of stocks into bonds until retirement, when a majority of your investments should be in the form of fixed income.

Bond Characteristics

Bonds have a number of characteristics of which you need to be aware. All of these factors play a role in determining the value of a bond and the extent to which it fits in your portfolio.

Face Value/Par Value

The face value (also known as the par value or principal) is the amount of money a holder will get back once a bond matures. A newly issued bond usually sells at the par value. Corporate bonds normally have a par value of $1,000, but this amount can be much greater for government bonds.

What confuses many people is that the par value is not the price of the bond. A bond's price fluctuates throughout its life in response to a number of variables (more on this later). When a bond trades at a price above the face value, it is said to be selling at a premium. When a bond sells below face value, it is said to be selling at a discount.

> ## ♣ It's A Fact!!
> ## Debt Versus Equity
>
> Bonds are debt, whereas stocks are equity. This is the important distinction between the two securities. By purchasing equity (stock) an investor becomes an owner in a corporation. Ownership comes with voting rights and the right to share in any future profits. By purchasing debt (bonds) an investor becomes a creditor to the corporation (or government). The primary advantage of being a creditor is that you have a higher claim on assets than shareholders do: that is, in the case of bankruptcy, a bondholder will get paid before a shareholder. However, the bondholder does not share in the profits if a company does well—he or she is entitled only to the principal plus interest.
>
> To sum up, there is generally less risk in owning bonds than in owning stocks, but this comes at the cost of a lower return.
>
> Source: © 2008 Investopedia, ULC.

Coupon (The Interest Rate)

The coupon is the amount the bondholder will receive as interest payments. It's called a "coupon" because sometimes there are physical coupons on the bond that you tear off and redeem for interest. However, this was more common in the past. Nowadays, records are more likely to be kept electronically.

As previously mentioned, most bonds pay interest every six months, but it's possible for them to pay monthly, quarterly, or annually. The coupon is expressed as a percentage of the par value. If a bond pays a coupon of 10% and its par value is $1,000, then it'll pay $100 of interest a year. A rate that stays as a fixed percentage of the par value like this is a fixed-rate bond. Another possibility is an adjustable interest payment, known as a floating-rate bond. In this case the interest rate is tied to market rates through an index, such as the rate on Treasury bills.

You might think investors will pay more for a high coupon than for a low coupon. All things being equal, a lower coupon means that the price of the bond will fluctuate more.

♣ It's A Fact!!
Callable Or Redeemable Bonds

Callable or redeemable bonds are bonds that can be redeemed or paid off by the issuer prior to the bonds' maturity date. When an issuer calls its bonds, it pays investors the call price (usually the face value of the bonds) together with accrued interest to date and, at that point, stops making interest payments. Call provisions are often part of corporate and municipal bonds, but usually not bonds issued by the federal government.

An issuer may choose to redeem a callable bond when current interest rates drop below the interest rate on the bond. That way the issuer can save money by paying off the bond and issuing another bond at a lower interest rate. This is similar to refinancing the mortgage on your house so you can make lower monthly payments. Callable bonds are more risky for investors than non-callable bonds because an investor whose bond has been called is often faced with reinvesting the money at a lower, less attractive rate. As a result, callable bonds often have a higher annual return to compensate for the risk that the bonds might be called early.

Source: Excerpted from "Callable or Redeemable Bonds," U.S. Securities and Exchange Commission (SEC), April 4, 2008.

♣ It's A Fact!!

The bond rating system helps investors determine a company's credit risk. Think of a bond rating as the report card for a company's credit rating. Blue-chip firms, which are safer investments, have a high rating, while risky companies have a low rating. Table 23.1 illustrates the different bond rating scales from the major rating agencies in the U.S.: Moody's, Standard and Poor's (S&P), and Fitch Ratings.

Table 23.1. Bond Rating Scales

Bond Rating

Moody's	S&P/Fitch	Grade	Risk
Aaa	AAA	Investment	Highest Quality
Aa	AA	Investment	High Quality
A	A	Investment	Strong
Baa	BBB	Investment	Medium Grade
Ba, B	BB, B	Junk	Speculative
Caa/Ca/C	CCC/CC/C	Junk	Highly Speculative
C	D	Junk	In Default

Notice that if the company falls below a certain credit rating, its grade changes from investment quality to junk status. Junk bonds are aptly named: they are the debt of companies in some sort of financial difficulty. Because they are so risky, they have to offer much higher yields than any other debt. This brings up an important point: not all bonds are inherently safer than stocks. Certain types of bonds can be just as risky, if not riskier, than stocks.

Source: © 2008 Investopedia, ULC.

Maturity

The maturity date is the date in the future on which the investor's principal will be repaid. Maturities can range from as little as one day to as long as 30 years (though terms of 100 years have been issued).

A bond that matures in one year is much more predictable and thus less risky than a bond that matures in 20 years. Therefore, in general, the longer the time to maturity, the higher the interest rate. Also, all things being equal, a longer term bond will fluctuate more than a shorter term bond.

Issuer

The issuer of a bond is a crucial factor to consider, as the issuer's stability is your main assurance of getting paid back. For example, the U.S. government is far more secure than any corporation. Its default risk (the chance of the debt not being paid back) is extremely small—so small that U.S. government securities are known as risk-free assets. The reason behind this is that a government will always be able to bring in future revenue through taxation. A company, on the other hand, must continue to make profits, which is far from guaranteed. This added risk means corporate bonds must offer a higher yield in order to entice investors—this is the risk/return tradeoff in action.

Yield, Price, And Other Confusion

Understanding the price fluctuation of bonds is probably the most confusing part of this lesson. In fact, many new investors are surprised to learn that a bond's price changes on a daily basis, just like that of any other publicly traded security. Up to this point, we've talked about bonds as if every investor holds them to maturity. It's true that if you do this you're guaranteed to get your principal back; however, a bond does not have to be held to maturity. At any time, a bond can be sold in the open market, where the price can fluctuate—sometimes dramatically. We'll get to how price changes in a bit. First, we need to introduce the concept of yield.

Measuring Return With Yield

Yield is a figure that shows the return you get on a bond. The simplest version of yield is calculated using the following formula: yield = coupon amount/price. When you buy a bond at par, yield is equal to the interest rate. When the price changes, so does the yield.

Let's demonstrate this with an example. If you buy a bond with a 10% coupon at its $1,000 par value, the yield is 10% ($100/$1,000). Pretty simple stuff. But if the price goes down to $800, then the yield goes up to 12.5%. This happens because you are getting the same guaranteed $100 on an asset that is worth $800 ($100/$800). Conversely, if the bond goes up in price to $1,200, the yield shrinks to 8.33% ($100/$1,200).

Yield To Maturity

Of course, these matters are always more complicated in real life. When bond investors refer to yield, they are usually referring to yield to maturity (YTM). YTM is a more advanced yield calculation that shows the total return you will receive if you hold the bond to maturity. It equals all the interest payments you will receive (and assumes that you will reinvest the interest payment at the same rate as the current yield on the bond) plus any gain (if you purchased at a discount) or loss (if you purchased at a premium).

Knowing how to calculate YTM isn't important right now. In fact, the calculation is rather sophisticated and beyond the scope of this chapter. The key point here is that YTM is more accurate and enables you to compare bonds with different maturities and coupons.

Putting It All Together: The Link Between Price And Yield

The relationship of yield to price can be summarized as follows: when price goes up, yield goes down and vice versa. Technically, you'd say the bond's price and its yield are inversely related.

Here's a commonly asked question: How can high yields and high prices both be good when they can't happen at the same time? The answer depends on your point of view. If you are a bond buyer, you want high yields. A buyer wants to pay $800 for the $1,000 bond, which gives the bond a high yield of 12.5%. On the other hand, if you already own a bond, you've locked in your interest rate, so you hope the price of the bond goes up. This way you can cash out by selling your bond in the future.

Price In The Market

So far we've discussed the factors of face value, coupon, maturity, issuers and yield. All of these characteristics of a bond play a role in its price. However, the factor that influences a bond more than any other is the level of prevailing interest rates in the economy. When interest rates rise, the prices of bonds in the market fall, thereby raising the yield of the older bonds and bringing them into line with newer bonds being issued with higher coupons. When interest rates fall, the prices of bonds in the market rise, thereby lowering the yield of the older bonds and bringing them into line with newer bonds being issued with lower coupons.

☞ **Remember!!**

You should research bonds just as you would stocks. We've gone over several factors you need to consider before loaning money to a government or company, so do your homework!

Source: © 2008 Investopedia, ULC.

How Do I Buy Bonds?

Most bond transactions can be completed through a full service or discount brokerage. You can also open an account with a bond broker, but be warned that most bond brokers require a minimum initial deposit of $5,000. If you cannot afford this amount, we suggest looking at a mutual fund that specializes in bonds (or a bond fund).

Some financial institutions will provide their clients with the service of transacting government securities. However, if your bank doesn't provide this service and you do not have a brokerage account, you can purchase government bonds through a government agency (this is true in most countries). In the U.S. you can buy bonds directly from the government through

TreasuryDirect at http://www.treasurydirect.gov. The Bureau of the Public Debt started TreasuryDirect so that individuals could buy bonds directly from the Treasury, thereby bypassing a broker. All transactions and interest payments are done electronically.

If you do decide to purchase a bond through your broker, he or she may tell you that the trade is commission free. Don't be fooled. What typically happens is that the broker will mark up the price slightly; this markup is really the same as a commission. To make sure that you are not being taken advantage of, simply look up the latest quote for the bond and determine whether the markup is acceptable.

Chapter 24

Understanding Savings Bonds

Introduction To Savings Bonds

Savings bonds have been called "the all American investment." They are an easy way to save money safely and get a good market return. Rates change every May and November based on either current market rates or inflation. Current rates can be found at the Savings Bond website, available online at http://www.treasurydirect.gov/indiv/products/products.htm.

There are two main types of bonds offered. The Inflation Indexed—or I Bond—is designed to offer all Americans a way to save that protects the purchasing power of their investment by assuring them a real rate of return over and above inflation. I Bonds have features that make them attractive to many investors. They are sold at face value in denominations of $50, $75, $100, $200, $500, $1,000, $5,000, and $10,000 and earn interest for as long as 30 years. I Bond earnings are added every month and interest is compounded semiannually. They are state and local income tax exempt and federal income tax on I Bond earnings can be deferred until the bonds are cashed

About This Chapter: This chapter includes information from the following documents produced by the U.S. Department of the Treasury (www.treas.gov and www.savingsbonds.gov): "Introduction to Savings Bonds," undated, accessed May 2008; "EE Savings Bonds In Depth," December 27, 2007; "Buy EE Savings Bonds," June 3, 2008; "Redeem EE/E Bonds and Savings Notes," October 18, 2006; "I Savings Bonds In Depth," December 27, 2007; "Buy I Savings Bonds," December 27, 2007; and "I and EE Savings Bond Comparison," December 27, 2007.

or stop earning interest after 30 years. Investors cashing I Bonds before five years are subject to a three-month earnings penalty.

The Series EE Savings Bonds pay interest equal to 90 percent of the average five-year Treasury securities yield for the preceding six months. This means that the rates on EE bonds are based on rates set by participants in the large government bond trading market. The Series I Bond, on the other hand, carries a fixed base rate plus a semi-annual calculation based on the rate of inflation as measured by the Consumer Price Index. The Series EE bond replaced the E bond, which is the one most associated with World War II war bonds.

> ♣ **It's A Fact!!**
> During World War II, many of Hollywood's most popular celebrities participated in bond drives to aid the war effort. The poster art used to advertise war bonds is still frequently seen in special exhibits in museums. The war bond campaign has been called a unique fusion of nationalism and consumerism. They offered Americans a financial and moral stake in the war.
>
> Source: "Introduction to Savings Bonds," U.S. Department of the Treasury.

EE Savings Bonds In Depth

An Easy And Safe Way To Save

EE Bonds are reliable, low-risk government-backed savings products that you can use toward financing education, supplemental retirement income, birthday and graduation gifts, and other special events. Series EE Bonds purchased on or after May 1, 2005, earn a fixed rate of return, letting you know what the bonds are worth at all times. EE Bonds purchased between May 1997 and April 30, 2005, are based on five-year Treasury security yields and earn a variable market-based rate of return.

Electronic EE Bonds

You can purchase, manage, and redeem electronic EE Bonds safely through a personal TreasuryDirect account. A new program called SmartExchange^{SM} allows TreasuryDirect account owners to convert their Series E, EE, and I paper savings bonds to electronic securities in a special Conversion Linked

Account in their online account. (NOTE: Paper EE Bonds are still available for purchase through most local financial institutions or participating employers' payroll deduction plans.)

Key Facts About Buying Electronic EE Bonds

- Sold at face value; that is, you pay $50 for a $50 bond and it's worth its full value when it's available for redemption

- Purchase in amounts of $25 or more, to the penny

- $5,000 maximum purchase in one calendar year

- Issued electronically to your designated account

Key Facts About Buying Paper EE Bonds

- Sold at half their face value; that is, you pay $25 for a $50 bond but it's not worth its face value until it has matured

- Purchase in denominations of $50, $75, $100, $200, $500, $1,000, and $5,000, and $10,000

- $5,000 maximum purchase in one calendar year

- Issued as paper bond certificates

✎ What's It Mean?

Series EE Bonds: These savings bonds replaced the Series E bonds. They are purchased at a discount of half their face value. You cannot buy more than $5,000 (face value) during any calendar year. EE bonds increase in value as the interest accrues or accumulates and pay interest for 30 years. When EE bonds "mature," or come due, you are paid your original investment plus all of the interest.

Source: Excerpted from "Savings Bonds," U.S. Securities and Exchange Commission (www.sec .gov), January 17, 2008.

Who Can Own Bonds

Individuals, corporations, associations, public or private organizations, and fiduciaries can own paper Series EE/E Bonds. At this time, only individuals can open a TreasuryDirect account and own electronic savings bonds.

You can own U.S. Savings Bonds if you have a Social Security number and you're a resident of the United States, citizen of the United States living abroad (must have U.S. address of record), civilian employee of the United States regardless of residence, or minor. Unlike other securities, minors may own U.S. Savings Bonds.

At this time, only individuals 18 or older can open TreasuryDirect accounts and purchase electronic savings bonds. Gift bonds purchased for minor children may be delivered to the minor linked account.

Buy EE Savings Bonds

Where To Buy

You can purchase electronic and paper EE Bonds through several sources:

- **TreasuryDirect:** This is the easiest, fastest way to buy Series EE bonds. The bonds are issued directly to you in your TreasuryDirect account. No paper bonds are issued. You have access to your account 24 hours a day, seven days a week. You can set up an automatic purchase schedule of as little as $25.

- **Banks And Other Financial Institutions:** The paper bond is printed to your instructions and mailed to you in 15 business days. Your bond's issue date reflects the date of purchase so that no interest is lost.

> ♣ **It's A Fact!!**
>
> **Chain Letters And Savings Bonds**
>
> Buying savings bonds as part of a chain letter or other pyramid scheme is prohibited.
>
> Source: "Buy EE Savings Bonds," U.S. Department of the Treasury, June 3, 2008.

- **Internet Banking Systems:** You can purchase paper bonds through online account access with many local financial institutions. See if a financial institution in your area offers this service.

- **Payroll Savings Plan:** You can buy EE Bonds through the Payroll Savings Plan if your employer offers it. Payroll for paper savings bonds and Electronic Payroll are available.

Purchase Limit

The purchase limit for both paper and electronic EE Bonds is $5,000 for each calendar year.

Identifying Information

Your Social Security number (SSN) is needed to buy a bond. The bond owner will be asked to provide his or her Social Security number for tax purposes when they cash the bond. But, if you're buying a gift and don't know the person's number, you can use your own. Using your SSN doesn't mean you will have a tax liability when the bond is cashed. The bond owner will be asked to provide his or her Social Security Number for tax purposes when they cash the bond.

Redeem EE/E Bonds And Savings Notes

- You can redeem your EE Bonds when the bonds are 12 months old.

- For Series EE/E Bonds and Savings Notes, you'll receive the purchase price of the bond plus accrued interest.

- If you redeem an EE Bond before it is five years old, you will lose three months of accrued interest.

Savings bonds are non-transferable. If you purchase a bond at an auction or find a bond belonging to someone else, you can't redeem it. The registration on the bond is a contractual relationship between the owner and the United States Treasury.

What Are Your Bonds Worth?

It's good to know what your bonds are worth before you redeem them. There are several options to help you determine the current redemption value of your bonds.

- Savings Bond Calculator is available online at http://www.treasury direct.gov/indiv/tools/tools_savingsbondcalc.htm and can help you determine the current redemption value of your bonds.

- Savings Bond Wizard is a free downloadable software program designed for individuals that want to maintain an inventory of their bonds (available online at http://www.treasurydirect.gov/indiv/tools/ tools_savingsbondwizard.htm.

- Savings Bonds Value Files are downloadable tables (available at http://www.treasurydirect.gov/indiv/tools/tools_savingsbondvalues.htm) to help you price your bonds.

- Simplified Savings Bond Redemption Tables are available for download (available at http://www.treasurydirect.gov/indiv/tools/ tools_redemptiontables.htm).

Redeem Bonds

To redeem electronic bonds purchased in TreasuryDirect, log in and follow the on-screen directions. Your checking or savings account will be credited with the redemption amount within one business day of the redemption date.

You can cash your EE/E Bonds and Savings Notes at most local financial institutions. Treasury doesn't maintain a listing of local banks that redeem bonds, so check with the banks in your area. When you present the bonds, you'll be asked to establish your identity. You can do this by being a customer with an active account open for at least six months at the financial institution that will be paying the bonds, or presenting documentary identification, such as a driver's license.

If you're not listed as the owner or co-owner on the bonds you're redeeming, you'll have to establish that you're entitled to redeem the bonds. It's always a good idea to check with your financial institution before presenting the bonds for payment to find out what identification and other documents you need.

Amount You Can Redeem At One Time

You may redeem up to $1,000 worth of bonds at one time based on documentary identification alone. If you want to redeem more than $1,000 worth of bonds, your servicing Treasury Retail Securities Site that handles savings bond transactions can help. In this instance, you'll need to sign the request for payment on the back of the bonds before a certifying officer at the bank, provide your Social Security number, and mail the bonds to the Treasury Retail Securities Site that services your area.

Tax Information

When a bond is redeemed, an IRS Form 1099-INT is issued, either at the time of redemption or at the end of the tax year, to the person who redeemed the bond.

Not Sure If You Already Redeemed A Bond?

If you have the serial numbers, The U.S. Treasury Department can look up the status of the securities, assuming they are U.S. Treasury securities. To do so, a signed request by the owner or co-owner must be received before the

---

♣ It's A Fact!!

The Patriot Savings Bond

The Patriot Bond is identical in every way to the paper EE Bond except that any EE Bond purchased through financial institutions after December 10, 2001 has the words "Patriot Bond" printed on the top half of the bond between the Social Security number and issue date. All EE Bond terms and conditions apply.

Patriot Bonds offer Americans one more way to express their support for our nation's anti-terrorism efforts. Proceeds are deposited into a general fund that includes contributions to anti-terrorism efforts and spent according to law.

Where To Buy: Patriot Bonds can only be purchased through financial institutions. EE Bonds purchased through the Payroll Savings Plan will not bear the Patriot Bond inscription, because they are processed by many different organizations using a variety of inscription techniques. As a result, this precludes TreasuryDirect from being able to offer the special inscription for payroll customers.

Source: From "Patriot Savings Bond," U.S. Department of the Treasury (www.savingsbonds.gov), August 4, 2006.

information can be provided. If the bond owner or both co-owners are deceased, then the person making the request needs to provide proof, such as a copy of the death certificate(s). Send the request to this address:

Bureau of the Public Debt
P.O. Box 7012
Parkersburg, WV 26106-7012

I Savings Bonds In Depth

I Bonds were once sold and redeemed solely as a paper security, but now they're also available in electronic form. As a TreasuryDirect account holder, you can buy, manage, and redeem I Bonds online.

A new program called SmartExchange℠ allows TreasuryDirect account owners to convert their Series E, EE, and I paper savings bonds to electronic securities in a special Conversion Linked Account within their online account.

Buying I Bonds Through TreasuryDirect

• Sold at face value; you pay $50 for a $50 bond.

• Purchased in amounts of $25 or more, to the penny.

• $5,000 maximum purchase in one calendar year.

• Issued electronically to your designated account.

Buying Paper I Bonds

• Sold at face value; that is, you pay $50 for a $50 bond.

• Purchased in denominations of $50, $75, $100, $200, $500, $1,000, and $5,000.

• $5,000 maximum purchase in one calendar year.

• Issued as paper bond certificates.

> ✎ **What's It Mean?**
>
> Series I Bonds: These bonds are sold at face value and grow with inflation-indexed earnings for up to 30 years. You can buy up to $5,000 in any calendar year.
>
> Source: Excerpted from "Savings Bonds," U.S. Securities and Exchange Commission (www.sec.gov), January 17, 2008.

If you redeem I Bonds within the first five years, you'll forfeit the three most recent months' interest; after five years, you won't be penalized.

Buy I Savings Bonds

The I Savings Bond is a security that increases in value until it's cashed or reaches final maturity in 30 years. It is available in paper and electronic format. You can buy electronic bonds through TreasuryDirect.

Where To Buy

It is easier to buy electronic and paper I Bonds than ever before. You can purchase them through:

- **TreasuryDirect:** This is the easiest, fastest way to buy Series I bonds. The bonds are issued directly in your TreasuryDirect account. No paper bonds are issued. You have access to your account 24 hours a day, seven days a week. You can set up an automatic purchase schedule of as little as $25.

- **Banks And Other Financial Institutions:** The bond is printed to your instructions and mailed to you within 15 business days. Your bond's issue date reflects the date of purchase so that no interest is lost.

- **Internet Banking Systems:** You can purchase paper bonds through online account access with many local financial institutions. See if a financial institution in your area offers this service.

- **Payroll Savings Plan:** You can buy I Bonds through the Payroll Savings Plan. Payroll for paper savings bonds and payroll for electronic bonds are available.

Purchase Limit

The purchase limit for both paper and electronic I Bonds is $5,000 per calendar year.

Identifying Information

Your Social Security Number (SSN) is needed to buy a bond. The bond owner will be asked to provide his or her Social Security number for tax purposes when they cash the bond. However, if you're buying a gift and don't know the recipient's SSN, you can use your own. Using your SSN doesn't mean you will have a tax liability when the bond is cashed. The bond owner will be asked to provide his or her Social Security number for tax purposes when they cash the bond.

Table 24.1. I And EE Savings Bond Comparison

	I Bonds	EE Bonds
Denominations	Any amount of $25 or more, including penny increments*	Any amount of $25 or more, including penny increments*
Purchase Price	Face value**	Face value**
Purchase Limit	$5,000 per Social Security Number***	$5,000 per Social Security Number***
Interest Earnings	A fixed rate of return and a variable semi-annual inflation rate (based on the Consumer Price Index for All Urban Consumers for March and September) are combined; interest compounds semiannually for 30 years	Bonds issued after May 2005 earn a fixed rate of return; Variable rates for bonds bought from May 1997 through April 2005 are based on 90% of the six-month averages of five-year Treasury Securities yields; interest compounds semiannually for 30 years
Redemption	Can be redeemed after 12 months	Can be redeemed after 12 months
Early Redemption Penalties	Three-month interest penalty if redeemed during the first five years	Three-month interest penalty if redeemed during the first five years

Who Can Own I Bonds

You can own I Bonds if you have a Social Security number and you're a United States resident or a United States citizen who lives abroad, a civilian employee of the United States regardless of where you live, or a minor (under age 18). Unlike other securities, minors may own U.S. Savings Bonds.

Table 24.1. Continued

	I Bonds	EE Bonds
Taxes	Exempt from state and local income tax; TreasuryDirect reports interest earnings; an online 1099-INT shows interest reportable for tax purposes; tax benefits available when used for education expenses	Exempt from state and local income tax; TreasuryDirect reports interest earnings; an online 1099-INT shows interest reportable for tax purposes; tax benefits available when used for education expenses

*On paper savings bonds issued or replaced on or after August 1, 2006, the first five digits of your Social Security number will be masked and replaced with asterisks. This is being done to protect your privacy and to prevent the information from being used for identity theft. Paper savings bonds can be purchased at financial institutions or through employer payroll savings plans.

** Paper I Bonds are offered in seven denominations—$50, $75, $100, $200, $500, $1,000, $5,000. They are purchased for their face value (for example, a $100 I bond costs $100). Paper EE Bonds are offered in eight denominations—$50, $75, $100, $200, $500, $1,000, $5,000, and $10,000. They are purchased for 50% of their face value (for example, a $100 EE bond costs $50). This means that they take longer to mature than electronic bonds, as their value is based on interest rates. They are guaranteed to reach face value in 20 years.

***You can purchase an additional $5,000 in paper EE Bonds or paper I Bonds per Social Security number.

In some cases, fiduciaries (such as trusts) can own I bonds.

At this time, only individuals 18 or older can open TreasuryDirect accounts and purchase electronic savings bonds. Gift bonds purchased for minor children may be delivered to the minor linked account.

I And EE Savings Bond Comparison

The U.S. Department of Treasury currently offer two series of savings bonds for purchase: EE and I. Both series are offered in electronic and paper format. Here is a comparison of I Bonds and EE Bonds.

Table 24.1 (see pages 252–253) applies to electronic bonds purchased through TreasuryDirect.

✎ What's It Mean?

Series HH Bonds: You can purchase Series HH bonds, but only in exchange for Series EE or E bonds and Savings Notes or with the proceeds from a matured Series HH bond. Unlike EE bonds, Series HH bonds are purchased at their face amount in $500 to $10,000 denominations, but there is no limit on the amount you can purchase. These bonds don't increase in value and have a maturity of 20 years.

Source: Excerpted from "Savings Bonds," U.S. Securities and Exchange Commission (www.sec.gov), January 17, 2008.

Chapter 25

Treasury Bonds And Other Treasury Instruments

Treasury Bonds

Treasury bonds are issued in terms of 30 years and pay interest every six months until they mature. When a Treasury bond matures, you are paid its face value.

The price and yield of a Treasury bond are determined at auction. The price may be greater than, less than, or equal to the face value of the bond.

Treasury bonds are sold in TreasuryDirect (www.treasurydirect.gov and by banks, brokers, and dealers. (Note: At this time, only individuals can hold accounts in TreasuryDirect.)

Bonds exist in either of two formats: as paper certificates (these are older bonds) or as electronic entries in accounts. Today the U.S. Department of Treasury issues Treasury bonds in electronic form, not paper. Paper bonds can be converted to electronic form.

About This Chapter: This chapter includes information from the following documents produced by the U.S. Department of the Treasury (www.treas.gov): "Treasury Bonds In Depth," March 28, 2008; "Treasury Bonds: FAQ," February 21, 2007; "TIPS In Depth," March 28, 2008; "Comparison of TIPS and Series I Savings Bonds," March 28, 2008; "Treasury Notes In Depth," March 28, 2008; and "Treasury Bills In Depth," April 14, 2008.

Frequently Asked Questions About Treasury Bonds

How do I know when Treasury bonds will be auctioned?

The U.S. Department of Treasury auctions Treasury bonds four times a year, in February, May, August, and November.

For specific dates, see the Tentative Auction Schedule (available online at http://www.treas.gov/offices/domestic-finance/debt-management/auctions/auctions.pdf), which shows auction dates months in advance, or "Upcoming Treasury Marketable Securities Auctions," (available online at http://www.treasury direct.gov/RI/OFAnnce) which shows auctions that have already officially been scheduled. (Auctions are officially scheduled only days before they are conducted.)

Also, you can sign up for e-mail notification of auctions.

Are Treasury bonds still issued paper form?

No. All Treasury bonds are now issued and held electronically.

Do some Treasury bonds still exist in paper form?

Yes. These are Treasury bonds that were issued in paper form and haven't matured. If you own one of these, you can convert it to electronic form and hold it in an account, or keep it in paper form.

What are reopenings, premiums, and accrued interest?

In a reopening, additional amounts of a previously issued security are auctioned.

☞ Remember!! Key Facts About Treasury Bonds

- The yield on a bond is determined at auction.

- Bonds are sold in increments of $100. The minimum purchase is $100.

- You can hold a Treasury bond until it matures or sell it before it matures.

- In a single auction, an investor can buy up to $5 million in bonds by non-competitive bidding or up to 35% of the initial offering amount by competitive bidding.

Source: From "Treasury Bonds In Depth," U.S. Department of the Treasury, March 28, 2008.

♣ It's A Fact!!

Two types of bids are accepted for Treasury bonds, Treasury inflation-protected securities (TIPS), Treasury notes, and Treasury bills:

- With a noncompetitive bid, you agree to accept the interest rate, yield, or discount rate determined at auction. With this bid, you are guaranteed to receive the bond, TIPS, note, or bill you want, and in the full amount you want.

- With a competitive bid, you specify the yield you are willing to accept. Your bid may be: 1) accepted in the full amount you want if your bid is equal to or less than the yield or discount rate determined at auction, 2) accepted in less than the full amount you want if your bid is equal to the high yield or discount rate, or 3) rejected if the yield you specify is higher than the yield or discount rate set at auction.

To place a noncompetitive bid, you may use TreasuryDirect, or a bank, broker, or dealer. To place a competitive bid, you must use a bank, broker, or dealer.

Source: U.S. Department of the Treasury, 2008.

Reopened securities have the same maturity date and interest rate as the original securities, but a different issue date and usually a different price.

When you buy a reopened security, you have to pay a premium if the price of the security at reopening is greater than the face value of the security. The price of the reopened security will be determined at auction. Because the security is being auctioned at two separate times, market conditions probably won't be the same and, therefore, the prices likely won't be the same either.

Also, when you buy a reopened security, regardless of its price, you may have to pay accrued interest—interest the security earns from the original issue date of the security until the date we issue the security to you. However, the U.S. Department of Treasury pays the accrued interest back to you in your first semiannual interest payment.

The Treasury bonds that are auctioned in May and November are reopenings.

Treasury Inflation-Protected Securities (TIPS) In Depth

Treasury inflation-protected securities (TIPS) are marketable securities whose principal is adjusted by changes in the Consumer Price Index. With inflation (a rise in the index), the principal increases. With a deflation (a drop in the index), the principal decreases.

The relationship between TIPS and the Consumer Price Index affects both the sum you are paid when your TIPS matures and the amount of interest that a TIPS pays you every six months. TIPS pay interest at a fixed rate. Because the rate is applied to the adjusted principal, however, interest payments can vary in amount from one period to the next. If inflation occurs, the interest payment increases. In the event of deflation, the interest payment decreases.

At the maturity of a TIPS, you receive the adjusted principal or the original principal, whichever is greater. This provision protects you against deflation.

The Treasury provides TIPS Inflation Index Ratios (available online at http://www.savingsbonds.gov/instit/annceresult/tipscpi/tipscpi.htm) to allow you to easily calculate the change to principal resulting from changes in the Consumer Price Index.

Methods Of Buying TIPS

TIPS are sold in TreasuryDirect and Legacy Treasury Direct, and through banks, brokers, and dealers.

The price of a TIPS can be less than, equal to, or greater than the face value.

You can bid for TIPS with a noncompetitive or competitive bid.

Comparison Of TIPS And Series I Savings Bonds

Type Of Investment

- **TIPS:** Marketable, can be bought and sold in the secondary securities market

- **I-Bonds:** Non-marketable, cannot be bought or sold in secondary securities market (registered in names of individuals or, for paper bonds only, their fiduciary estates)

How To Buy

- **TIPS:** At auction through TreasuryDirect, Legacy Treasury Direct, or through banks, brokers, and dealers (As of January 2007, 20-year TIPS are not available in Legacy Treasury Direct, but are available in TreasuryDirect.)

- **I-Bonds:** Electronically, anytime online from TreasuryDirect; paper, from most banks, credit unions, or savings institutions

Purchase Limits

- **TIPS:** At auction, non-competitive bidding up to $5 million; competitive bidding up to 35% of the offering amount

- **I-Bonds:** $5,000 per Social Security number per calendar year

Par Amount/Face Amount

- **TIPS:** Minimum purchase is $100; increments of $100

- **I-Bonds:** Electronically, purchased in amounts $25 or more, to the penny; paper, offered in eight denominations ($50, $75, $100, $200, $500, $1,000, and $5,000)

Inflation Indexing

- **TIPS:** Inflation adjustments measured by the Consumer Price Index for All Urban Consumers (CPI-U) published monthly

- **I-Bonds:** Semiannual inflation rate (based on CPI-U changes) announced in May and November

Discounts/Face Amount

- **TIPS:** Price and interest determined at auction

- **I-Bonds:** Electronic I Bonds, purchased in amounts of $25 or more, to the penny; paper bonds issued at face amount (a $100 I-Bond costs $100)

Earnings Rates

- **TIPS:** Principal increases/decreases with inflation/deflation; coupons calculated based upon adjusted principal; fixed coupon rate

- **I-Bonds:** Earnings rate is a combination of the fixed rate of return, set at the time of purchase, and a variable semiannual inflation rate.

Coupons/Interest

- **TIPS:** Semiannual interest payments at the coupon rate set at auction; inflation-adjusted principal is used to calculate the coupon amount.

- **I-Bonds:** Interest accrues over the life of the bond and is paid upon redemption

Tax Issues

☞ Remember!!
Key Facts About TIPS

- TIPS are issued in terms of five, 10, and 20 years. The 20-year TIPS is no longer sold in Legacy Treasury Direct, but it continues to be available in TreasuryDirect.

- The interest rate on a TIPS is determined at auction.

- TIPS are sold in increments of $100. The minimum purchase is $100.

- TIPS are issued in electronic form.

- You can hold a TIPS until it matures or sell it in the secondary market before it matures.

- In a single auction, an investor can buy up to $5 million in TIPS by non-competitive bidding or up to 35% of the initial offering amount by competitive bidding.

Source: From "TIPS In Depth," U.S. Department of the Treasury, March 28, 2008.

- **TIPS:** Semiannual interest payments and inflation adjustments that increase the principal are subject to federal tax in the year that they occur, but are exempt from state and local income taxes.

- **I-Bonds:** Tax reporting of interest can be deferred until redemption, final maturity, or other taxable disposition, whichever occurs first. Interest is subject to federal income tax, but exempt from state and local income taxes. Interest can also be claimed annually.

Life Span

- **TIPS:** Issued in terms of five, 10, and 20 years

- **I-Bonds:** Earn interest for up to 30 years

Disposal Before Maturity

• **TIPS:** Can be sold prior to maturity in the secondary market

• **I-Bonds:** Redeemable after 12 months with three months interest penalty; no penalty after five years

Treasury Notes

Treasury notes, or T-notes, are issued in terms of two, five, and 10 years, and pay interest every six months until they mature. The price of a note may be greater than, less than, or equal to the face value of the note. When a note matures, you are paid its face value. Notes are sold in TreasuryDirect and Legacy Treasury Direct, and by banks, brokers, and dealers.

You can bid for a note.

☞ Remember!!
Key Facts About T-Notes

• The yield on a note is determined at auction.

• Notes are sold in increments of $100. The minimum purchase is $100.

• Notes are issued in electronic form.

• You can hold a note until it matures or sell it before it matures.

• In a single auction, an investor can buy up to $5 million in notes by non-competitive bidding or up to 35% of the initial offering amount by competitive bidding.

Source: "Treasury Notes In Depth," U.S. Department of Treasury, March 28, 2008.

Treasury Bills

Treasury bills, or T-bills, are issued at a discount from their face value. For example, you might pay $990 for a $1,000 bill. When the bill matures, you would be paid its face value, $1,000. Your interest is the face value minus the purchase price—in this example, the interest is $10. The interest is determined by the discount rate, which is set when the bill is auctioned. You can buy a bill in TreasuryDirect or Legacy Treasury Direct, or through a bank, broker, or dealer.

☞ Remember!!
Key Facts About T-Bills

- Bills are sold at a discount. The discount rate is determined at auction.

- Bills pay interest only at maturity. The interest is equal to the face value minus the purchase price.

- Bills are sold in increments of $100. The minimum purchase is $100.

- All bills except cash management bills are auctioned every week. Cash management bills aren't auctioned on a regular schedule.

- Cash management bills are issued in variable terms, usually only a matter of days.

- Bills are issued in electronic form.

- You can hold a bill until it matures or sell it before it matures.

- In a single auction, an investor can buy up to $5 million in bills by non-competitive bidding or up to 35% of the initial offering amount by competitive bidding.

Source: "Treasury Bills In Depth," U.S. Department of Treasury, April 14, 2008.

Chapter 26

Municipal And Corporate Bonds

Frequently Asked Questions About Municipal Bonds

What are municipal bonds?

Municipal bonds ("muni bonds") are debt securities issued by state and local governments, or their authorized agencies, to borrow or raise money for public purposes such as building schools, highways, or hospitals. When you purchase a municipal bond, you lend money to the "issuer" (that is, the government entity that issued the bond), which, in turn, pays a set amount of interest while you hold the bond and returns your principal investment on a specified maturity date.

A primary feature of many municipal bonds is that the interest income an investor receives is generally exempt from federal income tax. The interest may also be exempt from state and local taxes if the investor lives in the state where the bond is issued. Municipal bonds, therefore, also are known as tax-exempt bonds.

Because they offer tax-free income, municipal bonds generally have annual yields below those of corporate bonds or U.S. Treasury bonds. These

About This Chapter: This chapter begins with "Frequently Asked Questions about Municipal Bonds," © 2008 Investment Company Institute (www.ici.org). Reprinted with permission. Additional information about corporate bonds from the Financial Industry Regulatory Authority is cited separately within the chapter.

low yields allow state and local governments to borrow money for public projects at below market rates.

How are municipal bonds traded?

The municipal, or "muni," market does not operate via a centralized exchange. Instead, it is an over-the-counter market—a network of dealers and brokers that connect buyers and sellers. Some bonds are "actively traded," meaning that they are traded on a regular basis. However, many investors buy and hold their bonds until they mature, so certain municipal bonds may not trade for months or years at a time.

Securities dealers that trade municipal securities must register with the Municipal Securities Rulemaking Board (MSRB), which sets the rules for the municipal bond market subject to the oversight of the U.S. Securities and Exchange Commission (SEC).

Who owns municipal bonds?

Individual, or "retail," investors are the largest holders of municipal securities. They hold 35 percent of municipal bonds directly and another 36 percent indirectly through mutual funds, closed-end funds, unit investment trusts (UITs), and exchange-traded funds (ETFs). According to the Investment Company Institute (ICI)'s most recent data, investment companies of all types hold $907 billion, or 36 percent, of the $2.5 trillion municipal bond market. Mutual funds alone account for 32 percent of all U.S. municipal securities, totaling over $809 billion. Closed-end funds hold 4 percent, totaling $89 billion; municipal bond UITs hold $8 billion; and ETFs that track municipal bond indices hold $575 million in assets.

♣ **It's A Fact!!**
How are municipal bonds regulated?

Unlike registered investment companies, issuers of municipal securities do not have to file registration statements with the U.S. Securities and Exchange Commission (SEC). However, information about these issuers, including details of their financial condition, is available from various sources.

Source: © 2008 Investment Company Institute.

What is the role of credit rating agencies related to municipal bonds?

One way to evaluate a municipal securities issuer is to examine its credit rating. Credit rating agencies assign credit ratings based on their analysis of an issuer's ability to make interest payments and repay principal in a timely manner. (Credit rating agencies also grade corporate bonds, but their analysis of corporate bonds differs from their analysis of municipal bonds.)

Bonds rated BBB or Baa, or better, are characterized as "investment grade," meaning that they have a high probability of being repaid and have few speculative features. Municipal bonds with lower or no ratings carry higher risks, but may also pay the investor higher interest rates to compensate for that risk.

In addition to the ratings provided by credit rating agencies, most institutional investors, including investment companies, conduct their own credit analysis.

What is bond insurance?

Bond insurance is a type of credit enhancement. A bond insurer unconditionally and irrevocably guarantees that interest and principal will be paid as scheduled—on time and in full—even if the bond issuer defaults. If a bond carries insurance, it typically is insured in the primary market, at the time of issuance, but it may be insured at any time in the secondary market. For some small municipal issuers, access to capital markets is made more affordable by the use of a credit enhancement like bond insurance.

Many of today's municipal bonds are insured by monoline insurers, or insurers that back debt securities only and are not exposed to risks from any other lines of business. They may, however, be exposed to other forms of risk (that is, interest rate risk, market risk, etc.) Monoline insurers must meet the requirements of insurance regulators in every state where they do business. They are closely monitored by the major credit rating agencies.

Monoline insurers conduct an underwriting process before insuring a municipal bond: the insurers examine the issuer's tax base (if applicable) and operations, regional economy, financial condition, existing debt, expected future borrowing, and spending requirements, as well as the legal provisions securing the bonds.

Bond issuers, or the investment banks and securities dealers that sell the bonds, typically pay the insurance premiums. There are no direct charges for investors, but the investor may earn less income than if the bond were not insured because of the added protection provided by the insurance.

Why do bond issuers buy insurance?

Bond issuers use bond insurance because it improves the credit quality of a bond, making it easier to sell. Bond insurance boosts credit quality by offering protection against default or downgrade if a bond issuer cannot meet its obligations to pay interest and principal to bondholders.

♣ **It's A Fact!!**
How are mono-line insurers rated?

Credit rating agencies frequently evaluate bond insurers' claims-paying ability—through detailed analyses of financial resources, operations, and exposures—and publish regular reports on each insurer. Credit rating agencies look at key indicators, including the quality of the insured portfolio, capital adequacy, financial performance, operating efficiency, risk management, liquidity of assets, reinsurance, business viability, ownership, and the skill and experience of management.

Source: © 2008 Investment Company Institute.

Insured municipal bonds are rated based on the credit of the insurer (based on its claims-paying ability) rather than the underlying credit of the issuer. Historically, this has improved the credit rating of the bond. A higher credit rating allows the issuer to benefit from lower financing costs because bonds with high ratings—and, therefore, greater security—pay lower interest rates. This also leads to enhanced liquidity for insured bonds because there is greater demand among investors for highly rated securities.

Accordingly, an issuer may seek bond insurance for a number of reasons. If a bond issuer's credit would not earn a high rating, bond insurance could improve the credit quality of the bond. But even highly rated bond issuers use bond insurance—to lower the costs of borrowing.

What happens if a monoline insurer is downgraded?

Because an insured bond carries the rating of the bond insurer, the bond's rating will be downgraded when a monoline insurer is downgraded. With a lower credit rating, the market value (that is, price) of the underlying municipal bond could fall because the perceived risk of owning the bond has increased. The presence of an insurance policy alone does not guarantee a municipal bond's price in the secondary market. As with any other security, the actual price is determined by the market at the time of resale. Municipal bonds sold prior to maturity may be worth more or less than their original cost. Generally, if the price of a municipal bond drops, higher yields will follow.

As noted above, however, some issuers obtain bond insurance primarily to lower their costs of borrowing. If these issuers carry a credit rating independent of the credit rating from the monoline insurer, market participants may "look through" or disregard the downgrade of the insurer. Depending on the market at the time of resale, this might enable the issuer to maintain a higher trading price.

Presently, the credit ratings of certain insurers are under review due to subprime lending exposure that threatens their ability to pay claims. This, in turn, has resulted in some rating downgrades. Municipal bond funds and money market funds holding municipal bonds face certain regulatory requirements regarding the quality of the securities held in their portfolios. These funds also state in their prospectuses that they will only hold securities of a certain quality. If these funds hold securities that have been downgraded because they are insured by downgraded monoline insurers, the funds may have to determine whether they can continue to hold those bonds.

In the long term, the inability of monoline insurers to maintain high credit ratings may restrict the supply of high quality, short-term securities for municipal money market funds and other municipal bond funds.

What is the credit quality of most of the underlying municipal bonds?

Monoline insurers typically insure only municipal bonds that are of investment-grade quality on their own. The underlying bonds may or may not be rated by a credit rating agency. A bond without a rating does not necessarily carry a higher level of risk; it simply means that the issuer did not apply for an underlying rating (a rating on the uninsured bond), possibly because it did not want to incur the additional cost.

What are variable rate demand obligations and tender option bonds?

Variable-rate demand obligations (VRDOs) are debt securities that bear interest at a floating, or variable, rate adjusted at specified intervals (daily, weekly, or monthly) according to a specific index or through a remarketing process. Holders can redeem these securities at designated times. Issuers offer VRDOs in order to access the

> ### ♣ It's A Fact!!
> ### What other types of municipal securities are insured by monoline insurers?
>
> In addition to traditional municipal bonds, monoline insurers provide insurance for variable-rate demand obligations (VRDOs) and tender option bonds (TOBs). Monoline insurers also insure structured finance bonds and certain international debt securities.
>
> Source: © 2008 Investment Company Institute.

short-term market to obtain lower interest rates. Tender option bonds (TOBs) are similar to VRDOs but are synthetically created by a bond dealer with long-term bonds purchased in either the primary or secondary markets. Both VRDOs and TOBs are short-term, tax-exempt instruments whose yield is reset daily or weekly based on an index of short-term municipal rates.

VRDOs and TOBs are purchased at par, the face value of the security. Each structure includes a liquidity facility which provides a "put" or demand feature. This allows the bondholder (for example, a fund) to put the security back to the remarketing agent and receive face value plus accrued interest with specified notice. A remarketing agent—a bank or other entity—helps to make a market for the securities and ensures that a holder's put is honored by reselling the products, holding them in its own inventory, or arranging for the holder to be paid from the bank liquidity facility. In addition to providing a source of cash to satisfy redemptions by fund shareholders, these liquidity features operate to shorten the long-term bonds' maturity and make them appropriate for a money market fund.

What is the credit quality of VRDOs and TOBs?

Most VRDOs and TOBs are highly rated due to credit enhancements (such as bond insurance or letters of credit), which guarantee timely principal and interest payments, as well as the liquidity facility, which provides payment for tendered bonds. In most cases, the liquidity facility requires that the municipal bonds maintain certain credit ratings. Consequently, like insured municipal bonds, VRDOs and TOBs may be affected when monoline insurers are downgraded. For example, a downgrade of the monoline insurer may trigger a "termination event" that releases the liquidity facility from its obligation to buy back the security.

Funds are taking action in advance of this possibility. Some funds are unloading the securities from their portfolios by exercising the put feature to the remarking agent, thereby receiving par and accrued interest for the security. Other funds are obtaining changes to their contracts with liquidity providers to preserve the liquidity facility regardless of the monoline insurer's rating, by linking the termination events to the credit rating of the underlying issuer and/or the monoline insurer.

A money market fund that holds VRDOs or TOBs in its portfolio may have to review whether it may continue to hold securities that are enhanced by the downgraded monoline insurer.

What is an auction rate security?

Auction rate securities (ARS) are municipal securities with a variable interest rate that is set periodically through a "Dutch Auction" process. Auctions are typically held every 7, 28, or 35 days, and interest on these securities is paid at the end of each auction period. ARS trade at par and are callable at par on any interest payment date at the option of the issuer. Although ARS are issued and rated as long-term municipal bonds (20 to 30 years), they are priced and traded as short-term instruments because of the liquidity provided through the interest rate reset mechanism.

During the auction, a broker-dealer submits bids, on behalf of current and prospective investors, to the auction agent—typically a bank. Based on the submitted bids, the auction agent will set the next interest rate by determining the "clearing rate," the lowest rate to clear the total outstanding amount of

ARS. The program documents for an ARS also define situations under which a "maximum rate" is used for the next interest rate period. Generally, the maximum rate is a multiple of a specified index or a fixed rate.

Unlike TOBs and VRDOs, ARS holders do not have the right to put their securities back to the issuer; so a bank liquidity facility is not required. As a result, money market funds cannot hold ARS because SEC rules restrict them to securities with a final maturity of 397 days or less. In addition, because ARS do not carry a "put" feature, they are very sensitive to changes in credit ratings and normally require the highest ratings to make them marketable. This is usually achieved with bond insurance. Thus, when a monoline insurer is downgraded, investors are less likely to participate in an auction for the ARS, reducing demand for the securities.

Typical investors of ARS include corporate and high net worth individuals, bond funds, and bank trust departments.

What is a failed auction?

An auction fails when there are more shares offered for sale in the auction than there are bids to buy shares, or if the clearing rate of the auction would be above the maximum rate defined in program documents. A failed auction does not mean the security goes into default, because the issuer continues to pay interest at the maximum rate; however, existing holders of the securities who wanted to sell them generally are not able to do so in that particular auction. Auction failures are the result of limited liquidity in the market for the particular ARS and not necessarily the result of an event of default by the issuer.

Corporate Bonds

From "Individual Bonds: Corporate Bonds," © 2008 Financial Industry Regulatory Authority, Inc. (FINRA). Reprinted with permission from FINRA.

Companies issue corporate bonds (or corporates) to raise money for capital expenditures, operations, and acquisitions. Corporates are issued by all types of businesses, and are segmented into major industry groups.

Corporate bondholders receive the equivalent of an IOU from the issuer of the bond. But unlike equity stockholders, the bondholder doesn't receive any ownership rights in the corporation. However, in the event that the corporation falls into bankruptcy and is liquidated, bondholders are more likely than common stockholders to receive some remuneration.

There are many types of corporate bonds, and investors have a wide-range of choices with respect to bond structures, coupon rates, maturity dates, and credit quality, among other characteristics. Most corporate bonds are issued with maturities ranging from one to 30 years (short-term debt that matures in 270 days or less is called "commercial paper"). Bondholders generally receive regular, predetermined interest payments (the "coupon"), set when the bond is issued. Interest payments are subject to federal and state income taxes, and capital gains and losses on the sale of corporate bonds are taxed at the same short- and long-term rates (for bonds held for less, or for more, than one year) that apply when an investor sells stock.

♣ It's A Fact!!

Bond Fact: The corporate debt market is approximately $4.6 trillion, making it larger than the U.S. Treasury bond and municipal bond markets combined (Securities Industry and Financial Markets Association).

Source: FINRA, 2008.

Sweeteners—Special Features That Often Come At A Price To Investors

In an effort to make bonds more attractive to investors, issuers sometimes add special features called "sweeteners" to a bond. For instance, bonds that have a survivor option, where the issuer agrees to repurchase the security at par from the investor's estate in the event of death, is one such sweetener that is gaining popularity. Survivor options are not all alike and may contain limitations and special conditions. The insurance feature of insured bonds is another type of sweetener. Investors should understand that sweeteners almost always come at a price—either as a direct cost to investors or a lower rate of return.

Most corporate bonds trade in the over-the-counter (OTC) market. The OTC market for corporates is decentralized, with bond dealers and brokers trading with each other around the country over the phone or electronically. Some bonds trade in small quantities (or odd lots) in the centralized environments of the New York Stock Exchange (NYSE) and American Stock Exchange (AMEX), and are also traded in the OTC market.

TRACE—Corporate Bond Trade Reporting Comes Of Age

TRACE (the Trade Reporting and Compliance Engine) was launched in 2002, as the first intraday consolidated tape in the U.S. OTC fixed-income markets. All broker-dealers that FINRA regulates are required to report corporate bond transactions to the TRACE system. TRACE enables individual investors to receive real-time information on the actual sale price of virtually all U.S. corporate bonds

Go to the TRACE Corporate Bond Data page on the internet at http://apps.finra.org/regulatory_systems/traceaggregates/1 for a snapshot of TRACE-reported corporate bond information.

Part Four

Stocks And Mutual Funds

Chapter 27

Understanding Stocks

Stocks Basics: Introduction

Wouldn't you love to be a business owner without ever having to show up at work? Imagine if you could sit back, watch your company grow, and collect the dividend checks as the money rolls in! This situation might sound like a pipe dream, but it's closer to reality than you might think.

As you've probably guessed, we're talking about owning stocks. This fabulous category of financial instruments is, without a doubt, one of the greatest tools ever invented for building wealth. Stocks are a part, if not the cornerstone, of nearly any investment portfolio. When you start on your road to financial freedom, you need to have a solid understanding of stocks and how they trade on the stock market.

Over the last few decades, the average person's interest in the stock market has grown exponentially. What was once a toy of the rich has now turned into the vehicle of choice for growing wealth. This demand coupled with advances in trading technology has opened up the markets so that nowadays nearly anybody can own stocks.

Types Of Stock

♣ **It's A Fact!!**

The two main categories of stocks are common stock and preferred stock. Preferred stockholders have priority over common stockholders in terms of dividend payout and in recouping their investment if the company fails or liquidates. However, preferred stockholders, unlike common stockholders, cannot vote for directors of the company.

There are five basic categories of stock:

- **Income Stocks** pay unusually large dividends that can be used as a means of generating income without selling the stock, but the price of the stock generally does not rise very quickly.

- **Blue-Chip Stocks** are issued by very solid and reliable companies with long histories of consistent growth and stability. Blue-chip stocks usually pay small but regular dividends and maintain a fairly steady price throughout market ups and downs.

- **Growth Stocks** are issued by young, entrepreneurial companies that are experiencing a faster growth rate than their general industries. These stocks normally pay little or no dividend because the company needs all of its earnings to finance expansion. Since they are issued by companies with no proven track record, growth stocks are riskier than other types of stocks but also offer more appreciation potential.

- **Cyclical Stocks** are issued by companies that are affected by general economic trends. The prices of these stocks tend to go down during recessionary periods and increase during economic booms. Examples of cyclical stock companies include automobile, heavy machinery, and home building.

- **Defensive Stocks** are the opposite of cyclical stocks. Defensive stocks—issued by companies producing staples such as food, beverages, drugs, and insurance—typically maintain their value during recessionary periods.

Despite their popularity, however, most people don't fully understand stocks. Much is learned from conversations around the water cooler with others who also don't know what they're talking about. Chances are you've already heard people say things like, "Bob's cousin made a killing in XYZ company, and now he's got another hot tip..." or "Watch out with stocks—you can lose your shirt in a matter of days!" So much of this misinformation is based on a get-rich-quick mentality, which was especially prevalent during the amazing dotcom market in the late '90s. People thought that stocks were the magic answer to instant wealth with no risk. The ensuing dotcom crash proved that this is not the case. Stocks can (and do) create massive amounts of wealth, but they aren't without risks. The only solution to this is education. The key to protecting yourself in the stock market is to understand where you are putting your money.

What Are Stocks?

Plain and simple, stock is a share in the ownership of a company. Stock represents a claim on the company's assets and earnings. As you acquire more stock, your ownership stake in the company becomes greater. Whether you say shares, equity, or stock, it all means the same thing.

Being An Owner

Holding a company's stock means that you are one of the many owners (shareholders) of a company and, as such, you have a claim (albeit usually very small) to everything the company owns. Yes, this means that technically you own a tiny sliver of every piece of furniture, every trademark, and every contract of the company. As an owner, you are entitled to your share of the company's earnings as well as any voting rights attached to the stock.

Being a shareholder of a public company does not mean you have a say in the day-to-day running of the business. Instead, one vote per share to elect the board of directors at annual meetings is the extent to which you have a say in the company. For instance, being a Microsoft shareholder doesn't mean you can call up Bill Gates and tell him how you think the company should be run.

The management of the company is supposed to increase the value of the firm for shareholders. If this doesn't happen, the shareholders can vote to have the management removed, at least in theory. In reality, individual investors

> **♣ It's A Fact!!**
>
> A stock is represented by a stock certificate. This is a fancy piece of paper that is proof of your ownership. In today's computer age, you won't actually get to see this document because your brokerage keeps these records electronically, which is also known as holding shares "in street name." This is done to make the shares easier to trade. In the past, when a person wanted to sell his or her shares, that person physically took the certificates down to the brokerage. Now, trading with a click of the mouse or a phone call makes life easier for everybody.
>
> Source: © 2008 Investopedia, ULC.

like you and I don't own enough shares to have a material influence on the company. It's really the big boys like large institutional investors and billionaire entrepreneurs who make the decisions.

For ordinary shareholders, not being able to manage the company isn't such a big deal. After all, the idea is that you don't want to have to work to make money, right? The importance of being a shareholder is that you are entitled to a portion of the company's profits and have a claim on assets. Profits are sometimes paid out in the form of dividends. The more shares you own, the larger the portion of the profits you get. Your claim on assets is only relevant if a company goes bankrupt. In case of liquidation, you'll receive what's left after all the creditors have been paid. This last point is worth repeating: the importance of stock ownership is your claim on assets and earnings. Without this, the stock wouldn't be worth the paper it's printed on.

Another extremely important feature of stock is its limited liability, which means that, as an owner of a stock, you are not personally liable if the company is not able to pay its debts. Other companies such as partnerships are set up so that if the partnership goes bankrupt the creditors can come after the partners (shareholders) personally and sell off their house, car, furniture, etc. Owning stock means that, no matter what, the maximum value you can lose is the value of your investment. Even if a company of which you are a shareholder goes bankrupt, you can never lose your personal assets.

Debt Vs. Equity

Why does a company issue stock? Why would the founders share the profits with thousands of people when they could keep profits to themselves? The reason is that at some point every company needs to raise money. To do this, companies can either borrow it from somebody or raise it by selling part of the company, which is known as issuing stock. A company can borrow by taking a loan from a bank or by issuing bonds. Both methods fit under the umbrella of debt financing. On the other hand, issuing stock is called equity financing. Issuing stock is advantageous for the company because it does not require the company to pay back the money or make interest payments along the way. All that the shareholders get in return for their money is the hope that the shares will someday be worth more than what they paid for them. The first sale of a stock, which is issued by the private company itself, is called the initial public offering (IPO).

It is important that you understand the distinction between a company financing through debt and financing through equity. When you buy a debt investment such as a bond, you are guaranteed the return of your money (the principal) along with promised interest payments. This isn't the case with an equity investment. By becoming an owner, you assume the risk of the company not being successful—just as a small business owner isn't guaranteed a return, neither is a shareholder. As an owner, your claim on assets is less than that of creditors. This means that if a company goes bankrupt and liquidates, you, as a shareholder, don't get any money until the banks and bondholders have been paid out; we call this absolute priority. Shareholders earn a lot if a company is successful, but they also stand to lose their entire investment if the company isn't successful.

Risk

It must be emphasized that there are no guarantees when it comes to individual stocks. Some companies pay out dividends, but many others do not. And there is no obligation to pay out dividends even for those firms that have traditionally given them. Without dividends, an investor can make money on a stock only through its appreciation in the open market. On the downside, any stock may go bankrupt, in which case your investment is worth nothing.

Although risk might sound all negative, there is also a bright side. Taking on greater risk demands a greater return on your investment. This is the reason why stocks have historically outperformed other investments such as bonds or savings accounts. Over the long term, an investment in stocks has historically had an average return of around 10–12%.

Different Types Of Stock

There are two main types of stocks: common stock and preferred stock.

✔ Quick Tip

How To Read Stock Tables

The traditional way to check basic stock information is by using the long columns of small print in a newspaper's business section. They might seem confusing at first glance, but these stock tables break down what is happening at each company listed on the stock exchanges and include stocks, bonds, money market funds and mutual funds. Once you adjust your eyes to the fine print, reading the stock tables is really quite simple.

The following information illustrates a sample stock table for a fictitious company called Future Comm. We break down each column and describe what it means. You can find the same information in online stock listings. In addition to the standard abbreviations, stock tables in print and online often include other symbols indicating a variety of factors, such as stock splits, dividend changes, first day of trading, new 52-week highs and lows, warrants and other relevant data.

| 52-Weeks | | | | | | | | | |
Hi	Lo	Stock	(Sym)	Div	Yld	PE	Vol 100s	Close	Net Chg
132.94	80.06	Fut Comm	(FTC)	.56	.6	21	100927	96.47	-0.12

52-Weeks Hi/Lo: The highest and lowest prices paid for Future Comm stock during the past year. The numbers used to be expressed in fractions but now all prices have been converted to decimals so they can be read as dollars and cents. In this case, the stock's price has been between $80.06 and $132.94 per share over the past year. Knowing the past year's high and low can help an investor evaluate a stock's current price.

Stock: The name of the company.

Sym: The stock's trading symbol. To avoid confusion and simplify the order process, every stock that is traded on a securities market is assigned a symbol.

Common Stock

Common stock is, well, common. When people talk about stocks they are usually referring to this type. In fact, the majority of stock is issued is in this form. We basically went over features of common stock in the previous section. Common shares represent ownership in a company and a claim (dividends) on a portion of profits. Investors get one vote per share to elect

---

Some newspapers do not provide the stock's trading symbol but instead provide an abbreviation of the company's name. Many financial websites let you type in a company's name and quickly find out its symbol.

Div: Short for dividend. For each share of stock owned, a Future Comm shareholder should receive 56 cents from the company's annual profits. Payment is usually made on a quarterly basis. Not all companies pay dividends all the time. The company's board of directors decides whether a dividend will be paid and its amount. When companies are just starting out they usually do not pay a dividend because if they are making a profit they are reinvesting it back into the company to accelerate growth.

Yld: The yield, or the rate of return, on a stockholder's investment. It is figured by dividing the annual dividend by the current price of the stock. Future Comm stockholders earn 0.6% of today's stock price from dividends.

PE: Short for price/earnings ratio. The price of a share of stock divided by the company's earnings per share for the last year.

Vol 100s: The total amount of stock traded during the previous day. On that day, 10,092,700 shares of Future Comm stock changed hands. The number does not include "odd lots," which are sales of less than 100 shares.

Close: The last price paid for this stock at the end of the previous day was $96.47.

Net Chg: The last price on the previous day, $96.47, was 12 cents less than the last price on the preceding day.

the board members, who oversee the major decisions made by management.

Over the long term, common stock, by means of capital growth, yields higher returns than almost every other investment. This higher return comes at a cost since common stocks entail the most risk. If a company goes bankrupt and liquidates, the common shareholders will not receive money until the creditors, bondholders, and preferred shareholders are paid.

Preferred Stock

Preferred stock represents some degree of ownership in a company but usually doesn't come with the same voting rights. (This may vary depending on the company.) With preferred shares, investors are usually guaranteed a fixed dividend forever. This is different than common stock, which has variable dividends that are never guaranteed. Another advantage is that in the event of liquidation, preferred shareholders are paid off before the common shareholder (but still after debt holders). Preferred stock may also be callable, meaning that the company has the option to purchase the shares from shareholders at anytime for any reason (usually for a premium).

Some people consider preferred stock to be more like debt than equity. A good way to think of these kinds of shares is to see them as being in between bonds and common shares.

Different Classes Of Stock

Common and preferred are the two main forms of stock; however, it's also possible for companies to customize different classes of stock in any way they want. The most common reason for this is the company wanting the voting power to remain with a certain group; therefore, different classes of shares are given different voting rights. For example, one class of shares would be held by a select group who are given ten votes per share while a second class would be issued to the majority of investors who are given one vote per share.

When there is more than one class of stock, the classes are traditionally designated as Class A and Class B. Berkshire Hathaway (ticker: BRK), has two classes of stock. The different forms are represented by placing the letter behind the ticker symbol in a form like this: "BRKa, BRKb" or "BRK.A, BRK.B".

Chapter 28

How The Stock Market Works

How Stocks Trade

Most stocks are traded on exchanges, which are places where buyers and sellers meet and decide on a price. Some exchanges are physical locations where transactions are carried out on a trading floor. You've probably seen pictures of a trading floor, in which traders are wildly throwing their arms up, waving, yelling, and signaling to each other. The other type of exchange is virtual, composed of a network of computers where trades are made electronically.

The purpose of a stock market is to facilitate the exchange of securities between buyers and sellers, reducing the risks of investing. Just imagine how difficult it would be to sell shares if you had to call around the neighborhood trying to find a buyer. Really, a stock market is nothing more than a super-sophisticated farmers' market linking buyers and sellers.

Before we go on, we should distinguish between the primary market and the secondary market. The primary market is where securities are created (by means of an IPO) while, in the secondary market, investors trade previously issued securities without the involvement of the issuing-companies.

About This Chapter: Text in this chapter is from "Stock Basics," reprinted with permission from Investopedia, ULC. © 2008 Investopedia.com. Additional from the U.S. Securities and Exchange Commission is cited separately within the chapter.

♣ **It's A Fact!!**

How A Stock Is Bought And Sold

1. Tom Smith of Sarasota, Florida decides to invest in the stock market.

1a. Diane Whitford of Hartford, Connecticut decides to sell 300 shares of XYZ Corp. (XYZ) stock to help pay for a new car.

2. Tom has been thinking of investing in the XYZ Corp. He calls his broker, who is a member of the New York Stock Exchange, to get a quote on XYZ; that is, to find out the highest bid to buy and the lowest offer to sell.

2a. Diane checks nyse.com to find out what price XYZ is trading at by typing in the company's ticker symbol, XYZ.

3. Tom's broker and Diane find out the current quote and price for XYZ from an electronic data system that continually updates information directly from the floor of the NYSE.

4. Taking into account what he already knows about XYZ—and after a discussion with his broker—Tom instructs his broker to purchase 300 shares of XYZ at the current market price.

4a. Diane logs into her online brokerage account, which is linked to a brokerage firm that is a member of the New York Stock Exchange, and places an order to sell her 300 shares at the current market price.

5. Both orders are sent electronically to the NYSE Trading Floor either via the SuperDOT® System to the specialist's workstation.

6. The customer can either use the auction market with the specialist or, to obtain an electronic execution, use NYSE Direct+ (a high-speed electronic connection between NYSE member firms and the Exchange that enables immediate electronic execution of customer orders).

7. At the specialist workstation both orders are represented as auction market orders in order to have the opportunity for price improvement. The specialist who handles XYZ makes sure the transactions are executed fairly and in an orderly manner.

8. After the transaction is executed, the specialist's workstation sends notice to the firms originating the orders and to the consolidated tape so that a written record is made of every transaction.

9. The transaction is reported by computer and appears on the consolidated tape displays across the country and around the world.

10. The transaction is processed electronically, crediting Tom's brokerage firm and debiting the account of Diane's brokerage firm. Tom's broker calls him and tells him at what price he bought 300 shares of XYZ. In a couple of days, Tom receives a written confirmation in the mail. Diane receives confirmation from her brokerage firm electronically on her computer within seconds. These confirmations describe the trade, its terms and conditions, and the exact amount to be paid or received.

11. Tom settles his account within three business days after the transaction by submitting payment to his brokerage firm for the 300 shares of XYZ, plus any applicable commissions.

11a. Diane's trade is also settled in three business days. Her account will be credited with the proceeds of the sale of stock, minus any applicable commissions.

The secondary market is what people are referring to when they talk about the stock market. It is important to understand that the trading of a company's stock does not directly involve that company.

The New York Stock Exchange

The most prestigious exchange in the world is the New York Stock Exchange (NYSE). The "Big Board" was founded over 200 years ago in 1792 with the signing of the Buttonwood Agreement by 24 New York City stockbrokers and merchants. Currently the NYSE, with stocks like General Electric, McDonald's, Citigroup, Coca-Cola, Gillette, and Wal-mart, is the market of choice for the largest companies in America.

The NYSE is the first type of exchange (as we referred to above), where much of the trading is done face-to-face on a trading floor. This is also referred to as a listed exchange. Orders come in through brokerage firms that are members of the exchange and flow down to floor brokers who go to a specific spot on the floor where the stock trades. At this location, known as the trading post, there is a specific person known as the specialist whose job is to match buyers and sellers. Prices are determined using an auction method: the current price is the highest amount any buyer is willing to pay and the lowest price at which someone is willing to sell. Once a trade has been made, the details are sent back to the brokerage firm, who then notifies the investor who placed the order. Although there is human contact in this process, don't think that the NYSE is still in the stone age: computers play a huge role in the process.

The Nasdaq

The second type of exchange is the virtual sort called an over-the-counter (OTC) market, of which the Nasdaq is the most popular. These markets have no central location or floor brokers whatsoever. Trading is done through a computer and telecommunications network of dealers. It used to be that the largest companies were listed only on the NYSE while all other second tier stocks traded on the other exchanges. The tech boom of the late '90s changed all this; now the Nasdaq is home to several big technology companies such as Microsoft, Cisco, Intel, Dell, and Oracle. This has resulted in the Nasdaq becoming a serious competitor to the NYSE.

On the Nasdaq brokerages act as market makers for various stocks. A market maker provides continuous bid and ask prices within a prescribed percentage spread for shares for which they are designated to make a market. They may match up buyers and sellers directly but usually they will maintain an inventory of shares to meet demands of investors.

Other Exchanges

The third largest exchange in the U.S. is the American Stock Exchange (AMEX). The AMEX used to be an alternative to the NYSE, but that role has since been filled by the Nasdaq. In fact, the National Association of Securities Dealers (NASD), which is the parent of Nasdaq, bought the AMEX in 1998. Almost all trading now on the AMEX is in small-cap stocks and derivatives.

There are many stock exchanges located in just about every country around the world. American markets are undoubtedly the largest, but they still represent only a fraction of total investment around the globe. The two other main financial hubs are London, home of the London Stock Exchange, and Hong Kong, home of the Hong Kong Stock Exchange.

The last place worth mentioning is the over-the-counter bulletin board (OTCBB). The Nasdaq is an over-the-counter market, but the term commonly refers to small public companies that don't meet the listing requirements of any of the regulated markets, including the Nasdaq. The OTCBB is home to penny stocks because there is little to no regulation. This makes investing in an OTCBB stock very risky.

What Causes Stock Prices To Change?

Stock prices change every day as a result of market forces. By this we mean that share prices change because of supply and demand. If more people want to buy a stock (demand) than sell it (supply), then the price moves up. Conversely, if more people wanted to sell a stock than buy it, there would be greater supply than demand, and the price would fall.

Understanding supply and demand is easy. What is difficult to comprehend is what makes people like a particular stock and dislike another stock.

This comes down to figuring out what news is positive for a company and what news is negative. There are many answers to this problem and just about any investor you ask has their own ideas and strategies.

That being said, the principal theory is that the price movement of a stock indicates what investors feel a company is worth. Don't equate a company's value with the stock price. The value of a company is its market capitalization, which is the stock price multiplied by the number of shares outstanding. For example, a company that trades at $100 per share and has 1 million shares outstanding has a lesser value than a company that trades at $50 that has 5 million shares outstanding ($100 x 1 million = $100 million while $50 x 5 million = $250 million). To further complicate things, the price of a stock doesn't only reflect a company's current value, it also reflects the growth that investors expect in the future.

The most important factor that affects the value of a company is its earnings. Earnings are the profit a company makes, and in the long run no company can survive without them. It makes sense when you think about it. If a company never makes money, it isn't going to stay in business. Public companies are required to report their earnings four times a year (once each quarter). Wall Street watches with rabid attention at these times, which are referred to as earnings seasons. The reason behind

☞ **Remember!!**

The important things to grasp about stock prices are the following:

1. At the most fundamental level, supply and demand in the market determines stock price.

2. Price times the number of shares outstanding (market capitalization) is the value of a company. Comparing just the share price of two companies is meaningless.

3. Theoretically, earnings are what affect investors' valuation of a company, but there are other indicators that investors use to predict stock price. Remember, it is investors' sentiments, attitudes, and expectations that ultimately affect stock prices.

4. There are many theories that try to explain the way stock prices move the way they do. Unfortunately, there is no one theory that can explain everything.

Source: © 2008 Investopedia, ULC.

this is that analysts base their future value of a company on their earnings projection. If a company's results surprise (are better than expected), the price jumps up. If a company's results disappoint (are worse than expected), then the price will fall.

Of course, it's not just earnings that can change the sentiment towards a stock (which, in turn, changes its price). It would be a rather simple world if this were the case! During the dotcom bubble, for example, dozens of internet companies rose to have market capitalizations in the billions of dollars without ever making even the smallest profit. As we all know, these valuations did not hold, and most internet companies saw their values shrink to a fraction of their highs. Still, the fact that prices did move that much demonstrates that there are factors other than current earnings that influence stocks. Investors have developed literally hundreds of these variables, ratios and indicators. Some you may have already heard of, such as the price/earnings ratio, while others are extremely complicated and obscure with names like Chaikin oscillator or moving average convergence divergence.

So, why do stock prices change? The best answer is that nobody really knows for sure. Some believe that it isn't possible to predict how stock prices will change, while others think that by drawing charts and looking at past price movements, you can determine when to buy and sell. The only thing we do know is that stocks are volatile and can change in price extremely rapidly.

Understanding Market Indices

Excerpted from "Market Indices," U.S. Securities and Exchange Commission (SEC), August 30, 2004.

If you open the financial pages of many newspapers, you will find a number of major market indices listed. Each of the indices tracks the performance of a specific "basket" of stocks considered to represent a particular market or sector of the U.S. stock market or the economy. For example, the Dow Jones Industrial Average (DJIA) is an index of 30 "blue chip" U.S. stocks of industrial companies (excluding transportation and utility companies). The S&P 500 Composite Stock Price Index is an index of 500 stocks from major industries of the U.S. economy. There are indices for almost every conceivable sector of the economy and stock market. The following are general descriptions of some of the many major market indices. (Please note that the SEC does not regulate the content of these indices).

Dow Jones Industrial Average (DJIA): The Dow Jones Industrial Average is an index of 30 "blue chip" stocks of U.S. "industrial" companies. The Index includes substantial industrial companies with a history of successful growth and wide investor interest. The Index includes a wide range of companies—from financial services companies, to computer companies, to retail companies—but does not include any transportation or utility companies, which are included in separate indices. The stocks included in the DJIA are not changed often. Unlike many other indices, the DJIA is not a "weighted" index (that is, the Index does not take market capitalization into account).

NYSE Composite Index: The NYSE Composite Index tracks the price movements of all common stocks listed on the New York Stock Exchange. The Index is "capitalization-weighted" (that is, each stock's weight in the Index is proportionate to the stock's market capitalization).

S&P 500 Composite Stock Price Index: The S&P 500 Composite Stock Price Index is a capitalization-weighted index of 500 stocks intended to be a representative sample of leading companies in leading industries within the U.S. economy. Stocks in the Index are chosen for market size (large-cap), liquidity, and industry group representation.

Wilshire 5000 Total Market Index: The Wilshire 5000 Total Market Index measures the performance of all U.S. headquartered equity securities with readily available price data. The Index is a capitalization-weighted Index. The Index includes all of the stocks contained in the S&P 500 Composite Stock Price Index. The Index is intended to measure the entire U.S. stock market.

Russell 2000® Index: The Russell 2000® Index is a capitalization-weighted index designed to measure the performance of a market consisting of the 2,000 smallest publicly traded U.S. companies (in terms of market capitalization) that are included in the Russell 3000® Index.

Nasdaq-100 Index: The Nasdaq-100 Index is a "modified capitalization-weighted" index designed to track the performance of a market consisting of the 100 largest and most actively traded non-financial domestic and international securities listed on The Nasdaq Stock Market, based on market capitalization. To be included in the Index, a stock must have a minimum average daily trading volume of 100,000 shares. Generally, companies on the

---

♣ It's A Fact!!

Closing Price

Many investors use closing prices reported in the newspapers to monitor their holdings. But not all closing prices are the same, and the differences may be important to you. Here's what you should know about closing prices:

"Closing price" generally refers to the last price at which a stock trades during a regular trading session. For many market centers, including the New York Stock Exchange, the American Stock Exchange, and the Nasdaq Stock Market, regular trading sessions run from 9:30 a.m. to 4:00 p.m. Eastern Time.

Because the closing price for the same stock may be reported differently among various media and market data vendors, investors should try to understand what the reported price is based on. For example:

- Does the newspaper or vendor indicate that the closing price is based on the regular trading session price established on the security's primary market, such as the New York Stock Exchange, the American Stock Exchange, or the Nasdaq Stock Market?

- Does the closing price reflect the last trade reported over the consolidated tape as of the close of the regular trading session at 4:00 p.m. Eastern Time?

- Does the closing price reflect the last trade reported over the consolidated tape in after-hours trading?

Investors may be able to find this information if their newspaper or vendor system describes how the closing price is being reported.

Source: Excerpted from "Closing Price," U.S. Securities and Exchange Commission (SEC), August 30, 2004.

Index also must have traded on Nasdaq, or been listed on another major exchange, for at least two years.

After-Hours Trading

Excerpted from "After-Hours Trading: Understanding the Risks," U.S. Securities and Exchange Commission (SEC), December 26, 2007.

The New York Stock Exchange and the Nasdaq Stock Market—the highest volume market centers in the U.S. today—have traditionally been open for business from 9:30 a.m. to 4:00 p.m. Eastern Time. Although trading outside that window—or "after-hours" trading—has occurred for some time, it used to be limited mostly to high net worth investors and institutional investors.

But that changed by the end of the last century. With the rise of Electronic Communications Networks, or ECNs, everyday individual investors can gain access to the after-hours markets. Before you decide to trade after-hours, you need to educate yourself about the differences between regular and extended trading hours, especially the risks. You should consult your broker and read any disclosure documents on this option.

While after-hours trading presents investing opportunities, there are also the following risks for those who want to participate:

Inability To See Or Act Upon Quotes: Some firms only allow investors to view quotes from the one trading system the firm uses for after-hours trading. Check with your broker to see whether your firm's system will permit you to access other quotes on other ECNs. But remember that just because you can get quotes on another ECN does not necessary mean you will be able to trade based on those quotes. You need to ask your firm if it will route your order for execution to the other ECN. If you are limited to the quotes within one system, you may not be able to complete a trade, even with a willing investor, at a different trading system.

Lack Of Liquidity: Liquidity refers to your ability to convert stock into cash. That ability depends on the existence of buyers and sellers and how easy it is to complete a trade. During regular trading hours, buyers and sellers of most stocks can trade readily with one another. During after-hours, there may be less trading volume for some stocks, making it more difficult to execute some of your trades. Some stocks may not trade at all during extended hours.

Larger Quote Spreads: Less trading activity could also mean wider spreads between the bid and ask prices. As a result, you may find it more difficult to get your order executed or to get as favorable a price as you could have during regular market hours.

Price Volatility: For stocks with limited trading activity, you may find greater price fluctuations than you would have seen during regular trading hours. News stories announced after-hours may have greater impacts on stock prices.

Uncertain Prices: The prices of some stocks traded during the after-hours session may not reflect the prices of those stocks during regular hours, either at the end of the regular trading session or upon the opening of regular trading the next business day.

Bias Toward Limit Orders: Many electronic trading systems currently accept only limit orders, where you must enter a price at which you would like your order executed. A limit order ensures you will not pay more than the price you entered or sell for less. If the market moves away from your price, your order will not be executed. Check with your broker to see whether orders not executed during the after-hours trading session will be canceled or whether they will be automatically entered when regular trading hours begin. Similarly, find out if an order you placed during regular hours will carry over to after-hours trading.

Competition With Professional Traders: Many of the after-hours traders are professionals with large institutions, such as mutual funds, who may have access to more information than individual investors.

Computer Delays: As with online trading, you may encounter during after-hours delays or failures in getting your order executed, including orders to cancel or change your trades. For some after-hours trades, your order will be routed from your brokerage firm to an electronic trading system. If a computer problem exists at your firm, this may prevent or delay your order from reaching the system. If you encounter significant delays, you should call your broker to determine the extent of the problem and what you can to get your order executed.

Chapter 29

Types Of Investment Companies

Investment Companies

Generally, an "investment company" is a company (corporation, business trust, partnership, or limited liability company) that issues securities and is primarily engaged in the business of investing in securities.

An investment company invests the money it receives from investors on a collective basis, and each investor shares in the profits and losses in proportion to the investor's interest in the investment company. The performance of the investment company will be based on (but it won't be identical to) the performance of the securities and other assets that the investment company owns.

The federal securities laws categorize investment companies into three basic types:

• Mutual funds (legally known as open-end companies)

• Closed-end funds (legally known as closed-end companies)

• UITs (legally known as unit investment trusts)

About This Chapter: This chapter includes information from the following documents produced by the U.S. Securities and Exchange Commission (www.sec.gov): "Investment Companies," May 14, 2007, "Mutual Funds," May 14, 2007, "Interval Funds," March 15, 2007, "Unit Investment Trusts (UITs)," May 8, 2007, "Closed-End Funds," May 7, 2007, and "Real Estate Investment Trusts," July 14, 2004.

Each type has its own unique features. For example, mutual fund and UIT shares are "redeemable" (meaning that when investors want to sell their shares, they sell them back to the fund or trust, or to a broker acting for the fund or trust, at their approximate net asset value). Closed-end fund shares, on the other hand, generally are not redeemable. Instead, when closed-end fund investors want to sell their shares, they generally sell them to other investors on the secondary market, at a price determined by the market. In addition, there are variations within each type of investment company, such as stock funds, bond funds, money market funds, index funds, interval funds, and exchange-traded funds (ETFs).

Some types of companies that might initially appear to be investment companies may actually be excluded under the federal securities laws. For example, private investment funds with no more than 100 investors and private investment funds whose investors each have a substantial amount of investment assets are not considered to be investment companies—even though they issue securities and are primarily engaged in the business of investing in securities. This may be because of the private nature of their offerings or the financial means and sophistication of their investors.

Before purchasing shares of an investment company, you should carefully read all of a fund's available information, including its prospectus and most recent shareholder report.

Investment companies are regulated primarily under the Investment Company Act of 1940 and the rules and registration forms adopted under that Act. Investment companies are also subject to the Securities Act of 1933 and the Securities Exchange Act of 1934. For the definition of "investment company," you should refer to Section 3 of the Investment Company Act of 1940 and the rules under that section.

Mutual Funds

A mutual fund is a company that pools money from many investors and invests the money in stocks, bonds, short-term money-market instruments, or other securities. Legally known as an "open-end company," a mutual fund is one of three basic types of investment company.

Here are some of the traditional and distinguishing characteristics of mutual funds:

- Investors purchase mutual fund shares from the fund itself (or through a broker for the fund), but are not able to purchase the shares from other investors on a secondary market, such as the New York Stock Exchange or Nasdaq Stock Market. The price investors pay for mutual fund shares is the fund's approximate per share net asset value (NAV) plus any shareholder fees that the fund imposes at purchase (such as sales loads).

♣ **It's A Fact!!**
Mutual funds come in many varieties. For example, there are index funds, stock funds, bond funds, money market funds, and more. Each of these may have a different investment objective and strategy and a different investment portfolio. Different mutual funds may also be subject to different risks, volatility, and fees and expenses.

Source: SEC, May 14, 2007.

- Mutual fund shares are "redeemable." This means that when mutual fund investors want to sell their fund shares, they sell them back to the fund (or to a broker acting for the fund) at their approximate per share NAV, minus any fees the fund imposes at that time (such as deferred sales loads or redemption fees).

- Mutual funds generally sell their shares on a continuous basis, although some funds will stop selling when, for example, they become too large.

- The investment portfolios of mutual funds typically are managed by separate entities known as "investment advisers" that are registered with the U.S. Securities and Exchange Commission (SEC).

All funds charge management fees for operating the fund. Some also charge for their distribution and service costs, commonly referred to as "12b-1" fees. Some funds may also impose sales charges or loads when you purchase or sell fund shares. In this regard, a fund may offer different "classes" of shares in the same portfolio, with certain fees and expenses varying among classes.

To figure out how the costs of a mutual fund add up over time and to compare the costs of different mutual funds, you should use the SEC's Mutual

Fund Cost Calculator (available online at http://www.sec.gov/investor/tools/ mfcc/get-started.htm). Some funds may reduce their sales charges depending on the amount you invest in the fund. At certain thresholds, known as breakpoints, you may receive increasingly lower sales charges as your investment increases.

Keep in mind that just because a fund had excellent performance last year does not necessarily mean that it will duplicate that performance. For example, market conditions can change and this year's winning fund might be next year's loser. That is why the SEC requires funds to tell investors that a fund's past performance does not necessarily predict future results. You should carefully read all of a fund's available information, including its prospectus, or profile if it has one, and most recent shareholder report.

Mutual funds are subject to SEC registration and regulation, and are subject to numerous requirements imposed for the protection of investors. Mutual funds are regulated primarily under the Investment Company Act of 1940 and the rules and registration forms adopted under that Act. Mutual funds are also subject to the Securities Act of 1933 and the Securities Exchange Act of 1934. You can find the definition of "open-end company" in Section 5 of the Investment Company Act of 1940.

Interval Funds

An interval fund is a type of investment company that periodically offers to repurchase its shares from shareholders. That is, the fund periodically offers to buy back a stated portion of its shares from shareholders. Shareholders are not required to accept these offers and sell their shares back to the fund.

Legally, interval funds are classified as closed-end funds, but they are very different from traditional closed-end funds in that:

- Their shares typically do not trade on the secondary market. Instead, their shares are subject to periodic repurchase offers by the fund at a price based on net asset value.

- They are permitted to (and many interval funds do) continuously offer their shares at a priced based on the fund's net asset value.

An interval fund will make periodic repurchase offers to its shareholders, generally every three, six, or twelve months, as disclosed in the fund's prospectus and annual report. The interval fund also will periodically notify its shareholders of the upcoming repurchase dates. When the fund makes a repurchase offer to its shareholders, it will specify a date by which shareholders must accept the repurchase offer. The actual repurchase will occur at a later, specified date.

♣ It's A Fact!!
Interval funds are regulated primarily under the Investment Company Act of 1940 and the rules adopted under that Act, in particular Rule 23c-3. Interval funds are also subject to the Securities Act of 1933 and the Securities Exchange Act of 1934.

Source: SEC, March 15, 2007.

The price that shareholders will receive on a repurchase will be based on the per share NAV determined as of a specified (and disclosed) date. This date will occur sometime after the close of business on the date that shareholders must submit their acceptances of the repurchase offer (but generally not more than 14 days after the acceptance date).

Note that interval funds are permitted to deduct a redemption fee from the repurchase proceeds, not to exceed 2% of the proceeds. The fee is paid to the fund, and generally is intended to compensate the fund for expenses directly related to the repurchase. Interval funds may charge other fees as well.

An interval fund's prospectus and annual report will disclose the various details of the repurchase offer. Before investing in an interval fund, you should carefully read all of the fund's available information, including its prospectus and most recent shareholder report.

Unit Investment Trusts (UITs)

A "unit investment trust," commonly referred to as a "UIT," is one of three basic types of investment company. Here are some of the traditional and distinguishing characteristics of UITs:

- A UIT typically issues redeemable securities (or "units"), like a mutual fund, which means that the UIT will buy back an investor's "units," at the investor's request, at their approximate net asset value (or NAV). Some exchange-traded funds (ETFs) are structured as UITs. Under SEC exemptive orders, shares of ETFs are only redeemable in very large blocks (blocks of 50,000 shares, for example) and are traded on a secondary market.

- A UIT typically will make a one-time "public offering" of only a specific, fixed number of units (like closed-end funds). Many UIT sponsors, however, will maintain a secondary market, which allows owners of UIT units to sell them back to the sponsors and allows other investors to buy UIT units from the sponsors.

- A UIT will have a termination date (a date when the UIT will terminate and dissolve) that is established when the UIT is created (although some may terminate more than fifty years after they are created). In the case of a UIT investing in bonds, for example, the termination date may be determined by the maturity date of the bond investments. When a UIT terminates, any remaining investment portfolio securities are sold and the proceeds are paid to the investors.

- A UIT does not actively trade its investment portfolio. That is, a UIT buys a relatively fixed portfolio of securities (for example, five, ten, or twenty specific stocks or bonds), and holds them with little or no change for the life of the UIT. Because the investment portfolio of a UIT generally is fixed, investors know more or less what they are investing in for the duration of their investment. Investors will find the portfolio securities held by the UIT listed in its prospectus.

- A UIT does not have a board of directors, corporate officers, or an investment adviser to render advice during the life of the trust.

✔ Quick Tip

Keep in mind that just because a UIT had excellent performance last year does not necessarily mean that it will duplicate that performance. For example, market conditions can change, and this year's winning UIT could be next year's loser.

Source: SEC, May 8, 2007.

UITs are regulated primarily under the Investment Company Act of 1940 and the rules adopted under that Act, in particular Section 4 and Section 26.

Closed-End Funds

A "closed-end fund," legally known as a "closed-end company," is one of three basic types of investment company. Here are some of the traditional and distinguishing characteristics of closed-end funds:

- Closed-end funds generally do not continuously offer their shares for sale. Rather, they sell a fixed number of shares at one time (in an initial public offering), after which the shares typically trade on a secondary market, such as the New York Stock Exchange or the Nasdaq Stock Market.

- The price of closed-end fund shares that trade on a secondary market after their initial public offering is determined by the market and may be greater or less than the shares' net asset value (NAV).

- Closed-end fund shares generally are not redeemable. That is, a closed-end fund is not required to buy its shares back from investors upon request. Some closed-end funds, commonly referred to as interval funds, offer to repurchase their shares at specified intervals.

- The investment portfolios of closed-end funds generally are managed by separate entities known as "investment advisers" that are registered with the SEC.

- Closed-end funds are permitted to invest in a greater amount of "illiquid" securities than are mutual funds. (An "illiquid" security generally is considered to be a security that cannot be sold within seven days at the approximate price used by the fund in determining NAV.) Because of this feature, funds that seek to invest in markets where the securities tend to be more illiquid are typically organized as closed-end funds.

Closed-end funds come in many varieties. They can have different investment objectives, strategies, and investment portfolios. They also can be subject to different risks, volatility, and fees and expenses.

Keep in mind that just because a fund had excellent performance last year does not necessarily mean that it will duplicate that performance. For example, market conditions can change and this year's winning fund could be next year's loser.

Closed-end funds are subject to SEC registration and regulation, which subjects them to numerous requirements imposed for the protection of investors. Closed-end funds are regulated primarily under the Investment Company Act of 1940 and the rules adopted under that Act. Closed-end funds are also subject to the Securities Act of 1933 and the Securities Exchange Act of 1934. You can find the definition of "closed-end company" in Section 5 of the Investment Company Act.

Real Estate Investment Trusts

Real estate investment trusts, known as REITs, are entities that invest in different kinds of real estate or real estate related assets, including shopping centers, office buildings, hotels, and mortgages secured by real estate. There are basically three types of REITS:

- Equity REITS, the most common type of REIT, invest in or own real estate and make money for investors from the rents they collect

- Mortgage REITS lend money to owners and developers or invest in financial instruments secured by mortgages on real estate

- Hybrid REITS are a combination of equity and mortgage REITS

> ♣ **It's A Fact!!**
> For more information about REITS, you can visit the website of the National Association of Real Estate Investment Trusts (available online at http://www.nareit.org), a trade organization for the REIT industry.
>
> Source: SEC, July 14, 2004.

The Internal Revenue Code lists the conditions a company must meet to qualify as a REIT. For example, the company must pay 90% of its taxable income to shareholders every year. It must also invest at least 75% of its total assets in real estate and generate 75% or more of its gross income from investments in or mortgages on real property.

Many REITs trade on national exchanges or in the over-the-counter market. REITs that are publicly traded must file reports with the SEC, such as quarterly and annual filings. You can find these reports on the SEC's EDGAR database.

Chapter 30

Understanding Mutual Funds

About Mutual Funds

What Is A Mutual Fund?

A mutual fund is a company that invests in a diversified portfolio of securities. People who buy shares of a mutual fund are its owners or shareholders. Their investments provide the money for a mutual fund to buy securities such as stocks and bonds. A mutual fund can make money from its securities in two ways: a security can pay dividends or interest to the fund, or a security can rise in value. A fund can also lose money and drop in value.

Different Funds, Different Features

There are three basic types of mutual funds—stock (also called equity), bond, and money market. Stock mutual funds invest primarily in shares of stock issued by U.S. or foreign companies. Bond mutual funds invest primarily in bonds. Money market mutual funds invest mainly in short-term securities issued by the U.S. government and its agencies, U.S. corporations, and state and local governments.

About This Chapter: Text in this chapter was excerpted from "A Guide to Understanding Mutual Funds," © 2008 Investment Company Institute (www.ici.org). Reprinted with permission.

Why Invest In A Mutual Fund?

Mutual funds make saving and investing simple, accessible, and affordable. The advantages of mutual funds include professional management, diversification, variety, liquidity, affordability, convenience, and ease of recordkeeping—as well as strict government regulation and full disclosure.

Professional Management: Even under the best of market conditions, it takes an astute, experienced investor to choose investments correctly, and a further commitment of time to continually monitor those investments.

✎ What's It Mean?

Annual And Semiannual Reports: Summaries that a mutual fund sends to its shareholders that discuss the fund's performance over a certain period and identify the securities in the fund's portfolio on a specific date.

Family Of Funds: A group of mutual funds, each typically with its own investment objective, managed and distributed by the same company.

Hybrid Fund: A mutual fund that invests in a mix of equity and fixed-income securities.

Load Fund: A fund that imposes a one-time fee—either when fund shares are purchased (front-end load) or redeemed (back-end load)—or a fund that charges a 12b-1 fee greater than 0.25 percent.

Net Asset Value (NAV): The per-share value of a mutual fund, found by subtracting the fund's liabilities from its assets and dividing by the number of shares outstanding. Mutual funds calculate their NAVs at least once daily.

No-Load Fund: A mutual fund whose shares are sold without a sales commission and without a 12b-1 fee of more than 0.25 percent per year.

Prospectus: The official document that describes a mutual fund to prospective investors. The prospectus contains information required by the U.S. Securities and Exchange Commission (SEC), such as investment objectives and policies, risks, services, and fees.

Statement Of Additional Information (SAI): The supplementary document to a prospectus that contains more detailed information about a mutual fund; also known as "Part B" of the prospectus.

With mutual funds, experienced professionals manage a portfolio of securities for you full-time, and decide which securities to buy and sell based on extensive research. A fund is usually managed by an individual or a team choosing investments that best match the fund's objectives. As economic conditions change, the managers often adjust the mix of the fund's investments to ensure it continues to meet the fund's objectives.

Diversification: Successful investors know that diversifying their investments can help reduce the adverse impact of a single investment. Mutual funds introduce diversification to your investment portfolio automatically by holding a wide variety of securities. Moreover, since you pool your assets with those of other investors, a mutual fund allows you to obtain a more diversified portfolio than you would probably be able to comfortably manage on your own—and at a fraction of the cost.

In short, funds allow you the opportunity to invest in many markets and sectors. That's the key benefit of diversification.

Variety: Within the broad categories of stock, bond, and money market funds, you can choose among a variety of investment approaches. Today, there are about 8,200 mutual funds available in the U.S., with goals and styles to fit most objectives and circumstances.

Low Costs: Mutual funds usually hold dozens or even hundreds of securities like stocks and bonds. The primary way you pay for this service is through a fee that is based on the total value of your account. Because the fund industry consists of hundreds of competing firms and thousands of funds, the actual level of fees can vary. But for most investors, mutual funds provide professional management and diversification at a fraction of the cost of making such investments independently.

Liquidity: Liquidity is the ability to readily access your money in an investment. Mutual fund shares are liquid investments that can be sold on any business day. Mutual funds are required by law to buy, or redeem, shares each business day. The price per share at which you can redeem shares is known as the fund's net asset value (NAV). NAV is the current market value of all the fund's assets, minus liabilities, divided by the total number of outstanding shares.

Convenience: You can purchase or sell fund shares directly from a fund or through a broker, financial planner, bank, or insurance agent, by mail, over the telephone, and increasingly by personal computer. You can also arrange for automatic reinvestment or periodic distribution of the dividends and capital gains paid by the fund. Funds may offer a wide variety of other services, including monthly or quarterly account statements, tax information, and 24-hour phone and computer access to fund and account information.

Protecting Investors: Not only are mutual funds subject to compliance with their self-imposed restrictions and limitations, they are also highly regulated by the federal government through the U.S. Securities and Exchange Commission (SEC). As part of this government regulation, all funds must meet certain operating standards, observe strict antifraud rules, and disclose complete information to current and potential investors. These laws are strictly enforced and designed to protect investors from fraud and abuse. But these laws obviously cannot help you pick the fund that is right for you or prevent a fund from losing money. You can still lose money by investing in a mutual fund. A mutual fund is not guaranteed or insured by the Federal Deposit Insurance Corporation (FDIC) or Securities Investor Protection Corporation (SIPC), even if fund shares are purchased through a bank.

Stock Funds

Stock funds invest primarily in stocks. A share of stock represents a unit of ownership in a company. If a company is successful, shareholders can profit in two ways: the stock may increase in value, or the company can pass its profits to shareholders in the form of dividends. If a company fails, a shareholder can lose the entire value of his or her shares; however, a shareholder is not liable for the debts of the company.

When you buy shares of a stock mutual fund, you essentially become a part owner of each of the securities in your fund's portfolio. Stock investments have historically been a great source for increasing individual wealth, even though the stocks of the most successful companies may experience periodic declines in value. Over time, stocks historically have performed better than other investments in securities, such as bonds and money market instruments. Of course, there is no guarantee that this historical trend will be true in the future. That's why stock funds are best used as long-term investments.

♣ It's A Fact!!
Volatility: Stock Market
Returns Fluctuate From Year To Year

The upswings and downturns of the stock market affect stock fund returns. Despite a history of outperforming other types of securities, stocks sometimes lose money. Sometimes these losses can be substantial and last for long periods. The average annual return on stocks from 1926 to 2005 is about 10.4 percent.

Bond Funds

Bond funds invest primarily in securities known as bonds. A bond is a type of security that resembles a loan. When a bond is purchased, money is lent to the company, municipality, or government agency that issued the bond. In exchange for the use of this money, the issuer promises to repay the amount loaned (the principal; also known as the face value of the bond) on a specific maturity date. In addition, the issuer typically promises to make periodic interest payments over the life of the loan.

A bond fund share represents ownership in a pool of bonds and other securities comprising the fund's portfolio. Although there have been past exceptions, bond funds tend to be less volatile than stock funds and often produce regular income. For these reasons, investors often use bond funds to diversify, provide a stream of income, or invest for intermediate-term goals. Like stock funds, bond funds have risks and can make or lose money.

Types Of Risk: After a bond is first issued, it may be traded. If a bond is traded before it matures, it may be worth more or less than the price paid for it. The price at which a bond trades can be affected by several types of risk.

• *Interest Rate Risk:* Think of the relationship between bond prices and interest rates as opposite ends of a seesaw. When interest rates fall, a bond's value usually rises. When interest rates rise, a bond's value usually falls. The longer a bond's maturity, the more its price tends to fluctuate as market interest rates change. However, while longer-term bonds tend to fluctuate in value more than shorter-term bonds, they also tend to have higher yields to compensate for this risk. Unlike a bond, a bond mutual fund does not have a fixed maturity. It does, however, have an average portfolio maturity—the average of all the

---

✔ Quick Tip
Are Tax-Free Bond Funds Right For You?

With most bond funds, the income you receive is taxable as ordinary income. However, some funds invest in bonds whose interest payments are free from federal income tax, while other funds invest in bonds that are free from both federal and state income tax. Tax-exempt funds may be subject to capital gains taxes.

The income tax benefit typically means that the income from these funds is lower than that of comparable taxable funds. But if you compare the yields after taxes, a tax-free fund may be a better choice, depending on your tax bracket. Table 30.1 shows how taxable and tax-free yields compare after taxes for investors in different tax brackets.

If you live in an area where there are state or local income taxes, you may be able to find a fund whose interest payments are free from these taxes as well as federal taxes.

Table 30.1. Tax Comparison

A Hypothetical Tax-Free Yield of:	4.0%	5.0%	6.0%	7.0%
Equals a Taxable Yield in the 28% Tax Bracket of:	5.56%	6.94%	8.33%	9.72%
Equals a Taxable Yield in the 31% Tax Bracket of:	5.80%	7.25%	8.70%	10.14%
Equals a Taxable Yield in the 36% Tax Bracket of:	6.25%	7.81%	9.38%	10.94%

maturity dates of the bonds in the fund's portfolio. In general, the longer a fund's average portfolio maturity, the more sensitive the fund's share price will be to changes in interest rates and the more the fund's shares will fluctuate in value.

- *Credit Risk:* Credit risk refers to the "creditworthiness" of the bond issuer and its expected ability to pay interest and to repay its debt. If a bond issuer is unable to repay principal or interest on time, the bond is said to be in default. A decline in an issuer's credit rating, or creditworthiness, can cause a bond's price to decline. Bond funds holding the bond could then experience a decline in their net asset value.

- *Prepayment Risk:* Prepayment risk is the possibility that a bond owner will receive his or her principal investment back from the issuer prior to the bond's maturity date. This can happen when interest rates fall, giving the issuer an opportunity to borrow money at a lower interest rate than the one currently being paid. (For example, a homeowner who refinances a home mortgage to take advantage of decreasing interest rates has prepaid the mortgage.) As a consequence, the bond's owner will not receive any more interest payments from the investment. This also forces any reinvestment to be made in a market where prevailing interest rates are lower than when the initial investment was made. If a bond fund held a bond that has been prepaid, the fund may have to reinvest the money in a bond that will have a lower yield.

Money Market Funds

A money market fund invests in a pool of short-term, interest-bearing securities. A money market instrument is a short-term IOU issued by the U.S. government, U.S. corporations, and state and local governments. Money market instruments have maturity dates of less than 13 months. These instruments are relatively stable because of their short maturities and high quality.

Money market funds are most appropriate for short-term investment and savings goals or in situations where you seek to preserve the value of your investment while still earning income. In general, money market funds are useful as part of a diversified personal financial program that includes long-term investments.

Money Market Fund Risks: The short-term nature of money market investments makes money market funds less volatile than any other type of fund. Money market funds seek to maintain a $1-per-share price to preserve your investment principal while generating dividend income.

To help preserve the value of your principal investment, money market funds must meet stringent credit quality, maturity, and diversification standards. Most money market funds are required to invest at least 95 percent of their assets in U.S. Treasury issues and privately issued securities carrying the highest credit rating by at least two of the five major credit rating agencies. A money market fund generally cannot invest in any security with a maturity greater than 397 days, nor can its average maturity exceed 90 days. All of these factors help minimize risk. However, money market funds do not guarantee that you will receive all your money back. Money market funds are not insured by the U.S. government.

"Inflation risk"—that is, the risk your investment return fails to keep pace with the inflation rate—is another concern if you choose to invest in money market funds or any other short-term investments.

Investing Internationally

International stock and bond mutual funds provide a convenient, low-cost way for you to invest in foreign securities markets compared with investing in these markets directly. Investing internationally offers diversification and the opportunity for higher returns. But these investments also have risks that are usually not present with investments in U.S. stocks and bonds.

For example, U.S. investors usually buy foreign securities in the other country's currency, making the investments subject to changes in the currency

**✔ Quick Tip
Thinking Of Investing Internationally?**

From year to year, investments overseas rarely perform the same as investments in U.S. markets. There are times when each type of investment outperforms the other. The key point is that a diversified investment strategy that incorporates both domestic and foreign securities can help improve your potential return and offset the risks of downturns in either market.

exchange rate. Fluctuations in currency exchange rates can have a significant effect on an investor's return. If your fund's investment in a Malaysian stock increased by 10 percent during a six-month period while the value of the Malaysian ringgit declined 10 percent during the same period, you would break even on the investment. Some international funds try to offset this effect by performing "hedging transactions."

Investing in foreign markets may involve additional costs due to the unique operational requirements of an overseas fund, and may also involve volatile political and economic situations—especially in emerging markets.

How Mutual Funds Are Structured

A mutual fund is usually either a corporation or a business trust (which is like a corporation). Like any corporation, a mutual fund is owned by its shareholders. Virtually all mutual funds are externally managed; they do not have employees of their own. Instead, their operations are conducted by affiliated organizations and independent contractors.

Other Types Of Investment Companies

Mutual funds are one of three types of investment companies; the other two are closed-end funds and unit investment trusts.

A closed-end fund is an investment company whose shares are publicly traded like stocks. As a result, the price of a closed-end fund share fluctuates based on supply and demand. If the share price is more than the value of its assets, then the fund is trading at a premium; if the share price is less, then it is trading at a discount. The assets of a closed-end fund are managed by a professional or a group of professionals choosing investments such as stocks and bonds to match the fund's objectives.

A unit investment trust (UIT) is an investment company that buys a fixed portfolio of stocks or bonds. A UIT holds its securities until the trust's termination date. When a trust is dissolved, proceeds from the securities are paid to shareholders. UITs often have a fixed number of shares or "units" that are sold to investors in an initial public offering. If some shareholders redeem units, the UIT or its sponsor may purchase them and reoffer them to the public.

Becoming An Informed Investor

The Mutual Fund Prospectus And Shareholder Reports

To protect investors, all mutual funds are highly regulated by the federal government through the U.S. Securities and Exchange Commission (SEC). Federal law requires that all funds provide two types of documents to current and potential investors free of charge: a prospectus and a shareholder report.

A mutual fund's prospectus describes in plain English the fund's goals, fees and expenses, investment strategies and risks, as well as information on how to buy and sell shares. You can get a copy of a fund's current prospectus from the fund or your broker or financial planner. Many funds also make prospectuses available on their websites. The SEC requires a fund to provide a full prospectus either before you invest or together with the confirmation statement for your initial investment.

> ♣ **It's A Fact!!**
> **The Fund Profile**
> Some mutual funds offer a streamlined version of a fund prospectus called a fund profile. The fund profile contains the answers to key questions to consider before investing in a mutual fund. If you find you need more information, a fund stands ready to send you a prospectus, shareholder reports, and other helpful documents. Once you invest, the fund automatically sends you the prospectus.

Annual and semiannual shareholder reports document the fund's recent performance and include other important information. By examining these reports, you can learn if a fund has been effective in meeting the goals and investment strategies described in the fund's prospectus.

What To Look For In A Shareholder Report

Shareholder reports typically include two main types of information:

• The fund's financial statements and performance

• A list of the securities the fund held in its portfolio at the end of the most recent accounting period

The annual report discusses the factors and investment strategies that affected the fund's performance during the period covered by the report. Also included in a fund's annual report (with the exception of money market funds) is information comparing the fund's performance at the end of each of the past 10 years (or since the first year the fund was in operation) with one or more market indices, such as the S&P 500 Stock Index or the Lehman Brothers Corporate Bond Index. Charts and tables assume a $10,000 investment was made at the beginning of the first fiscal year. (The SEC requires that the performance discussion and chart be included in either the shareholder report or the prospectus; most funds include it in their shareholder reports.)

Evaluating Fund Performance: A fund's annual report or prospectus contains charts and tables, like the one shown in Table 30.2, allowing for an easy comparison of the fund's performance versus a similar market index. When comparing mutual fund performance with that of an index, remember that your fund's performance is calculated after fees and expenses have been deducted; the performance of the index does not reflect the costs associated with constructing and maintaining an identical portfolio.

Table 30.2. Comparing A Fund's Performance

	Past 1 Year	Past 5 Years[2]	Past 10 Years[2]
Index Fund	30.29%	6.70%	10.99%
S&P 500 Index[1]	28.68%	-0.57%	11.07%

[1]The S&P 500 is the Standard & Poor's Composite Index of 500 Stocks, a widely recognized, unmanaged index of common stock price.

[2]Average annual return.

Publications And Websites

In addition to fund prospectuses and shareholder reports, there are many other sources of mutual fund information available to you. However, none can substitute for reading the prospectus and shareholder reports.

Information found in newspapers, magazines, independent reports, websites, and other outside sources of information can be valuable because they provide third-party views and comparisons of different funds.

Newspapers And Magazines: Many newspapers, business magazines, and financial publications cover mutual funds. They can be a source of information on industry trends, expense ratios, rankings, and profiles of various funds.

Newspapers can be a good way to track mutual fund performance. Most major dailies publish the latest mutual fund share prices and performance.

In some papers, the share price (NAV) is identified as the sell, or bid price, which is the amount per share you would receive if you sell a share (less any deferred sales charges or redemption fees). Also listed in the paper is the offering price, sometimes called the buy, or asked, price which is the price investors pay to purchase shares. The offering price is the share price plus any sales charges.

♣ **It's A Fact!!**
Online Information

Many fund companies have internet websites. You can usually access fund information and download prospectuses and annual reports from these sites. Some companies use the internet to provide educational material and to allow shareholder transactions. Fund information can also be found on the SEC's website (http://www.sec.gov).

How To Read A Mutual Fund Fee Table

There are two basic types of costs associated with mutual funds. Some funds charge shareholder fees when you purchase or redeem shares of the fund, that is, sales commissions. In addition, all funds have operating expenses, which represent the costs of running the fund. A mutual fund's fees and expenses are required by law to be clearly disclosed to investors in a fee table at the front of the fund's prospectus.

Mutual funds compete vigorously to keep costs low, since the performance figures reported by the fund, and the total value of your mutual fund account, are provided after all fees and expenses have been deducted. For example, the fund returns published in newspapers, advertisements, and official fund documents already are "net" of any fees the fund charges you. Thus, any time you consider a fund's past performance, your decision reflects the impact fees have had on the fund in the past.

Particularly important to your assessment of costs is the fund's expense ratio. The availability of this figure in all fund prospectuses allows you to easily compare how much more or less one fund costs versus another—an important part of making an informed investment decision.

The Statement Of Additional Information

After reviewing the prospectus, if you want more information, ask the fund for its Statement of Additional Information (SAI), which the fund will send you free of charge. Most SAIs are lengthy and fairly technical but include many additional details about the fund, such as:

• more information about the fund's securities, risks, and policies;

• the fund's audited financial statements;

• the fund's portfolio securities as of the date of the SAI; and

• information about anyone who owns five percent or more of the fund's shares.

Should Fund Fees Affect Your Decision?

If two funds were *identical*, except for the fees and expenses they charge, the lower-cost fund would be a better option.

But rarely, if ever, are funds identical. For example, stock funds typically cost more than bond and money market funds, but stock funds historically have provided a significantly higher return—even after expenses are deducted. Even different types of stock funds, U.S. or foreign, typically vary in cost.

Table 30.3. Mutual Fund Fee Table Required by Federal Law (example is hypothetical; estimated expenses are based on the U.S. Securities and Exchange Commission's Mutual Fund Cost Calculator, www.sec.gov/investor/tools/mfcc/get-started.htm)

Shareholder Fees

A	Maximum Sales Charge (Load) Imposed on Purchases (as a percentage of offering price)	4.5%
B	Maximum Deferred Sales Charge (Load)	None
C	Maximum Sales Charge (Load) on Reinvested Dividends	None
D	Redemption Fee	None
E	Exchange Fee	None
F	Annual Account Maintenance Fee	None

Annual Fund Operating Expenses

G	Management Fee	0.52%
H	Distribution (12b-1) Fee	0.25%
I	Other Expenses	0.20%
J	Total Annual Fund Operating Expenses (Expense Ratio)	0.97%

K Example: This example is intended to help an investor compare the cost of investing in different funds. The example assumes a $10,000 investment in the fund for one, three, five, and 10 years and then a redemption of all fund shares at the end of those periods. The example also assumes that an investment returns 5 percent each year and that the fund's operating expenses remain the same. Although actual costs may be higher or lower, based on these assumptions an investor's estimated expenses would be:

1 year: $547	5 years: $977
3 years: $754	10 years: $1,617

Shareholder Fees are charged directly to an investor for a specific transaction, such as a purchase, redemption, or exchange:

A—Maximum Sales Charge (Load) Imposed on Purchases: The maximum "front-end load" or sales charge that may be attached to the purchase of mutual fund shares. This fee compensates a financial professional for his or her services. By law, this charge may not exceed 8.5 percent of the investment, although most fund families charge less than the maximum.

B—Maximum Deferred Sales Charge (Load): The maximum "back-end load" or sales charge that a fund may impose when shares are redeemed or sold; an alternative way to compensate financial professionals for their services. A common type of deferred sales charge is a "contingent deferred sales charge," which typically applies for the first few years of ownership, declining until it disappears.

C—Maximum Sales Charge (Load) on Reinvested Dividends: The maximum fee charged by a fund when dividends are reinvested in the purchase of additional shares. Most funds do not charge a fee for this service. Beginning in April 2000, new funds were prohibited from charging this fee.

D—Redemption Fee: Like a contingent deferred sales charge, this fee is another type of back-end charge when an investor redeems shares. Unlike contingent deferred sales charges, this fee is paid to the fund. It covers costs, other than sales costs, involved with a redemption. The fee is expressed as a dollar amount or as a percentage of the redemption price.

E—Exchange Fee: This fee may be charged when an investor transfers money from one fund to another within the same fund family.

F—Annual Account Maintenance Fee: This fee may be charged by some funds, for example, to maintain low-balance accounts.

Annual Fund Operating Expenses reflect the normal costs of operating a fund. Unlike transaction fees, these expenses are not charged directly to an investor but are deducted from fund assets before earnings are distributed to shareholders.

G—Management Fee: This is a fee charged by a fund's investment adviser for managing the fund's portfolio of securities and providing related services.

H—Distribution (12b-1) Fee: This fee, if charged, is deducted from fund assets to pay marketing and advertising expenses or, more commonly, to compensate sales professionals. By law, 12b-1 fees cannot exceed one percent of a fund's average net assets per year. The 12b-1 fee may include a service fee of up to 0.25 percent of average net assets per year to compensate sales professionals for providing services or maintaining shareholder accounts.

I—Other Expenses: These expenses include, for example, fees paid to a fund's transfer agent for providing fund shareholder services, such as toll-free phone communications, computerized account services, website services, recordkeeping, printing, and mailing.

J—Total Annual Fund Operating Expenses (Expense Ratio: This represents the sum of all a fund's annual operating costs, expressed as a percentage of average net assets. Total annual fund operating expenses are also known as the fund's expense ratio.

K—Example of the effect of expenses on a $10,000 investment: This is a hypothetical illustration required by the SEC in every fund's fee table. It is presented in a standardized format and based on specified assumptions (five percent annual return, expenses unchanged) in order to make it easier for investors to compare different funds' fees.

✔ **Quick Tip**
How To Calculate The Annual Fund Fees You Pay

It's easy to compare the annual costs of two or more funds. Costs are displayed prominently at the front of each fund's prospectus in a standardized fee table. The fund fee table displays annual costs as a percentage of fund assets—the expense ratio. The expense ratio allows you to make simple but exact comparisons of annual fees. Finally—and equally important—the fee table includes a hypothetical example that tells you in dollars and cents what a $10,000 investment would cost based on a five percent return. This cost includes transactional charges, if any, and the fund's annual fees. Thus, in the hypothetical $10,000 investment example, a fund with a 0.75 operating expense ratio would cost a shareholder $6.25 a month.

You can also perform cost calculations and comparisons on your own based on your own investments. Some websites offer cost calculators, like the one found on the Securities and Exchange Commission website (at www.sec.gov/mfcc/mfcc-int.htm), that supply you with dollars-and-cents cost comparisons.

In short, there are many factors that affect the fees and expenses a fund charges. Only after weighing all of the relative benefits of different funds, including an analysis of their costs, can you decide if owning a particular fund is acceptable to you. A fund with higher costs may make more money for you, even after accounting for the costs you pay, than a fund with a lower cost. The opposite may also be true.

Chapter 31

How Mutual Fund And Other Investment Companies Operate

The Origins Of Pooled Investing

The investment company concept dates to Europe in the late 1700s, according to K. Geert Rouwenhorst in *The Origins of Mutual Funds*, when "a Dutch merchant and broker...invited subscriptions from investors to form a trust...to provide an opportunity to diversify for small investors with limited means."

The emergence of "investment pooling" in England in the 1800s brought the concept closer to U.S. shores. The enactment of two British laws, the Joint Stock Companies Acts of 1862 and 1867, permitted investors to share in the profits of an investment enterprise and limited investor liability to the amount of investment capital devoted to the enterprise. Shortly thereafter, in 1868, the Foreign and Colonial Government Trust formed in London. This trust resembled the U.S. fund model in basic structure, providing "the investor of moderate means the same advantages as the large capitalists...by spreading the investment over a number of different stocks."

Perhaps more importantly, the British fund model established a direct link with U.S. securities markets, helping finance the development of the

About This Chapter: Text in this is excerpted from "2008 Investment Company Fact Book, 48th Edition," © 2008 Investment Company Institute (www.ici.org). Reprinted with permission.

post-Civil War U.S. economy. The Scottish American Investment Trust, formed on February 1, 1873 by fund pioneer Robert Fleming, invested in the economic potential of the United States, chiefly through American railroad bonds. Many other trusts followed that targeted not only investment in America, but led to the introduction of the fund investing concept on U.S. shores in the late 1800s and early 1900s.

The first mutual, or "open-end," fund was introduced in Boston in March of 1924. The Massachusetts Investors Trust, formed as a common law trust, introduced important innovations to the investment company concept by establishing a simplified capital structure, continuous offering of shares, the ability to redeem shares rather than hold them until dissolution of the fund, and a set of clear investment restrictions and policies.

The Stock Market Crash of 1929 and the Great

♣ **It's A Fact!!**
Four Principal Securities Laws Govern Investment Companies

The Investment Company Act of 1940: Regulates the structure and operations of investment companies by imposing restrictions on investments and requiring investment companies, among other things, to maintain detailed books and records, safeguard their portfolio securities, and file semiannual reports with the U.S. Securities and Exchange Commission (SEC).

The Securities Act of 1933: Requires federal registration of all public offerings of securities, including investment company shares or units. The 1933 Act also requires that all investors receive a current prospectus describing the fund.

The Securities Exchange Act of 1934: Regulates broker-dealers, including investment company principal underwriters and other entities and persons that sell mutual fund shares, and requires them to register with the SEC. Among other things, the 1934 Act requires registered broker-dealers to maintain extensive books and records, segregate customer securities in adequate custodial accounts, and file detailed, annual financial reports.

The Investment Advisers Act of 1940: Requires federal registration of all investment advisers, including those to mutual funds and other investment companies. The Advisers Act contains provisions requiring fund advisers to meet recordkeeping, custodial, reporting, and other regulatory responsibilities.

Depression that followed greatly hampered the growth of pooled investments until a succession of landmark securities laws, beginning with the Securities Act of 1933 and concluding with the Investment Company Act of 1940, reinvigorated investor confidence. Renewed investor confidence and many innovations led to relatively steady growth in industry assets and number of accounts.

The Different Types of U.S. Investment Companies

An investment company is a corporation, trust, or partnership organized under state law that invests pooled shareholder dollars in securities appropriate to the entity's—and its shareholders'—investment objective. The main types of investment companies are: mutual, or "open-end," funds, closed-end funds, unit investment trusts, and exchange-traded funds, a relatively recent adaptation of the investment company concept.

A mutual fund is an investment company that buys a portfolio of securities selected by a professional investment adviser to meet a specified financial goal. Investors buy fund shares, which represent proportionate ownership in all the fund's securities. There is no limit on the number of shares issued by a mutual fund. A mutual fund is referred to as an "open-end" fund for two main reasons: 1) it is required to redeem (or buy back) outstanding shares at any time, at their current net asset value, which is the total market value of the fund's investment portfolio, minus its liabilities and divided by the number of shares outstanding; and 2) virtually all mutual funds continuously offer their shares to the public.

A closed-end fund is an investment company that issues a fixed number of shares that trade on a stock exchange or in the over-the-counter market. Assets of a closed-end fund are professionally managed in accordance with the fund's investment objectives and policies and may be invested in stocks, bonds, or other securities. The vast majority of closed-end funds are externally managed, like mutual funds. As with other publicly traded securities, the market price of closed-end fund shares fluctuates and is determined by supply and demand in the marketplace.

A unit investment trust (UIT) is an investment company that buys and holds a generally fixed portfolio of stocks, bonds, or other securities, and issues a fixed number of units for sale. Unit investment trusts are also externally managed. "Units" in the trust are sold to investors, or "unit holders," who, during the life of the trust, receive their proportionate share of dividends or interest paid by the trust. Unlike other investment companies, a UIT has a stated date for termination, which varies according to the investments held in its portfolio. At termination, investors receive their proportionate share of the UIT's net assets.

Another fund available to investors is an exchange-traded fund (ETF). Although an ETF is an investment company (either an open-end fund or UIT), its structure and the trading of its shares differ significantly from traditional mutual funds or UITs. Indeed, unlike with other mutual funds or UITs, ETF shares are traded intraday on stock exchanges at market-determined prices. As such, an ETF has the features of an investment company (diversified portfolio, professional management), but its shares trade in the retail market like an equity security. Unlike mutual funds, investors must buy or sell ETF shares through a broker just as they would the shares of any publicly traded company.

> ## ♣ It's A Fact!!
>
> With 92 percent of industry assets, mutual funds are the most common type of investment company. The other types of investment companies—closed-end funds, unit investment trusts, and exchange-traded funds—can differ from mutual funds in terms of structure, service providers, the roles and responsibilities of the investment company's entities, earnings, pricing and listing procedures, and taxation. Visit the Investment Company Institute's website (www.ici.org) for more detailed information about each type of investment company.

The Organization Of A Mutual Fund

Individuals and institutions invest in a mutual fund by purchasing shares issued by the fund. It is through these sales of shares that a mutual fund raises the cash used to invest in its portfolio of stocks, bonds, and other investments. Each investor owns a pro-rata share of the fund's investments and shares in the returns from the fund's portfolio while benefiting from professional investment management, diversification, and liquidity. Mutual funds may offer other benefits and services, such as asset allocation programs or money market sweep accounts.

A mutual fund is organized under state law either as a corporation or a business trust. Mutual funds have officers and directors or trustees. In this way, mutual funds are like any other type of operating company, such as IBM or General Motors.

Unlike other companies, however, a mutual fund is typically externally managed: it is not an operating company and it has no employees in the traditional sense. Instead, a fund relies upon third parties or service providers, either affiliated organizations or independent contractors, to invest fund assets and carry out other business activities. Figure 31.1 shows the types of service providers usually relied upon by a fund.

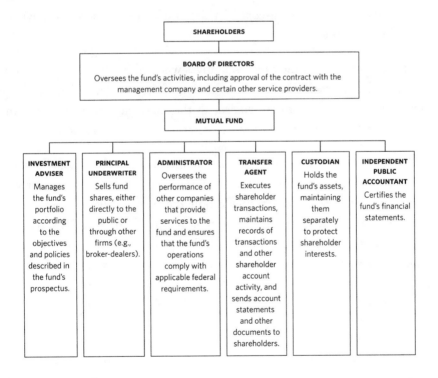

Figure 31.1. Structure Of A Mutual Fund. Note: Closed-end funds, UITs, and ETFs can differ from mutual funds and from each other with respect to structure.

How A Fund Is Created

Setting up a mutual fund is a complicated process performed by the fund's sponsor, typically the fund's investment adviser, administrator, or principal underwriter (also known as its distributor).

The fund sponsor has a variety of responsibilities. For example, it must assemble the group of third parties needed to launch the fund, including the persons or entities charged with managing and operating the fund. The sponsor provides officers and affiliated directors to oversee the fund, and recruits unaffiliated persons to serve as independent directors. It must also register the fund under state law as either a business trust or corporation. In addition, to sell its shares to the public, the fund must first register those shares with the SEC by filing a federal registration statement pursuant to the Securities Act of 1933 and, unless otherwise exempt from doing so, make filings and pay fees to each state (except Florida) in which the fund's shares will be offered to the public.

Broker-dealers and their representatives who sell fund shares to the public are subject to registration and regulation under the Securities Exchange Act of 1934. The investment adviser to the fund must register under the Investment Advisers Act of 1940 and comply with the Act's provisions.

Preparing the federal registration statement, contracts, filings for individual states, and corporate documents typically costs the fund sponsor several hundred thousand dollars. In addition, the Investment Company Act of 1940, a federal statute expressly governing mutual fund operations, requires that a mutual fund register with the SEC as an investment company. It also requires that each new fund have at least $100,000 of seed capital before distributing its shares to the public; this capital is usually contributed by the adviser or other sponsor in the form of an initial investment.

Mutual funds incur fees and expenses in their ongoing operations, including the servicing of shareholder accounts. In addition to management fees (that is, the fees paid to the fund's investment adviser to manage the fund's portfolio and perform other services), funds regularly incur transfer agent, custodian, accounting, and other business and brokerage expenses.

Status as a registered investment company allows the fund to be treated as a "pass-through" investment vehicle for tax purposes. In other words, the fund's income flows through to shareholders without being taxed at the fund level. Although a mutual fund is created from the seed money of a fund sponsor, it is managed for the benefit of all those investors who decide to buy shares once the fund is created and its shares offered to the public.

Shareholders

Investors are given comprehensive information about the fund to help them make informed decisions. A mutual fund's prospectus describes the fund's investment goals and objectives, fees and expenses, investment strategies and risks, and informs investors how to buy and sell shares. The SEC requires a fund to provide a prospectus either before an investor makes his or her initial investment or together with the confirmation statement of an initial investment. In addition, periodic shareholder reports, which are provided to investors at least every six months, discuss the fund's recent performance and include other important information, such as the fund's financial statements. By examining these reports and other publicly available information, an investor can learn if a fund has been effective in meeting the goals and investment strategies described in the fund's prospectus.

Like shareholders of other companies, mutual fund shareholders have specific voting rights. These include the right to elect directors at meetings called for that purpose (subject to a limited exception for filling vacancies). Shareholders must also approve material changes in the terms of a fund's contract with its investment adviser, the entity that manages the fund's assets. For example, a fund's management fee can be increased only when a majority of shareholders vote to approve the increase. Furthermore, funds seeking to change investment objectives or fundamental policies must first obtain the approval of the holders of a majority of the fund's outstanding voting securities.

Fund Entities And Service Providers

Boards Of Directors

A fund's board of directors is elected by the fund's shareholders to govern the fund, and its role is primarily one of oversight. The board of directors typically is not involved in the day-to-day management of the fund company. Instead, day-to-day management of the fund is handled by the fund's investment adviser or administrator pursuant to a contract with the fund.

Investment company directors must exercise the care that a reasonably prudent person would take with his or her own business. They are expected to exercise sound business judgment, approve policies and procedures to ensure the fund's compliance with the federal securities laws, and undertake oversight and review of the performance of the fund's operations, as well as of the operations of the fund's service providers with respect to the services they provide to the fund.

As part of this duty, a director is expected to obtain adequate information about issues that come before the board in order to exercise his or her "business judgment," a legal concept that involves a good-faith effort by the director.

Independent Directors: Mutual funds are required by law to have independent directors on their boards in order to better enable the board to provide an independent check on the fund's operations. Independent directors cannot have any significant relationship with the fund's adviser or underwriter.

Investment Advisers

As noted above, a fund's investment adviser is often the fund's initial sponsor and its initial shareholder through the "seed money" it invests to create the fund. The investment adviser invests the fund's assets in accordance with the fund's investment objectives and policies as stated in the registration statement it files with the SEC.

As a professional money manager, the investment adviser also provides a level of money management expertise usually beyond the scope of the average individual investor. The investment adviser has its own employees—typically, a team of experienced investment professionals—who work on behalf of the fund's shareholders and determine which securities to buy and sell in the fund's portfolio.

An adviser's investment decisions are based on a variety of factors, including the fund's investment objectives, its risk parameters, and extensive research of the market and financial performance of specific securities (for example, the performance and risks associated with a particular company's securities). To protect investors from the adviser's self-dealings, a fund's investment adviser and the adviser's employees are subject to numerous standards and legal restrictions, including restrictions on transactions between the adviser and the fund it advises.

A primary function of the investment adviser is to ensure that the fund's investments are appropriately diversified as required by federal laws and/or as disclosed in the fund's prospectus. Diversification of the fund's investment portfolio reduces the risk that the poor performance of any one security will dramatically reduce the value of the fund's entire portfolio. The allocation of a fund's assets among investments is constantly monitored and adjusted by the fund's investment adviser to protect the interests of shareholders in the fund as dictated by its investment objectives.

Administrators

A fund's administrator can be either an affiliate of the fund, typically the investment adviser, or an unaffiliated third party. The services it provides to the fund include overseeing other companies that provide services to the fund, as well as ensuring that the fund's operations comply with applicable federal requirements. Fund administrators typically pay for office space, equipment, personnel, and facilities; provide general accounting services; and help establish and maintain compliance procedures and internal controls. Often, they also assume responsibility for preparing and filing SEC, tax, shareholder, and other reports. For these services, they are compensated by the fund.

Principal Underwriters

Investors buy and redeem fund shares either directly or indirectly through the principal underwriter, also known as the fund's distributor. Principal underwriters are registered under the Securities Exchange Act of 1934 as broker-dealers, and, as such, are subject to strict rules governing how they offer and sell securities to investors.

The principal underwriter contracts with the fund to purchase and then resell fund shares to the public. A majority of both the fund's independent directors and the entire fund board must approve the initial contract with the underwriter.

The role of the principal underwriter is crucial to a fund's success and viability, in large part, because the principal underwriter is charged with attracting investors to the fund. Although many investors are long-term investors, an industry that competes on service and performance—combined with a shareholder's ability to redeem on demand—makes attracting new shareholders crucial.

Custodians

Mutual funds are required by law to protect their portfolio securities by placing them with a custodian. Nearly all mutual funds use banks as their custodians. The SEC requires any bank acting as a mutual fund custodian to comply with various regulatory requirements designed to protect the fund's assets, including provisions requiring the bank to segregate mutual fund portfolio securities from other bank assets.

Transfer Agents

Mutual funds and their shareholders also rely on the services of transfer agents to maintain records of shareholder accounts, calculate and distribute dividends and capital gains, and prepare and mail shareholder account statements, federal income tax information, and other shareholder notices. Some transfer agents also prepare and mail statements confirming shareholder transactions and account balances, and maintain customer service departments, including call centers, to respond to shareholder inquiries.

Fund Pricing: Net Asset Value And The Pricing Process

By law, investors are able to redeem mutual fund shares each business day. As a result, fund shares are very liquid investments. Most mutual funds also continually offer new shares to investors. Many fund companies also allow shareholders to transfer money—or make "exchanges"—from one fund to another within the same fund family. Mutual funds process investors' sales, redemptions, and exchanges as a normal part of daily business activity and must ensure that all transactions receive the appropriate price.

♣ It's A Fact!!
Determining Share Price

Fund X owns a portfolio of stocks worth $6 million; its liabilities are $60,000; its shareholders own 500,000 shares.

- Share Price or Net Asset Value (NAV) $11.88 = Market Value in Dollars of Securities Minus Liabilities ($6,000,000 minus $60,000) divided by the Number of Investor Shares Outstanding (500,000)

Share prices appear in the financial pages of most major newspapers.

A share price can also be found in semi-annual and annual reports.

The price per share at which shares are redeemed is known as the net asset value (NAV). NAV is the current market value of all the fund's assets, minus liabilities (for example, fund expenses), divided by the total number of outstanding shares. This calculation ensures that the value of each share in the fund is identical. An investor may determine the value of his or her pro rata share of the mutual fund by multiplying the number of shares held by the fund's NAV. Federal law requires that a fund's NAV be calculated each trading day.

The price at which a fund's shares may be purchased is its NAV per share plus any applicable front-end sales charge (the offering price of a fund without a sales charge would be the same as its NAV per share). The 1940 Act requires "forward pricing," meaning that shareholders who purchase or redeem shares must receive the next computed share price (NAV) following the fund's receipt of the transaction order. Under forward pricing, orders received prior to 4:00 p.m. receive the price determined that same day at 4:00 p.m.; orders received after 4:00 p.m. receive the price determined at 4:00 p.m. on the next business day.

The NAV must reflect the current value of the fund's securities. The value of these securities is determined either by a market quotation for those securities in which a market quotation is readily available, or if a market quotation is not readily available, at fair value as determined in good faith by the fund.

Most funds price their securities at 4:00 p.m. Eastern time, when the New York Stock Exchange closes. A mutual fund typically obtains the prices for securities it holds from a market data vendor, which is a company that collects prices on a wide variety of securities. Fund accounting agents internally validate the prices received from a vendor by subjecting them to various control procedures. In many instances, funds may use more than one pricing service either to ensure accuracy or to receive prices for a wide variety of securities held in its portfolio (for example, stocks or bonds).

The vast majority of mutual funds submit their daily NAVs to Nasdaq by 6:00 p.m. Eastern time so they may be published in the next day's morning newspapers. As Nasdaq receives prices, they are instantaneously transmitted to newswire services and other subscribers. Daily fund prices are available in newspapers and other sources, such as through a fund's toll-free telephone service or website.

Tax Features Of Funds

Unlike most corporations, a mutual fund generally distributes all of its earnings to shareholders each year and is taxed only on amounts it retains. This specialized "pass-through" tax treatment was established under the

♣ It's A Fact!!
Tax-Exempt Funds

Tax-exempt bond funds pay dividends earned from municipal bond interest. This income is exempt from federal income tax and, in some cases, state and local taxes as well. Tax-exempt money market funds invest in short-term municipal securities or equivalent instruments and also pay exempt-interest dividends. Even though income from these funds is generally tax-exempt, investors must report it on their income tax returns. Tax-exempt funds provide investors with this information in a year-end statement, and typically explain how to handle tax-exempt dividends on a state-by-state basis. For some taxpayers, portions of income earned by tax-exempt funds may also be subject to the federal alternative minimum tax.

Revenue Act of 1936 and endures today under Subchapter M of the Internal Revenue Code of 1986.

To qualify for specialized tax treatment under the Code, mutual funds must meet, among other conditions, various investment diversification standards and pass a test regarding the source of their income.

The Code's asset tests require that at least 50 percent of the fund's assets must be invested in cash, cash items, government securities, securities of other funds, and investments in other securities which, with respect to any one issuer, do not represent more than 5 percent of the assets of the fund nor more than 10 percent of the voting securities of the issuer. Furthermore, not more than 25 percent of the fund's assets may be invested in the securities of any one issuer (other than government securities or the securities of other funds) or of one or more qualified publicly traded partnerships.

Types Of Distributions

Mutual funds make two types of taxable distributions to shareholders: ordinary dividends and capital gains.

Dividend distributions come primarily from the interest and dividends earned by the securities in a fund's portfolio and net short-term gains, if any, after expenses are paid by the fund. These distributions must be reported as dividends on an investor's tax return. Legislation enacted in 2003 lowered the top tax rate on qualified dividend income to 15 percent, and legislation enacted in 2006 extended these lower rates through 2010.

Long-term capital gain distributions represent a fund's net gains, if any, from the sale of securities held in its portfolio for more than one year. The 2003 legislation also lowered the long-term capital gains tax paid by fund shareholders; in general, these gains are taxed at a 15 percent rate, although a lower rate applies to some taxpayers.

Fund investors are ultimately responsible for paying tax on a fund's earnings, whether they receive the distributions in cash or reinvest them in additional fund shares. To help mutual fund shareholders understand the impact of taxes on the returns generated by their investments, the SEC requires mutual funds to disclose standardized after-tax returns for one-, five-, and 10-year periods. After-tax returns, which accompany before-tax returns in fund prospectuses, are presented in two ways:

- After taxes on fund distributions only (pre-liquidation)

- After taxes on fund distributions and an assumed redemption of fund shares (post-liquidation)

Types Of Taxable Shareholder Transactions

An investor who sells mutual fund shares usually incurs a capital gain or loss in the year the shares are sold; an exchange of shares between funds in the same fund family also results in either a capital gain or loss.

Investors are liable for tax on any capital gain arising from the sale of fund shares, just as they would be if they sold a stock, bond, or other security. Capital losses from mutual fund share sales and exchanges, like capital losses from other investments, may be used to offset other gains in the current year and thereafter.

The amount of a shareholder's gain or loss on fund shares is determined by the difference between the "cost basis" of the shares (generally, the purchase price—including sales loads—for shares, whether acquired with cash or reinvested dividends) and the sale price. Many funds provide cost basis information to shareholders or compute gains and losses for shares sold.

Chapter 32

Exchange Traded Funds And Index Funds

A Guide To Exchange-Traded Funds

Exchange-traded funds (ETFs) are a relatively recent innovation to the investment company concept. Like more traditional mutual funds and other investment company offerings, ETFs offer investors, including those of moderate means, the opportunity to purchase shares in a diversified pool of securities at a competitive price.

ETFs make use of the basic premise underlying the investment company concept: a fund pools investor assets and employs investment diversification with an objective of meeting or beating market returns. But ETFs also offer features that differentiate them from the most common type of investment company—the mutual fund.

This chapter provides an introduction to ETF investing, explaining how ETFs work, their unique features and operations, and other characteristics.

What is an exchange-traded fund?

An exchange-traded fund is an investment company that offers investors a proportionate share in a portfolio of stocks, bonds, or other securities. Like

About This Chapter: From "A Guide to Exchange-Traded Funds," © 2007 Investment Company Institute (www.ici.org); reprinted with permission.

individual equity securities, ETFs are traded on a stock exchange and can be bought and sold throughout the day through a broker-dealer.

Most ETFs attempt to achieve the same investment return as that of a particular market index, such as the Dow Jones Industrial Average, Standard & Poor's 500 Index, or the Nasdaq Composite Index. To mirror the performance of a market index, an ETF invests either in all of the securities in the index or a representative sample of securities in the index.

Traditional index mutual funds are like ETFs in that they both hold investment portfolios that match a designated market index and attempt to achieve the same investment return as that index. But there are several important differences as well.

> ♣ It's A Fact!!
> The Origination Of The Investment Company Concept
>
> **1893:** First closed-end fund is started in Belgium.
>
> **1924:** First open-end mutual funds are established in Boston.
>
> **1961:** First tax-free unit investment trust is offered.
>
> **1976:** First retail index fund is introduced.
>
> **1993:** First exchange-traded fund shares are issued.
>
> Source: © 2007 Investment Company Institute.

How do ETFs work?

ETFs originate with a fund sponsor, which chooses the ETF's target index, determines which securities will be included in the "basket" of securities, and decides how many ETF shares will be offered to investors.

Say, for example, a fund sponsor wants to create an ETF that tracks the S&P 500 Index. Because of the expense involved in acquiring the basket of securities that represent the securities listed on the S&P 500—which can run into the millions of dollars—the fund sponsor typically contacts an institutional investor to obtain and deposit with the fund the basket of securities. In turn, the ETF issues to the institutional investor a "creation unit," which typically represents between 50,000 and 100,000 ETF shares. (Note that, unlike shares in a traditional mutual fund that are purchased with cash, ETF sponsors require its investors to deposit securities with the fund.)

Each ETF share represents a stake in every company listed on the S&P 500 Index. The institutional investor that holds the creation unit (the "creation unit holder") is then free to either keep the ETF shares or to sell all or part of them on the open market. ETF shares are listed on a number of stock exchanges (NYSE, Nasdaq, Amex, etc.) where investors can purchase them through a broker-dealer. Like other exchange-listed securities, a retail investor who purchases an ETF can liquidate its investment by selling its ETF shares at the then-current price. By contrast, a creation unit is liquidated when an institutional investor returns to the ETF the specified number of shares in the creation unit; in return, the institutional investor receives a basket of securities reflecting the current composition of the ETF.

The basket of securities deposited by the institutional investor with the fund sponsor has been predetermined by the sponsor to track a particular index. When changes are made to the index (a stock is added to or dropped from the index), the fund sponsor notifies the creation unit holders that changes need to be made to the basket of securities originally deposited with the fund to ensure that the basket continues to track the composition of the index.

How do ETFs generate returns for investors?

The price of an ETF share depends on the forces of supply and demand in the market and on the performance of the underlying index. Of course, the performance of the index is determined by the performance of each component stock.

In some ways, holding a share in an ETF is like holding a share of any company's stock. If an investor buys a share of XYZ Company's stock for $10 on Monday and sells when the share price rises to $20 on Wednesday, he or she has made a $10 profit. But if that investor sells on Friday, when the price of the stock has fallen to $8, he or she will experience a $2 loss. The same holds true for ETFs.

Pricing, however, differs between mutual funds and ETFs. For a mutual fund, the price at which investors buy and sell shares is equal to the fund's net asset value (NAV), less any commissions. The NAVs of both mutual funds and ETFs are calculated daily at the close of the markets. While investors can buy and sell mutual fund shares are any time throughout the day, all investors will receive the same transaction price (the NAV). In contrast, the price of an ETF share is continuously determined on a stock exchange. Consequently, the price at which investors buy and sell ETF shares may not necessarily equal the NAV of the portfolio of securities in the ETF. In addition,

---

♣ It's A Fact!!

How An ETF Comes To Market

Retail investors who purchase an interest in an ETF do not directly own a pro-rata interest in the ETF's portfolio. Rather, the investor owns a share in a "creation unit," which is issued by the ETF sponsor to a creation unit holder in return for a basket of securities. In other words, there is a person—typically an institutional investor—interposed between the retail ETF owner and the ETF sponsor.

Step One: A fund sponsor sets an investment objective (for example, create an ETF that tracks the S&P 500 Index) and develops the list of the basket securities that can be exchanged for ETF shares.

Step Two: The fund sponsor forms participation agreements with entities that want to become creation unit holders (for example, securities firm or institutional adviser).

Step Three: The participating companies assemble a basket of securities that contains shares of every company listed on the S&P 500 based on their relative weighting and deposit the basket of securities with the fund sponsor.

Step Four: In return for the basket of securities, the fund sponsor provides the participating entities with a "creation unit," which can contain thousands of individual ETF shares.

Step Five: The creation unit holder can either hold the ETF shares or sell all or part of them.

Step Six: Retail investors can purchase the individual ETF shares through a broker-dealer.

Source: © 2007 Investment Company Institute.

two investors selling the same ETF shares at different times on the same day may receive different prices for their shares, both of which may differ from the ETF's new asset value.

The price of an ETF share on a stock exchange is influenced by the forces of supply and demand. For example, when investor demand for an ETF increases, the ETF's share price will rise, perhaps exceeding the ETF's net asset value. ETFs are structured, however, so that large differences between their share prices and their NAVs are unlikely to persist. Third parties calculate and disseminate every 15 seconds a measure often called the Interday Indicative Value (IIV), which is a real-time estimate of a fund's NAV. When an ETF's share price is substantially above this indicative value, institutional investors may find it profitable to deliver the appropriate basket of securities to the ETF in exchange for ETF shares. Retail investors may find it profitable to take a short position in the ETF's shares. When an ETF's share price is substantially below its indicative value, institutional investors may find it profitable to return ETF shares to the fund in exchange for the ETF's basket of securities. Retail investors may find it profitable to take a long position in the ETF's shares. These actions by investors help keep the market-determined price of an ETF's shares close to the NAV of its underlying portfolio.

Dividends And Capital Gains: Dividends are paid on a quarterly or annual basis. Some ETFs allow their shareholders to reinvest their dividends in the purchase of additional ETF shares. Any profit realized in conjunction with the sale of any investment is called a "capital gain." Because ETF investors can see the value of their investment change throughout the day, they can sell their ETF shares when the price is higher, earning an investment return. However, when an ETF investor sells their ETF shares for a profit and realizes capital gains, the investor incurs a capital gains tax liability.

Are ETFs similar to index mutual funds?

ETFs and index mutual funds are similar in that they typically seek to match the return of a market index and both are good choices for investors with a long-term investment strategy. There are important differences between the two investment options, however.

♣ It's A Fact!!

Index Funds

An "index fund" describes a type of mutual fund or unit investment trust (UIT) whose investment objective typically is to achieve approximately the same return as a particular market index, such as the S&P 500 Composite Stock Price Index, the Russell 2000 Index or the Wilshire 5000 Total Market Index. An index fund will attempt to achieve its investment objective primarily by investing in the securities (stocks or bonds) of companies that are included in a selected index. Some index funds may also use derivatives (such as options or futures) to help achieve their investment objective. Some index funds invest in all of the companies included in an index; other index funds invest in a representative sample of the companies included in an index.

The management of index funds is more "passive" than the management of non-index funds, because an index fund manager only needs to track a relatively fixed index of securities. This usually translates into less trading of the fund's portfolio, more favorable income tax consequences (lower realized capital gains), and lower fees and expenses than more actively managed funds.

Because the investment objectives, policies, and strategies of an index fund require it to purchase primarily the securities contained in an index, the fund will be subject to the same general risks as the securities that are contained in the index. Those general risks are discussed in the descriptions of stock funds and bond funds. In addition, because an index fund tracks the securities on a particular index, it may have less flexibility than a non-index fund to react to price declines in the securities contained in the index.

Another type of investment company that attempts to track the performance of a market index is an exchange-traded fund (ETF). ETFs are legally classified as either UITs or open-end companies, but they differ from traditional UITs and open-end companies in a number of respects. For example, pursuant to SEC exemptive orders, shares issued by ETFs trade on a secondary market and are only redeemable in very large blocks (blocks of 50,000 shares, for example). ETFs are not considered to be, and may not call themselves, mutual funds.

Before investing in an index fund, you should carefully read all of the fund's available information, including its prospectus and most recent shareholder report.

Source: U.S. Securities and Exchange Commission (SEC), May 14, 2007.

ETF

- *Ownership:* ETF investors own a share in a "creation unit."

- *Method Of Purchase:* Investors can buy ETF shares only through a broker-dealer.

- *Pricing:* ETFs are priced continuously and investors can buy and sell their ETF shares throughout the day at the current offering price. As a result, two investors selling ETF shares at different times on the same day may receive different prices for their shares.

- *Management Style:* Passive. ETF managers only make changes to the ETF portfolio when there is a change in the underlying index.

- *Transaction Costs:* Because ETFs are purchased through a broker-dealer, an ETF investor pays a brokerage commission when buying or selling ETF shares. In addition to any commissions charged, ETF investors also may pay a management fee, which is deducted from the ETF's assets.

Index Fund

- *Ownership:* Index fund investors purchase a pro-rata interest in the securities that make up the fund's portfolio.

- *Method Of Purchase:* Index funds can be purchased through a variety of distribution channels, including through a broker-dealer or directly from a fund company.

- *Pricing:* Traditional mutual funds are priced at the close of the markets each day. While an investor may purchase or sell traditional mutual fund shares at any time on a trading day, the price the investor receives will be the price determined at the end of that trading date, which will be the same for all shareholders in the fund.

- *Management Style:* Passive. Fund managers only make changes to the fund portfolio when there is a change in the underlying index.

- *Transaction Costs:* Depending upon the distribution channel, an investor in a traditional mutual fund may be required to pay a commission when buying or selling shares. In addition to any commissions charged, mutual fund shareholders also pay an ongoing management fee, which is deducted from the fund's assets.

What kinds of ETFs are available for purchase?

There are ETFs that track almost every U.S. stock market index, as well as ETFs that track individual U.S. stock market sectors, international indices, and bond indices. The main categories of ETFs are as follows:

- **Broad-Based Equity Index Shares:** These ETFs track indices like the S&P 500 Index, the NASDAQ Composite Index, as well as large-, mid-, and small-cap indices.

- **Sector/Industry Equity Index Shares:** These ETFs track indices that focus on specific sectors such as energy, financial services, healthcare, real estate, technology, industrial, transportation, and consumer goods, to name a few.

♣ **It's A Fact!!**
**What are the risks
of investing in ETFs?**

All investments, including ETFs, involve varying degrees and types of risk, including the potential loss of money. While investment diversification mitigates the effect of a decline in the value of any one security in an ETF portfolio, an ETF's value could decline due to larger economic events or policy changes affecting the underlying index (for example, a recession). This is known as market risk. ETFs tracking a bond index are also subject to interest rate risk, which is the possibility that changes in interest rates will lower the price of bonds and reduce the value of an ETF's portfolio.

Source: © 2007 Investment Company Institute.

- **Global/International Equity Index Shares:** These ETFs track indices focusing on a specific country or region.

- **Bond Index Shares:** These ETFs track U.S. Treasury bond and corporate bond indices.

Who regulates ETFs?

The vast majority of exchange-traded funds are registered with the Securities and Exchange Commission (SEC) and must comply with the applicable provisions of the Investment Company Act, except to the extent the fund or trust has received exemptive relief from the Act. Exchange-traded funds have obtained exemptive relief to (1) allow them to register as mutual funds under the Act even though their shares are not individually redeemable (ETFs are, however, prohibited from referring to themselves as mutual funds.); (2) permit affiliated entities to purchase and redeem shares in kind rather than in cash; and (3) enable their shares to trade at negotiated prices on an exchange rather than at a current offering price described in the prospectus or at a price based on net asset value (NAV).

As of 2006, about three percent of ETF assets were not registered with or regulated by the SEC under the Investment Company Act. These ETFs are commodity-based. Those ETFs that invest in commodity futures are regulated by the Commodity Futures Trading Commission (CFTC), while the ETFs that invest solely in physical commodities are not regulated by the CFTC.

Where can I get more information on ETFs?

- U.S. Securities and Exchange Commission, Exchange Traded Funds (available online at http://www.sec.gov/answers/etf.htm)

- The American Stock Exchange, Exchange Traded Funds (available online at http://www.amex.com/?href=/etf/EtMain.jsp)

- The NASDAQ Stock Market, Exchange Traded Funds (available online at http://www.nasdaq.com/indexshares/about_funds.stm)

- ETFConnect, Know Your Funds (available online at http://www.etfconnect.com/education/fundamentals_etf.asp)

In addition, the Investment Company Institute provides answers to a series of frequently asked questions about exchange traded funds through its website at www.ici.org.

Chapter 33

What Is A Hedge Fund?

What are hedge funds?

Like mutual funds, hedge funds pool investors' money and invest those funds in financial instruments in an effort to make a positive return. Many hedge funds seek to profit in all kinds of markets by pursuing leveraging and other speculative investment practices that may increase the risk of investment loss.

Unlike mutual funds, however, hedge funds are not required to register with the U.S. Securities and Exchange Commission (SEC). Hedge funds typically issue securities in "private offerings" that are not registered with the SEC under the Securities Act of 1933. In addition, hedge funds are not required to make periodic reports under the Securities Exchange Act of 1934. But hedge funds are subject to the same prohibitions against fraud as are other market participants, and their managers have the same fiduciary duties as other investment advisers.

What are "funds of hedge funds?"

A fund of hedge funds is an investment company that invests in hedge funds—rather than investing in individual securities. Some funds of hedge

About This Chapter: From "Hedging Your Bets: A Heads Up on Hedge Funds and Funds of Hedge Funds," U.S. Securities and Exchange Commission (www.sec.gov), March 26, 2008.

funds register their securities with the SEC. These funds of hedge funds must provide investors with a prospectus and must file certain reports quarterly with the SEC.

Many registered funds of hedge funds have much lower investment minimums (for example, $25,000) than individual hedge funds. Thus, some investors that would be unable to invest in a hedge fund directly may be able to purchase shares of registered funds of hedge funds.

> **☞ Remember!!**
> Not all funds of hedge funds register with the SEC.

What information should I seek if I am considering investing in a hedge fund or a fund of hedge funds?

- Read a fund's prospectus or offering memorandum and related materials. Make sure you understand the level of risk involved in the fund's investment strategies and ensure that they are suitable to your personal investing goals, time horizons, and risk tolerance. As with any investment, the higher the potential returns, the higher the risks you must assume.

- Understand how a fund's assets are valued. Funds of hedge funds and hedge funds may invest in highly illiquid securities that may be difficult to value. Moreover, many hedge funds give themselves significant discretion in valuing securities. You should understand a fund's valuation process and know the extent to which a fund's securities are valued by independent sources.

- Ask questions about fees. Fees impact your return on investment. Hedge funds typically charge an asset management fee of 1–2% of assets, plus a "performance fee" of 20% of a hedge fund's profits. A performance fee could motivate a hedge fund manager to take greater risks in the hope of generating a larger return. Funds of hedge funds typically charge a fee for managing your assets, and some may also include a performance fee based on profits. These fees are charged in addition to any fees paid to the underlying hedge funds.

- Understand any limitations on your right to redeem your shares. Hedge funds typically limit opportunities to redeem, or cash in, your shares (for example, to four times a year), and often impose a "lock-up" period of one year or more, during which you cannot cash in your shares.

- Research the backgrounds of hedge fund managers. Know with whom you are investing. Make sure hedge fund managers are qualified to manage your money, and find out whether they have a disciplinary history within the securities industry. You can get this information (and more) by reviewing the adviser's Form ADV. You can search for and view a firm's Form ADV using the SEC's Investment Adviser Public Disclosure (IAPD) website (available online at http://www.adviserinfo.sec.gov/IAPD/Content/IapdMain/iapd_SiteMap.aspx). You also can get copies of Form ADV for individual advisers and firms from the investment adviser, the SEC's Public Reference Room, or (for advisers with less than $25 million in assets under management) the state securities regulator where the adviser's principal place of business is located. If you don't find the investment adviser firm in the SEC's IAPD database, be sure to call your state securities regulator or search the FINRA's BrokerCheck database (available online at http://www.finra.org/InvestorInformation/InvestorProtection/p005882?ssSourceNodeId=5) for any information they may have.

- Don't be afraid to ask questions. You are entrusting your money to someone else. You should know where your money is going, who is managing it, how it is being invested, how you can get it back, what protections are placed on your investment, and what your rights are as an investor. In addition, you may wish to read FINRA's investor alert, which describes some of the high costs and risks of investing in funds of hedge funds.

✔ Quick Tip

If you invest in hedge funds through a fund of hedge funds, you will pay two layers of fees: the fees of the fund of hedge funds and the fees charged by the underlying hedge funds.

What protections do I have if I purchase a hedge fund?

Hedge fund investors do not receive all of the federal and state law protections that commonly apply to most registered investments. For example, you won't get the same level of disclosures from a hedge fund that you'll get from registered investments. Without the disclosures that the securities laws require for most registered investments, it can be quite difficult to verify representations you may receive from a hedge fund. You should also be aware that, while the SEC may conduct examinations of any hedge fund manager that is registered as an investment adviser under the Investment Advisers Act, the SEC and other securities regulators generally have limited ability to check routinely on hedge fund activities.

The SEC can take action against a hedge fund that defrauds investors, and we have brought a number of fraud cases involving hedge funds. Commonly in these cases, hedge fund advisers misrepresented their experience and the fund's track record. Other cases were classic "Ponzi schemes," where early investors were paid off to make the scheme look legitimate. In some of the cases, the hedge funds sent phony account statements to investors to camouflage the fact that their money had been stolen. That's why it is extremely important to thoroughly check out every aspect of any hedge fund you might consider as an investment.

What should I do if I have a complaint about a hedge fund or a fund of hedge funds?

If you encounter a problem with your hedge fund or fund of hedge funds, you can send the SEC your complaint using their online complaint form at www.sec.gov/complaint.shtml. You can also reach them by regular mail at:

Securities and Exchange Commission
Office of Investor Education and Advocacy
100 F Street, NE
Washington, DC 20549-0213

Chapter 34

What To Expect When You Invest In Stocks

Expectations are so important. If you've heard from many people that a film you're about to see is stupendous and amazing, well... it had better be! If it's just pretty good, you'll be disappointed. If, on the other hand, you've heard nothing about it, or maybe one friend trashed it, then you'll probably be pleased if it seems pretty good. Same movie, different outcomes—just because of expectations.

Expectations play a critical role in finances, too. There are many adults who have never invested in stocks because they remember the stock market crash of 1929 and the Great Depression that followed. Others did invest in stocks, but they got burned once and never returned. If only they'd known what to expect.

Below are a bunch of different things that you need to understand before you jump into investing in the stock market. The more you know, the more realistic your expectations will be, and the better you'll likely do.

Expect A Risk-And-Return Tradeoff

Some people avoid the stock market because "it's too risky." But it can be riskier to not invest. If you put all your savings under your mattress, it probably won't be enough to sustain you in retirement. If it's all in a bank account earning 3% per year, on average, then that will barely keep up with inflation, at most. You can do better than that.

A key concept to understand is the tradeoff between risk and return. If you have a large and heavy fireproof safe, and you keep all your money in it, it's close to 100% secure. But what return are you getting on it—how quickly will that money grow? It won't grow. So

Table 34.1. Average yearly performance for various investments, 1925–2000

Type	Percent
Small-company Stocks	12.4%
Large-company Stocks	11.0%
Long-term Government Bonds	5.3%
Treasury Bills	3.8%
Inflation	3.1%

Source: Ibbotson

the tradeoff there is (just about): 100% reliable, 0% return. At the other end of the spectrum are options like the lottery. With a major lottery, you have more than a 99.999% chance of losing the money you "invest" in it, but if, against all odds, you win the jackpot, you get an incredible return on your "investment." This shouldn't be a very appealing proposition, either.

Reasonable people should aim for something in the middle. You should be willing to take on a little risk in order to make a decent return. Your most safe options include bank accounts, money market funds, CDs, and government bonds. Most bank accounts are insured (your bank is most likely protected by insurance, but you can ask, just to be sure). Government bonds are backed by the governments that issue them. As long as you have faith in the United States, U.S. bonds should be considered very safe. But... these investments don't offer the best potential returns.

The best place for long-term money is in the stock market. You do take on some risk with stocks, as all stocks go up and down. But over the long run, the market has gone up and so have most stocks in solid companies.

Table 34.1 has a summary of how various investments have performed on average each year, between 1925 and 2000.

If you invest in the stock market for just a year or two, don't expect to earn exactly 11% or 12.4%. You might earn 19%—or you might lose 23%. Over the long run, though, the stock market has averaged just about 11%, and over many years, you'll likely earn an average annual return that's somewhat close to that—perhaps 9% or 13%. Long-term money should grow fastest in stocks.

Expect Stock Prices To Go Up And Down

When you invest in shares of stock, expect the prices of those shares to go up and down. They will, every day, sometimes for understandable reasons, sometimes for no apparent reason. Here are some of many reasons why a stock price will move significantly up or down.

Why Stocks Go Up

- Increasing sales and profits

- A great new executive is hired to run the company

- An exciting new product or service is introduced

- Additional exciting new products or services are expected

- The company lands a big new contract

- A great review or flattering coverage in the media

- Scientists discover the product is good for something important

- A famous investor is buying shares

- Lots of people are buying shares

- An analyst upgrades the company, changing her recommendation from, for instance, "buy" to "strong buy"

- Other stocks in the same industry go up

- Most of the stock market is up

✔ Quick Tip
Expect To Wait

With sensible investing, it usually takes time for you to see significant results. Don't jump in, see your holdings drop a bit or not move much for a while, and then jump out, in an impatient huff. Engage in long-term, not short-term, thinking. Expect to wait. Investing is a marathon, not a sprint.

Expect To Own Pieces Of Companies   ♣ It's A Fact!!

Many people think of stocks just as pieces of paper that change in value from day to day. Wrong.

A share of stock represents real ownership in a company. If you own a share of the Gap, you literally own a piece of the company. If Gap introduces a new kind of jeans, and they're flying off the shelves, then the company will make more money and will be worth more money. If so, your share will be worth more, too. If you own shares of Philip Morris, which is a major cigarette manufacturer, and the government outlaws cigarettes, the company will suddenly be worth a lot less, and so will your shares.

You can buy shares of stock in any company that is "public" (public means the firm's stock is publicly traded). Almost any major company that you can think of is public. Here are some and their ticker symbols:

- Coca-Cola (NYSE: KO)
- PepsiCo (NYSE: PEP)
- Abercrombie & Fitch (NYSE: ANF)
- Starbucks (Nasdaq: SBUX)
- Apple Computer (Nasdaq: AAPL)
- Dell Computer (Nasdaq: DELL)
- Microsoft (Nasdaq: MSFT)
- Intel (Nasdaq: INTC)
- AOL Time Warner (NYSE: AOL)
- Ford Motor Company (NYSE: F)
- General Motors (NYSE: GM)
- Boeing (NYSE: BA)
- Nike (NYSE: NKE)
- Callaway Golf (NYSE: ELY)
- Wal-Mart (NYSE: WMT)
- Home Depot (NYSE: HD)
- Scholastic (Nasdaq: SCHL)
- General Electric (NYSE: GE)
- General Mills (NYSE: GIS)
- Kellogg (NYSE: K)
- Viacom (NYSE: VIA)
- Eastman Kodak (NYSE: EK)
- ExxonMobil (NYSE: XOM)
- McDonald's (NYSE: MCD)
- Wendy's (NYSE: WEN)
- Johnson & Johnson (NYSE: JNJ)

There are many, many more.

- A competitor's factory burns down
- The company wins a lawsuit
- More people are buying the product or service
- The company expands globally, and starts selling in other countries
- The industry is "hot"—people expect big things for good reasons
- The industry is "hot"—people don't understand much about it, but they're buying anyway
- The company is bought by another company
- The company might be bought by another company
- The company is going to "spin-off" part of itself as a new company
- Rumors
- For no reason at all

Why Stocks Go Down

- Profits and/or sales are slipping
- Top executives leave the company
- A famous investor sells shares of the company
- An analyst downgrades his recommendation of the stock, maybe from "buy" to "hold"
- The company loses a major customer
- Lots of people are selling shares
- A factory burns down
- Other stocks in the same industry go down
- Most of the stock market is down—perhaps in a temporary recession or bear market
- Another company introduces a better product
- There's a supply shortage, so not enough of the product can be made
- A big lawsuit is filed against the company
- Scientists discover the product is not safe

- Fewer people are buying the product
- The industry used to be "hot," but now another industry is more popular
- Some new law might hurt sales or profits
- A powerful company becomes a competitor
- Rumors
- For no reason at all

Expect Growth

You can expect that your money, invested in the overall American stock market, will increase in value—over the long term. You can expect a long-term average annual return of around 11%, give or take a percentage point or two, for the stock market as a whole, if the decades ahead are like the decades past.

You can expect your wealth to compound. With compounding, expect the growth to start out slowly, but then begin to snowball as the years go by.

Expect Volatility

One thing that often throws new investors for a loop is volatility. Volatility refers to how much a stock's price tends to jump up and down from day to day. The stock of some companies (often sleepy ones, such as cement firms or real estate enterprises) tends to go up or down by a fraction of a percent on most days. Companies with more volatile stock (often ones in fast-changing and heavily technology-dependent industries) often see their prices move by a few percentage points each day.

Over a few days or weeks, a volatile stock might surge by 50% or drop by 40%. These are big swings and they can frighten uninformed investors into selling when they sometimes shouldn't. Look at the stock price of Microsoft over the years, for example:

- October 1989: $1
- November 1990: $2
- December 1991: $4
- August 1994: $7
- January 1995: $7
- March 1995: $9

- March 1996: $13
- January 1997: $26
- March 1997: $22
- March 1998: $45
- January 1999: $87
- February 1999: $72
- December 1999: $119

- April 2000: $65
- June 2000: $82
- March 2001: $50
- June 2001: $65
- September 2001: $56
- January 2002: $70
- May 2002: $50

(The prices above are "split-adjusted." That means although the price wasn't really $1 in 1989, that's the correct value of the shares at that time, because there have been "splits" since then. Don't let yourself get distracted by the concept of stock splits now—you can learn about them later.)

Imagine yourself owning stock in Microsoft at various times. If you owned it from August 1994 to January 1995, and the stock wasn't gaining in value much, would you get impatient and sell? If you did, you'd have missed out on significant gains after that.

Expect volatility with some stocks. Don't stress out too much about how much the shares swing up and down. As long as you have faith in the company (based on ongoing research, not just a whim), the company's long-term performance is what counts. Microsoft's stock has gone up and down a lot, but just about anyone hanging on for five or more years has made good money.

Expect To Lose Some Money

This might be alarming or depressing to hear, but if you invest in the stock market, be ready to lose some of your money. If you invest in the overall market and not in individual stocks, then over many years, if not a few years, you should come out ahead and not lose money.

With stock in individual companies, though, you could lose money on some of them. It happens to the best of investors.

The more you know, the fewer losses you'll probably end up having, but some losses here and there are inevitable. As long as your money is divided between a handful of stocks, and not parked just in two, you'll minimize your risk. If you own stock in seven companies, and one or two tank, the others could gain enough to more than make up for your losses.

Expect Conflicting Information And Advice

Be prepared to be confused a little, if you choose to learn more about investing. You'll run across people giving you conflicting advice. Some will tell you to always have all your long-term money sitting in stocks. Others will say that it's okay to keep a lot of your money in cash, waiting for the right time to invest it. Some will tell you not to buy more shares of a stock if it starts falling. Others will counter that if you still believe in the stock, you might want to buy more shares, as the price is lower.

Don't let these and other contradictions throw you. Expect them, think about them, and invest in ways that make sense to you. Many times, investors can do well using either or both of two conflicting principles.

Expect Work—And Fun

Investing can be pretty simple. But if you want to take things a step further and shoot for maximum returns, then you'll need to do a little work. If you choose to invest in stocks of individual companies, to do well you'll need to learn a lot about each company you consider.

The good news, though, is that it can be a lot of fun. Especially if you invest in companies that interest you. If you love Starbucks, how painful would it really be to get to know how the company operates? If you're fascinated by airplanes, then learning a lot about Boeing or Southwest Airlines and their competitors shouldn't be too boring.

Not only can the research be fun—the investing can be, too. You get to watch your holdings grow in value. You might even compare how you're doing with friends or siblings. You'll follow how your companies do over time and get to know them even better. You'll root for your home teams— your companies. It can be work, but fun work.

—by Selena Maranjian

Chapter 35

What Happens When You Place An Order To Buy Or Sell Stock?

When you place an order to buy or sell stock, you might not think about where or how your broker will execute the trade. But where and how your order is executed can impact the overall costs of the transaction, including the price you pay for the stock. Here's what you should know about trade execution:

Trade Execution Isn't Instantaneous

Many investors who trade through online brokerage accounts assume they have a direct connection to the securities markets. But they don't. When you push that enter key, your order is sent over the Internet to your broker—who in turn decides which market to send it to for execution. A similar process occurs when you call your broker to place a trade.

While trade execution is usually seamless and quick, it does take time. And prices can change quickly, especially in fast-moving markets. Because price quotes are only for a specific number of shares, investors may not always receive the price they saw on their screen or the price their broker quoted over

About This Chapter: This chapter includes information from "Trade Execution: What Every Investor Should Know," U.S. Securities and Exchange Commission (www.sec.gov), June 22, 2004.

the phone. By the time your order reaches the market, the price of the stock could be slightly—or very—different.

No U.S. Securities and Exchange Commission (SEC) regulations require a trade to be executed within a set period of time. But if firms advertise their speed of execution, they must not exaggerate or fail to tell investors about the possibility of significant delays.

Your Broker Has Options For Executing Your Trade

Just as you have a choice of brokers, your broker generally has a choice of markets to execute your trade:

- For a stock that is listed on an exchange, such as the New York Stock Exchange (NYSE), your broker may direct the order to that exchange, to another exchange (such as a regional exchange), or to a firm called a "third market maker." A "third market maker" is a firm that stands ready to buy or sell a stock listed on an exchange at publicly quoted prices. As a way to attract orders from brokers, some regional exchanges or third market makers will pay your broker for routing your order to that exchange or market maker—perhaps a penny or more per share for your order. This is called "payment for order flow."

✎ What's It Mean?

Electronic Communications Network (ECN): An electronic communications network (ECN) is an electronic trading system that automatically matches buy and sell orders at specified prices.

Exchange: An exchange is a marketplace where traders can buy or sell stocks and bonds. For a stock that's listed on an exchange, such as the New York Stock Exchange (NYSE), your broker may direct the order to that exchange, to another exchange (such as a regional exchange), or to a firm called a "third market maker."

Market Maker: A "market maker" is a firm that stands ready to buy or sell a stock at publicly quoted prices. Market makers in exchange-listed stocks are known as "third market makers." Market makers in stocks that trade in over-the-counter (OTC) markets, such as the Nasdaq, are known as "Nasdaq market makers" or simply "market makers."

Source: From "Market Centers: Buying and Selling Stock," U.S. Securities and Exchange Commission (www.sec.gov), January 26, 2000.

- For a stock that trades in an over-the-counter (OTC) market, such as the Nasdaq, your broker may send the order to a "Nasdaq market maker" in the stock. Many Nasdaq market makers also pay brokers for order flow.

- Your broker may route your order—especially a "limit order"—to an electronic communications network (ECN) that automatically matches buy and sell orders at specified prices. A "limit order" is an order to buy or sell a stock at a specific price.

- Your broker may decide to send your order to another division of your broker's firm to be filled out of the firm's own inventory. This is called "internalization." In this way, your broker's firm may make money on the "spread"—which is the difference between the purchase price and the sale price.

Your Broker Has A Duty Of "Best Execution"

Many firms use automated systems to handle the orders they receive from their customers. In deciding how to execute orders, your broker has a duty to seek the best execution that is reasonably available for its customers' orders. That means your broker must evaluate the orders it receives from all customers in the aggregate and periodically assess which competing markets, market makers, or ECNs offer the most favorable terms of execution.

The opportunity for "price improvement"—which is the opportunity, but not the guarantee, for an order to be executed at a better price than what is currently quoted publicly—is an important factor a broker should consider in executing its customers' orders. Other factors include the speed and the likelihood of execution.

Here's an example of how price improvement can work: Let's say you enter a market order to sell 500 shares of a stock. The current quote is $20. Your broker may be able to send your order to a market or a market maker where your order would have the possibility of getting a price better than $20. If your order is executed at $20.05, you would receive $10,025.00 for the sale of your stock—$25.00 more than if your broker had only been able to get the current quote for you.

Of course, the additional time it takes some markets to execute orders may result in your getting a worse price than the current quote—especially in a fast-moving market. So, your broker is required to consider whether there is a trade-off between providing its customers' orders with the possibility—but not the guarantee—of better prices and the extra time it may take to do so.

✔ Quick Tip
If you're comparing firms, ask each how often it gets price improvement on customers' orders. And then consider that information in deciding with which firm you will do business.

Source: U.S. Securities and Exchange Commission, June 22, 2004.

You Have Options For Directing Trades

If for any reason you want to direct your trade to a particular exchange, market maker, or ECN, you may be able to call your broker and ask him or her to do this. But some brokers may charge for that service. Some brokers offer active traders the ability to direct orders in Nasdaq stocks to the market maker or ECN of their choice.

SEC rules aimed at improving public disclosure of order execution and routing practices require all market centers that trade national market system securities to make monthly, electronic disclosures of basic information concerning their quality of executions on a stock-by-stock basis, including how market orders of various sizes are executed relative to the public quotes. These reports must also disclose information about effective spreads—the spreads actually paid by investors whose orders are routed to a particular market center. In addition, market centers must disclose the extent to which they provide executions at prices better than the public quotes to investors using limit orders.

These rules also require brokers that route orders on behalf of customers to disclose, on a quarterly basis, the identity of the market centers to which they route a significant percentage of their orders. In addition, brokers must respond to the requests of customers interested in learning where their individual orders were routed for execution during the previous six months.

With this information readily available, you can learn where and how your firm executes its customers' orders and what steps it takes to assure best execution. Ask your broker about the firm's policies on payment for order flow, internalization, or other routing practices—or look for that information in your new account agreement. You can also write to your broker to find out the nature and source of any payment for order flow it may have received for a particular order.

Chapter 36

What Are Direct Investment Plans?

Want a simple, low-cost way to invest in a firm?

One approach is to go straight to the source. Currently, over 430 companies in the U.S. offer direct purchase plans, allowing you to buy shares directly from the company without a broker. In addition, a growing number of foreign firms also offer direct purchase plans through their ADR [American Depositary Receipt] programs.

Direct purchase plans are a form of dividend reinvestment plan, but in a traditional dividend reinvestment plan you must first enroll in the plan in order to participate, which means buying your initial shares through a broker.

Direct purchase plans allow you to completely bypass brokers. And they offer a low-cost means of investing directly in a company for even very modest sums of money.

The Dividend Advantage

The attraction of dividend-paying stocks has increased since dividends started to receive preferential tax treatment in 2003, and it should continue now that that treatment will be extended through 2010. Reinvesting dividends

About This Chapter: From "Buying Straight From the Source: AAII's 2008 Direct Purchase Plan Guide," by Maria Crawford Scott and Cara Scatizzi, © 2008 American Association of Individual Investors (www.aaii.com). Reprinted with permission.

✎ What's It Mean?

Many companies allow you to buy or sell shares directly through a direct stock plan (DSP). You can also have the cash dividends you receive from the company automatically reinvested into more shares through a dividend reinvestment plan (DRIP).

Here are descriptions of the two different types of plans:

• <u>Direct Stock Plans:</u> Some companies allow you to purchase or sell stock directly through them without your having to use or pay commissions to a broker. But you may have to pay a fee for using the plan's services. Some companies require that you already own stock in the company or are employed by the company before you may participate in their direct stock plans. You may be able to buy stock by investing a specific dollar amount rather than having to pay for an entire share. In that case, you could have your checking account debited on a regular basis to make investments in the plan. Some plans require a minimum amount of investment or require you to maintain specific minimums in your account.

• <u>Dividend Reinvestment Plans:</u> Dividend reinvestment plans let you take advantage of the power of compounding. Instead of receiving cash dividends from the company, you may purchase more of a company's stock by having the dividends reinvested. You must sign an agreement with the company for this to be done. If you have a brokerage account or mutual fund, your firm may also have a dividend reinvestment plan. You should check with your firm or the company to see whether you will be charged for this service.

Source: Excerpted from "Direct Investment Plans: Buying Stock Directly from the Company," U.S. Securities and Exchange Commission (SEC), March 2002.

allows you to build up your position in a company and keeps your money working for you over time. But keeping costs low is important, which is one of the attractions of a direct purchase plan.

Of course, a number of major discount brokerage firms offer their own dividend reinvestment plans, which allow you to reinvest the dividends of the stocks you own through the brokerage firm with no fees attached. This is an advantage because the amount of many dividend payments would otherwise typically entail the purchase of odd-lot sizes, which often have higher transaction charges.

However, many corporate direct purchase plans allow participants to make additional cash purchases of shares at little or no cost—a feature no brokerage firm can match. And, direct purchase plans typically have lower minimum investments than most brokers.

Direct purchase plans are custom-made for long-term, buy-and-hold investors. While they are not on their own a reason to buy a stock, they serve as a shareholder bonus on a company with promising long-term growth prospects.

How Do You Join?

Currently, around 438 companies offer direct purchase plans, with minimums ranging from $10 to $2,500, with $250 a typical minimum. In a few cases, direct purchase plans are offered even though no cash dividend is paid.

Direct purchase plans are described in a plan prospectus, which you can receive by contacting either the company's shareholder relations department or the plan administrator. You should read the plan prospectus or description carefully. While the overall structure of most direct purchase plans is similar, they vary in the details. The prospectus or plan description will provide information on such items as: eligibility requirements, plan options, costs, how and when purchases are made, how and when certificates will be issued, and what participants should do when withdrawing from the plan.

How Direct Purchase And Dividend Reinvestment Plans Work

A company's direct purchase or dividend reinvestment plan will be described in the plan's prospectus, which you should read carefully. While the overall structure of most dividend reinvestment plans is similar, they vary in the details.

Administration

Most companies appoint an outside agent to serve as the administrator for their dividend reinvestment plan. The administrator maintains records, sends account statements to participants, furnishes certificates for shares upon request and liquidates participants' shares when they leave the plan. The agent also is responsible for the purchase of company shares for the plan. When you join a plan, you will sign a card that authorizes the agent to make purchases on your behalf.

Joining The Plan

Direct purchase plans allow you to buy the shares directly from the plan administrator. Dividend reinvestment plans without the direct purchase feature require that you own at least one share (and sometimes more) registered in your name—you are a shareholder "of record." That means your name appears on the corporate records as the owner of the shares rather than the nominee name ("street name") of the broker or bank that may have purchased the shares for you (and who may be safekeeping them for you). If your shares are held in street name, you should ask your broker to transfer the shares to your own name.

Shares purchased under a direct purchase or dividend reinvestment plan are held by the plan and registered in the nominee name of the agent or plan trustee on behalf of the participants, each of whom has an account under the plan. For participants in dividend reinvestment plans, that means you may hold the company's shares in two places—your original registered shares, with the certificates either held by you or in custody at a bank or brokerage firm, and the shares purchased through the dividend reinvestment plan, held by the plan.

Many dividend reinvestment plans will allow participants to deposit certificates of shares registered in their own name into their dividend reinvestment plan account for safekeeping at no charge or for a modest fee; these shares are then treated in the same way as the other shares in the participant's account.

Certificates for shares purchased under the plan are usually issued only upon written request, although often at no charge. Certificates are also issued when a participant no longer wants to participate in the plan.

Plan Options

Aside from the initial purchase, direct investment plan and dividend reinvestment plan mechanics are the same. The basic plan offers reinvestment of dividends on all shares of stock registered in the participant's name. This is often referred to as "full reinvestment."

Under most plans, it isn't necessary to reinvest all dividends. Instead, participants are allowed to reinvest dividends on a portion of their registered shares while receiving cash dividends on the remaining shares. This is usually referred to as a "partial reinvestment option." Most plans also allow participants to purchase additional shares by making cash payments directly to the plan. This option is often referred to as "optional cash payment," and since the allowable amounts can be large, it offers participants a low-cost way to build a sizable holding in a company. The payments are optional—participants are not committed to making periodic cash investments.

However, usually there are minimums for each payment made, and often there is a maximum.

It is also important to note the frequency with which the plan invests cash payments, since interest is not paid on payments received in advance of actual investment.

A twist on the cash payment option is that some companies will allow registered shareholders to make cash investments without requiring them to reinvest dividends on the shares they are holding, although they may do so if they want. This is frequently referred to as the "cash payment only option."

An added convenience for participants who wish to make systematic cash investments is an automatic investment feature that is offered by most of the companies. The company or the plan agent automatically debits the investor's checking or savings account at regular intervals to purchase additional shares.

The Costs

Participant costs usually come in two forms: service charges and prorated brokerage commissions. Service charges cover administrative costs and are generally levied on each transaction; participants can hold costs down by combining a cash payment with a dividend reinvestment transaction, since usually the charges are capped (a $5.00 per transaction maximum is typical). Brokerage commissions levied on open market shares are at institutional rates (since the number of shares purchased is large), and are therefore considerably lower than the rate an investor would pay on his own.

Many companies cover all of the costs for share purchases from both reinvested dividends and optional cash payments. Some companies levy service charges, others prorate brokerage costs, and still others charge participants for both—there are many variations, so check the prospectus or plan description carefully.

When participation is terminated, some dividend reinvestment plans will sell plan shares for you, if you prefer, instead of sending you certificates. The cost to the participant is usually any prorated brokerage commissions, a lower-cost alternative than selling through a broker. Some plans will sell plan shares for you even if you are not terminating. Check the prospectus or plan description.

Share Purchases

The source of share purchases under a dividend reinvestment plan is spelled out in the plan description and prospectus.

The most common source is the secondary market-through an exchange where the shares are traded, in the over-the-counter market, or through negotiated transactions. Another source for some purchases is the company itself, using authorized but unissued shares of common stock or shares held in the company's treasury.

In plans that prorate brokerage commissions among participants, the source of share purchases is a concern. When shares are purchased directly from the company, there are no brokerage expenses to prorate.

When shares are purchased directly from the company, the prospectus will describe how the share price is determined. Usually, it is based on an average of the high and low or the closing price for the stock as reported by a specified source.

♣ It's A Fact!!
A Note About Taxes

Direct purchase and dividend reinvestment plans have many advantages, but their tax status is not one of them—unless you are investing through an IRA (offered by a few of the companies). Whether you receive your dividends in cash or have them reinvested, a taxable event has occurred, although the tax treatment now is lower than it was previously.

In addition, if you reinvest dividends, the IRS considers the "dividend" to be equal to the fair market value of shares acquired with reinvested dividends. The fair market price is the price on the exchange or market where shares are traded, not any discounted price. Furthermore, any brokerage commissions paid by the company in open market purchases to acquire the shares are considered additional dividend income to the participant.

When shares are sold, the tax basis is the fair market value as of the date the shares were acquired, plus any brokerage commissions paid by the company, and it is treated as income to the participant. Participants receive 1099-DIV forms each year from the company detailing dividends to be treated as income as reported to the IRS.

Source: American Association of Individual Investors, 2008.

Some companies offer participants discounts on the share price, but there is wide variation in how this is offered. Most often, the discounts are available only on shares purchased with reinvested dividends, but sometimes discounts apply to shares purchased both with reinvested dividends and with cash payments. Discounts are described in detail in plan prospectuses.

Where To Get Information

Companies with direct purchase plans appoint an outside agent to serve as the administrator for their plan. These administrators maintain plan records, send account statements to participants, furnish certificates for shares upon request—and handle the purchases and sales of the shares.

Four major firms serve as administrators for U.S.–based direct purchase plans and dividend reinvestment plans: American Stock Transfer & Trust; Computershare; Bank of New York Mellon; and Wells Fargo.

To find plan information from a company directly, go to the company website and look in the Investor Relations area.

Chapter 37

Investing In Foreign Stocks

As investors have learned recently, the market value of investments can change suddenly. This is true in the U. S. securities markets, but the changes may be even more dramatic in markets outside the United States. The world's economies are becoming more interrelated, and dramatic changes in stock value in one market can spread quickly to other markets.

Keep in mind that even if you only invest in stocks of U.S. companies you already may have some international exposure in your investment portfolio. Many of the factors that affect foreign companies also affect the foreign business operations of U.S. companies. The fear that economic problems around the globe will hurt the operations of U.S. companies can cause dramatic changes in U.S. stock prices.

Sudden changes in market value are only one important consideration in international investing. Changes in foreign currency exchange rates will affect all international investments, and there are other special risks you should consider before deciding whether to invest. The degree of risk may vary, depending on the type of investment and the market. For example, international mutual funds may be less risky than direct investments in foreign markets, and investing in developed economies may avoid some of the risks of investing in emerging markets.

About This Chapter: Excerpted from "International Investing," U.S. Securities and Exchange Commission (www.sec.gov), August 1, 2007.

Why do many Americans invest in foreign markets?

There are two of the chief reasons why people invest internationally:

• **Diversification:** Spreading your investment risk among foreign companies and markets that are different than the U.S. economy

• **Growth:** Taking advantage of the potential for growth in some foreign economies, particularly in emerging markets

By including exposure to both domestic and foreign stocks in your portfolio, you'll reduce the risk that you'll lose money and your portfolio's overall investment returns will have a smoother ride. That's because international investment returns sometimes move in a different direction than U.S. market returns. Even when international and U.S. investments move in the same direction the degree of change may be very different. When you compare the returns from emerging international markets with U.S. market returns you may see even wider swings in value.

Of course, you have to balance these considerations against the possibility of higher costs, sudden changes in value, and the special risks of international investing.

What are the special risks in international investing?

Although you take risks when you invest in any stock, international investing has some special risks:

• **Changes In Currency Exchange Rates:** When the exchange rate between the foreign currency of an international investment and the U.S. dollar changes, it can increase or reduce your investment return. How does this work? Foreign companies trade and pay dividends in the currency of their local market. When you receive dividends or sell your international investment, you will need to convert the cash you receive into U.S. dollars. During a period when the foreign currency is strong compared to the U.S. dollar, this strength increases your investment return because your foreign earnings translate into more dollars. If the foreign currency weakens compared to the U.S. dollar, this weakness reduces your investment return because your earnings translate into fewer dollars. In addition to exchange rates, you should be aware that some countries may impose foreign currency controls that restrict or delay you from moving currency out of a country.

- **Dramatic Changes In Market Value:** Foreign markets, like all markets, can experience dramatic changes in market value. One way to reduce the impact of these price changes is to invest for the long term and try to ride out sharp upswings and downturns in the market.

- **Political, Economic, And Social Events:** It is difficult for investors to understand all the political, economic, and social factors that influence foreign markets. These factors provide diversification, but they also contribute to the risk of international investing.

- **Lack Of Liquidity:** Foreign markets may have lower trading volumes and fewer listed companies. They may only be open a few hours a day. Some countries restrict the amount or type of stocks that foreign investors may purchase. You may have to pay premium prices to buy a foreign security and have difficulty finding a buyer when you want to sell.

- **Less Information:** Many foreign companies do not provide investors with the same type of information as U.S. public companies. It may be difficult to locate up-to-date information, and the information the company publishes may not be in English.

- **Reliance On Foreign Legal Remedies:** If you have a problem with your investment, you may not be able to sue the company in the United States. Even if you sue successfully in a U.S. court, you may not be able to collect on a U.S. judgment against a foreign company. You may have to rely on whatever legal remedies are available in the company's home country.

- **Different Market Operations:** Foreign markets often operate differently from the major U.S. trading markets. For example, there may be different periods for clearance and settlement of securities transactions. Some foreign markets may not report stock trades as quickly as U.S. markets. Rules providing for the safekeeping of shares held by custodian banks or depositories may not be as well developed in some foreign markets, with the risk that your shares may not be protected if the custodian has credit problems or fails.

What are the costs of international investments?

International investing can be more expensive than investing in U.S. companies. In smaller markets, you may have to pay a premium to purchase shares of popular companies. In some countries there may be unexpected taxes, such as withholding taxes on dividends. Transaction costs such as fees, broker's commissions, and taxes often are higher than in U.S. markets. Mutual funds that invest abroad often have higher fees and expenses than funds that invest in U.S. stocks, in part because of the extra expense of trading in foreign markets.

What are the different ways to invest internationally?

Mutual Funds: One way to invest internationally is through mutual funds. There are different kinds of funds that invest in foreign stocks.

• Global funds invest primarily in foreign companies, but may also invest in U.S. companies.

• International funds generally limit their investments to companies outside the United States.

• Regional or country funds invest principally in companies located in a particular geographical region (such as Europe or Latin America) or in a single country. Some funds invest only in emerging markets, while others concentrate on more developed markets.

✎ What's It Mean?

Index: An index is a group of stocks representing a particular segment of a market, or in some cases the entire market. For example, the Standard & Poor's 500 index represents a specific segment of the U.S. capital markets. Foreign stock markets also may be represented by an index, such as the MSCI EAFE index, a well-known index in more developed foreign markets, the Nikkei index of large Japanese companies, or the CAC 40 index of large French companies. The components of an index can change over time, as new stocks are added and old ones are dropped.

- International index funds try to track the results of a particular foreign market index. Index funds differ from actively managed funds, whose managers pick stocks based on research about the companies.

- International investing through mutual funds can reduce some of the risks mentioned earlier. Mutual funds provide more diversification than most investors could achieve on their own. The fund manager also should be familiar with international investing and have the resources to research foreign companies. The fund will handle currency conversions and pay any foreign taxes, and is likely to understand the different operations of foreign markets.

Like other international investments, mutual funds that invest internationally probably will have higher costs than funds that invest only in U.S. stocks.

Exchange-Traded Funds: An exchange-traded fund is a type of investment company whose investment objective is to achieve the same return as a particular market index. Increasingly popular with investors, ETFs are listed on stock exchanges and, like stocks (and in contrast to mutual funds), trade throughout the trading day. A share in an ETF that tracks an international index gives an exposure to the performance of the underlying stock or bond portfolio along with the ability to trade that share like any other security.

American Depositary Receipts: The stocks of most foreign companies that trade in the U.S. markets are traded as American Depositary Receipts (ADRs) issued by U.S. depositary banks.

Each ADR represents one or more shares of a foreign stock or a fraction of a share. If you own an ADR you have the right to obtain the foreign stock it represents, but U.S. investors usually find it more convenient to own the ADR. The price of an ADR corresponds to the price of the foreign stock in its home market, adjusted for the ratio of ADRs to foreign company shares.

Owning ADRs has some advantages compared to owning foreign shares directly:

- When you buy and sell ADRs you are trading in the U.S. market. Your trade will clear and settle in U.S. dollars.

- The depositary bank will convert any dividends or other cash payments into U.S. dollars before sending them to you.

- The depositary bank may arrange to vote your shares for you as you instruct.

On the other hand, there are some disadvantages:

- It may take a long time for you to receive information from the company because it must pass through an extra pair of hands. You may receive information about shareholder meetings only a few days before the meeting, well past the time when you could vote your shares.

- Depositary banks charge fees for their services and will deduct these fees from the dividends and other distributions on your shares. The depositary bank also will incur expenses, such as for converting foreign currency into U.S. dollars, and usually will pass those expenses on to you.

> ♣ **It's A Fact!!**
> **ADRs or ADSs?**
> Sometimes the terms "ADR" and "ADS" (American Depositary Share) are used interchangeably. An ADR is actually the negotiable physical certificate that evidences ADSs (in much the same way a stock certificate evidences shares of stock), and an ADS is the security that represents an ownership interest in deposited securities (in much the same way a share of stock represents an ownership interest in the corporation). ADRs are the instruments actually traded in the market.

U.S. Traded Foreign Stocks: Although most foreign stocks trade in the U.S. markets as ADRs, some foreign stocks trade here in the same form as in their local market. For example, Canadian stocks trade in the same form in the United States as they do in the Canadian markets, rather than as ADRs.

Stocks Trading On Foreign Markets: If you want to buy or sell stock in a company that only trades on a foreign stock market, your broker may be able to process your order for you. These foreign companies do not file reports with the U.S. Securities and Exchange Commission (SEC), however, so you will need to do additional research to get the information you need to make

✤ It's A Fact!! International Stock Scams

Whether it's foreign currency trading, "prime European bank" securities or fictitious coconut plantations in Costa Rica, you should be skeptical about exotic-sounding international invest-ment "opportunities" offering returns that sound too good to be true. They usually are. In the past, con artists have used the names of well-known European banks or the International Chamber of Commerce—without their knowledge or permission—to convince unsophisticated investors to part with their money.

Some promoters based in the United States try to make their investment schemes sound more enticing by giving them an inter-national flavor. Other promoters actually operate from outside the United States and use the internet to reach potential investors around the globe. Remember that when you invest abroad and something goes wrong, it's more difficult to find out what hap-pened and locate your money. As with any investment opportunity that promises quick profits or a high rate of return, you should stop, ask questions, and investi-gate before you invest.

an investment decision. Always make sure any broker you deal with is regis-tered with the SEC. It is against the law for unregistered foreign brokers to call you and solicit your investment.

What should I do if I want to invest?

Like any other investment, you should learn as much as you can about a company before you invest. Try to learn about the political, economic, and social conditions in the company's home coun-try, so you will understand better the fac-tors that affect the company's financial results and stock price. If you invest in-ternationally through mutual funds, make sure you know the countries where the fund invests and understand the kinds of investments it makes.

Here are some sources of informa-tion:

SEC Reports: Many foreign compa-nies file reports with the SEC. The SEC requires foreign companies to file electroni-cally, so their reports usually are available through the SEC's website at www.sec .gov/edgar.shtml at no charge. You can get paper copies for a fee from the SEC's Public Reference Branch by calling 202-551-8090 or sending a request to:

Public Reference Branch
U.S. Securities and Exchange Commission
100 F Street, N.E.
Washington, DC 20549

International Regulators: You might be able to learn more about a particular company by contacting the securities regulator that oversees the markets in which that company's securities trade. Many international securities regulators post issuer information on their websites, including audited financial statements. You'll find a list of international securities regulators on the website of the International Organization of Securities Commissions (IOSCO) at http://www.iosco.org.

Mutual Fund Firms: You can get the prospectus for a particular mutual fund directly from the mutual fund firm. Many firms also have websites that provide helpful information about international investing.

Remember!!

Tracking down information on international investments requires some extra effort, but it will make you a more informed investor. One of the most important things to remember is to read and understand the information before you invest.

The Company: Foreign companies often prepare annual reports, and some companies also publish an English language version of their annual report. Ask your broker for copies of the company's reports or check to see if they are available from the SEC. Some foreign companies post their annual reports and other financial information on their websites.

Broker-Dealers: Your broker may have research reports on particular foreign companies, individual countries, or geographic regions. Ask whether updated reports are available on a regular basis. Your broker also may be able to get copies of SEC reports and other information for you.

Publications: Many financial publications and international business newspapers provide extensive news coverage of foreign companies and markets.

Internet Resources: Various government, commercial, and media websites offer information about foreign companies and markets. However, as with any investment opportunity, you should be extremely wary of "hot tips," overblown statements, and information posted on the internet from unfamiliar sources. For tips on how to spot and avoid internet fraud, please visit the "Investor Information" section of our website at www.sec.gov/investor.shtml.

Chapter 38

Microcap Stocks: Among The Most Risky

Information is the investor's best tool when it comes to investing wisely. But accurate information about "microcap stocks"—low-priced stocks issued by the smallest of companies—may be difficult to find. Many microcap companies do not file financial reports with the U.S. Securities and Exchange Commission (SEC), so it's hard for investors to get the facts about the company's management, products, services, and finances. When reliable information is scarce, fraudsters can easily spread false information about microcap companies, making profits while creating losses for unsuspecting investors.

In the battle against microcap fraud, the SEC has toughened its rules and taken actions against wrongdoers, but can't stop every microcap fraud. Your help is needed in winning the battle. Before you consider investing in a microcap company, arm yourself first with information. The information in this chapter alert tells you about microcap stocks, how to find information, what "red flags" to consider, and where to turn if you run into trouble.

What is a microcap stock?

The term "microcap stock" applies to companies with low or "micro" capitalizations, meaning the total value of the company's stock. Microcap

About This Chapter: Text in this chapter is excerpted from "Microcap Stock: A Guide for Investors," U.S. Securities and Exchange Commission (www.sec.gov), February 22, 2006.

companies typically have limited assets. For example, in cases where the SEC suspended trading in microcap stocks, the average company had only $6 million in net tangible assets—and nearly half had less than $1.25 million. Microcap stocks tend to be low priced and trade in low volumes.

Where do microcap stocks trade?

Many microcap stocks trade in the "over-the-counter" (OTC) market and are quoted on OTC systems, such as the OTC Bulletin Board (OTCBB) or the "Pink Sheets."

- **OTC Bulletin Board:** The OTCBB is an electronic quotation system that displays real-time quotes, last-sale prices, and volume information for many OTC securities that are not listed on the Nasdaq Stock Market or a national securities exchange. Brokers who subscribe to the system can use the OTCBB to look up prices or enter quotes for OTC securities. Although the NASD oversees the OTCBB, the OTCBB is not part of the Nasdaq Stock Market. Fraudsters often claim that an OTCBB company is a Nasdaq company to mislead investors into thinking that the company is bigger than it is.

- **The "Pink Sheets":** The Pink Sheets—named for the color of paper on which they've historically been printed—are listings of price quotes for companies that trade in the over-the-counter market (OTC market). "Market makers"—the brokers who commit to buying and selling the securities of OTC issuers-can use the pink sheets to publish bid and ask prices. A company named Pink Sheets LLC, formerly known as the National Quotation Bureau, publishes the pink sheets in both hard copy and electronic format. Pink Sheets LLC is not registered with the SEC as a stock exchange, nor does the SEC regulate its activities.

How are microcap stocks different from other stocks?

- **Lack Of Public Information:** Information about microcap companies can be extremely difficult to find, making them more vulnerable to investment fraud schemes.

- **No Minimum Listing Standards:** Companies on the OTCBB or the Pink Sheets do not have to meet any minimum standards.

• **Risk:** While all investments involve risk, microcap stocks are among the most risky. Many microcap companies tend to be new and have no proven track record. Some of these companies have no assets or operations. Others have products and services that are still in development or have yet to be tested in the market. Another risk that pertains to microcap stocks involves the low volumes of trades. Because microcap stocks trade in low volumes, any size of trade can have a large percentage impact on the price of the stock.

How do I get information about microcap companies?

If you're working with a broker or an investment adviser, you can ask your investment professional if the company files reports with the SEC and to get you written information about the company and its business, finances, and management. Be sure to carefully read the prospectus and the company's latest financial reports. You can also get information on your own from the company, from the SEC, from reference books and commercial databases, and from state and other government regulators.

☞ Remember!!

Remember that unsolicited e-mails, message board postings, and company news releases should never be used as the sole basis for your investment decisions.

Your state securities regulator (look in the government section of your phone book or visit the website of the North American Securities Administrators Association at http://www.nasaa.org/QuickLinks/ContactYourRegulator.cfm) will tell you whether the company has been legally cleared to sell securities in your state. Many investors could easily have avoided heavy and painful financial losses if they only called their state securities regulator before they bought stock. Also, contact the secretary of state where the company is incorporated to find out whether the company is a corporation in good standing. (Visit the National Association of Secretaries of State website at http://www.nass.org for contact information regarding a particular Secretary of State.)

What if I want to invest in microcap stocks?

To invest wisely and avoid investment scams, research each investment opportunity thoroughly and ask questions. These simple steps can make the difference between profits and losses:

1. Find out whether the company has registered its securities with the SEC or your state's securities regulators.

2. Make sure you understand the company's business and its products or services.

3. Read carefully the most recent reports the company has filed with its regulators and pay attention to the company's financial statements, particularly if they are not audited or not certified by an accountant. If the company does not file reports with the SEC, be sure to ask your broker for what's called the "Rule 15c2-11 file" on the company. That file will contain important information about the company.

> ✔ **Quick Tip**
> If you've been asked to invest in a company but you can't find any record that the company has registered its securities with the SEC or your state, or that it's exempt from registration, call or write your state's securities regulator or the SEC immediately with all the details. You may have come face to face with a scam.

4. Check out the people running the company with your state securities regulator, and find out if they've ever made money for investors before. Also ask whether the people running the company have had run-ins with the regulators or other investors.

5. Make sure the broker and his or her firm are registered with the SEC and licensed to do business in your state. And ask your state securities regulator whether the broker and the firm have ever been disciplined or have complaints against them.

Make sure to ask lots of questions about any of your concerns. When you ask these questions, write down the answers you received and what you decided to do. If something goes wrong, your notes can help to establish what was said. Let your broker or investment adviser know you're taking notes. They'll know you're a serious investor and may tell you more—or give up trying to scam you.

Also, watch out for these "red flags":

- **SEC Trading Suspensions:** The SEC has the power to suspend trading in any stock for up to 10 days when it believes that information about the company is inaccurate or unreliable. Think twice before investing in a company that's been the subject of an SEC trading suspension. You'll find information about trading suspensions on the SEC's website.

- **High Pressure Sales Tactics:** Beware of brokers who pressure you to buy before you have a chance to think about and investigate the "opportunity." Dishonest brokers may try to tell you about a "once-in-a-lifetime" opportunity or one that's based on "inside" or "confidential" information. Don't fall for brokers who promise spectacular profits or "guaranteed" returns. These are the hallmarks of fraud. If the deal sounds too good to be true, then it probably is.

- **Assets Are Large But Revenues Are Small:** Microcap companies sometimes assign high values on their financial statements to assets that have nothing to do with their business. Find out whether there's a valid explanation for low revenues, especially when the company claims to have large assets.

- **Odd Items In The Footnotes To The Financial Statements:** Many microcap fraud schemes involve unusual transactions among individuals connected to the company. These can be unusual loans or the exchange of questionable assets for company stock that may be discussed in the footnotes.

- **Unusual Auditing Issues:** Be wary when a company's auditors have refused to certify the company's financial statements or if they've stated that the company may not have enough money to continue operating. Also question any change of accountants.

- **Insiders Own Large Amounts Of The Stock:** In many microcap fraud cases—especially "pump and dump" schemes—the company's officers and promoters own significant amounts of the stock. When one person or group controls most of the stock, they can more easily manipulate the stock's price at your expense. You can ask your broker or the company whether one person or group controls most of the company's stock, but if the company is the subject of a scam, you may not get an honest answer.

✔ **Quick Tip**

Don't deal with brokers who refuse to provide you with written information about the investments they're promoting. Never tell a cold caller your social security number or numbers for your banking and securities accounts. And be extra wary if someone you don't know and trust recommends foreign investments.

What if I run into trouble?

Act promptly! By law, you only have a limited time to take legal action. Follow these steps to solve your problem:

1. Talk to your broker and explain the problem. What happened? Who said what, and when? Were communications clear? What did the broker tell you? Did you take notes about what your broker said at the time? If so, what do your notes say?

   Note: If you believe your broker engaged in unauthorized transactions or other serious frauds, be sure to put your complaint in writing right away and send it to the firm. Your written complaint may be the only way to prove that you complained to the firm about unauthorized transactions.

2. If your broker can't resolve your problem, then talk to the broker's branch manager.

3. If the problem is still not resolved, put your complaint in writing and send it to the compliance department at the firm's main office. Explain your problem clearly, and tell the firm how you want it resolved. Ask the compliance office to respond to you in writing within 30 days.

4. If you're still not satisfied, then send a letter to your state securities regulator and attach copies of any letters you've sent already to the firm. Or send your complaint to the SEC using our online complaint form.

The SEC will forward your complaint to the firm's compliance department and ask that they look into the problem and respond to you in writing.

Please note that sometimes a complaint can be successfully resolved. But in many cases, the firm denies wrongdoing, and it comes down to one person's word against another's. In that case, the SEC cannot do anything more to help resolve the complaint. They cannot act as a judge or an arbitrator to establish wrongdoing and force the firm to satisfy your claim. And they cannot act as your lawyer.

Chapter 39

Day Trading: Your Dollars At Risk

Day traders rapidly buy and sell stocks throughout the day in the hope that their stocks will continue climbing or falling in value for the seconds to minutes they own the stock, allowing them to lock in quick profits. Day traders usually buy on borrowed money, hoping that they will reap higher profits through leverage, but running the risk of higher losses too.

While day trading is neither illegal nor is it unethical, it can be highly risky. Most individual investors do not have the wealth, the time, or the temperament to make money and to sustain the devastating losses that day trading can bring.

Here are some of the facts that every investor should know about day trading:

• Be prepared to suffer severe financial losses. Day traders typically suffer severe financial losses in their first months of trading, and many never graduate to profit-making status. Given these outcomes, it's clear: day traders should only risk money they can afford to lose. They should never use money they will need for daily living expenses, retirement, take out a second mortgage, or use their student loan money for day trading.

About This Chapter: Text in this chapter is from "Day Trading: Your Dollars at Risk," U.S. Securities and Exchange Commission (www.sec.gov), April 20, 2005.

- Day traders do not "invest." Day traders sit in front of computer screens and look for a stock that is either moving up or down in value. They want to ride the momentum of the stock and get out of the stock before it changes course. They do not know for certain how the stock will move, they are hoping that it will move in one direction, either up or down in value. True day traders do not own any stocks overnight because of the extreme risk that prices will change radically from one day to the next, leading to large losses.

- Day trading is an extremely stressful and expensive full-time job. Day traders must watch the market continuously during the day at their computer terminals. It's extremely difficult and demands great concentration to watch dozens of ticker quotes and price fluctuations to spot market trends. Day traders also have high expenses, paying their firms large amounts in commissions, for training, and for computers. Any day trader should know up front how much they need to make to cover expenses and break even.

- Day traders depend heavily on borrowing money or buying stocks on margin. Borrowing money to trade in stocks is always a risky business. Day trading strategies demand using the leverage of borrowed money to make profits. This is why many day traders lose all their money and may end up in debt as well. Day traders should understand how margin works, how much time they'll have to meet a margin call, and the potential for getting in over their heads.

- Don't believe claims of easy profits. Don't believe advertising claims that promise quick and sure profits from day trading. Before you start trading with a firm, make sure you know how many clients have lost money and how many have made profits. If the firm does not know, or will not tell you, think twice about the risks you take in the face of ignorance.

- Watch out for "hot tips" and "expert advice" from newsletters and websites catering to day traders. Some websites have sought to profit from day traders by offering them hot tips and stock picks for a fee. Once again, don't believe any claims that trumpet the easy profits of day trading. Check out these sources thoroughly and ask them if they have been paid to make their recommendations.

- Remember that "educational" seminars, classes, and books about day trading may not be objective. Find out whether a seminar speaker, an instructor teaching a class, or an author of a publication about day trading stands to profit if you start day trading.

✔ Quick Tip
**Check Out Day Trading Firms
With Your State Securities Regulator**

Like all broker-dealers, day trading firms must register with the U.S. Securities and Exchange Commission (SEC) and the states in which they do business. Confirm registration by calling your state securities regulator and at the same time ask if the firm has a record of problems with regulators or their customers. You can find the telephone number for your state securities regulator in the government section of your phone book or by calling the North American Securities Administrators Association at 202-737-0900. NASAA also provides this information on its website at http://www.nasaa.org/QuickLinks/ContactYourRegulator.cfm.

Part Five

If You Need More Information

Chapter 40

Directory Of Savings And Investment Organizations

Information For Savers And Investors

America Saves

Consumer Federation of America
1620 I Street, N.W., Suite 200
Washington, DC 20006
Phone: 202-387-6121
Website: http://
www.americasaves.org
E-mail:
information@americasaves.org

American Association of Individual Investors

625 North Michigan Avenue
Suite 1900
Chicago, IL 60611
Toll-Free: 800-428-2244
Phone: 312-280-0170
Fax: 312-280-9883
Website: http://www.aaii.com
E-mail: members@aaii.com

American Financial Services Association

AFSA Education Foundation
919 18th Street, N.W., Suite 300
Washington, DC 20006
Phone: 202-296-5544
Fax: 202-223-0321
Website: http://www.afsaef.org
E-mail: info@afsaef.org

About This Chapter: Information in this chapter was compiled from many sources deemed accurate. Inclusion not constitute endorsement, and there is no implication associated with omission. Contact information was verified July 2008.

**American Institute of
Certified Public Accountants**
Professional Ethics Division
Harborside Financial Center
220 Leigh Farm Road
Durham, NC 27707
Toll free: 888-777-7077
Website: http://www.aicpa.org/
Consumer+Information
E-mail: ethics@aicpa.org

**American Savings Education
Council**
1100 13th Street, N.W., Suite 875
Washington, DC 20005
Phone: 202-659-0670
Fax: 202-775-6312
Website: http://www.asec.org
E-mail: info@asec.org

American Stock Exchange
86 Trinity Place
New York, NY 10006
Phone: 212-306-1000
Website: http://www.amex.com
E-mail: amexfeedback@amex.com

Bankrate.com
11760 U.S. Highway 1, Suite 200
North Palm Beach, FL 33408
Phone: 561-630-2400
Fax: 561-625-4540
Website: http://www.bankrate.com

Better Investing Community
National Association of Investors
Corp.
P.O. Box 220
Royal Oak, MI 48068
Toll-Free: 877-275-6242
Phone: 248-583-6242
Fax: 248-583-4880
Website:
http://www.better-investing.org
E-mail:
service@better-investing.org

Choose to Save
2121 K Street N.W.
Suite 600
Washington, DC 20037-1896
Phone: 202-659-0670
Fax: 202-775-6312
Website: http://
www.choosetosave.org
E-mail: info@choosetosave.org

**Dominion Bond Rating
Service**
DBRS Tower
181 University Avenue
Suite 700
Toronto, ON M5H 3M7
Phone: 416-593-5577
Fax: 416-593-8432
Website: http://www.dbrs.com

Federal Citizen Information Center

1800 F Street, N.W.
Room G-142, (XCC)
Washington, DC 20405
Toll-Free: 888-8-PUEBLO
(878-3256)
Phone: 202-501-1794
Website: http://
www.pueblo.gsa.gov

Federal Deposit Insurance Corporation (FDIC)

550 17th Street, N.W.
Washington, DC 20429
Toll-Free: 877-ASK-FDIC
(877-275-3342)
TDD Toll-Free: 800-925-4618
Phone: 703-562-2222
Website: http://www.fdic.gov

Financial Planning Association

4100 East Mississippi Avenue
 Suite 400
Denver, CO 80246-3053
Toll-Free: 800-647-6340
or 800-322-4237
Fax: 303-759-0749
Website: http://www.fpanet.org
E-mail: fpa@fpanet.org

InCharge Education Foundation

2101 Park Center Dr.
Suite 310
Orlando, FL 32835
Phone: 407-291-7770
Website: http://
education.incharge.org

Institute for Financial Literacy

P.O. Box 1842
Portland, ME 04104
Toll-Free: 866-662-4932
Phone: 207-221-3600
TTY: 866-662-4937
Fax: 207-221-3691
Website: http://
www.financiallit.org

Insurance Information Institute

Consumer Affairs
110 William Street
New York, NY 10038
Toll-Free: 800-331-9146
Phone: 212-346-5500
Website: http://www.iii.org

Investment Company Institute

1401 H Street, N.W.
Washington, DC, 20005
Phone: 202-326-5800
Website: http://www.ici.org

Investor Protection Trust

919 18ᵗʰ Street N.W., Suite 300
Washington, DC 20006-5517
Phone: 202-775-2111
Website: http://
www.investorprotection.org
E-mail:
iptinfo@investorprotection.org

Investors Alliance, Inc.

P.O. Box 10136
Pompano Beach, FL 33061-9951
Toll-Free: 866-627-9090
Website: http://
www.investorsalliance.info
E-mail: info@powerinvestor.com

Iowa State University Cooperative Extension

2150 Beardshear Hall
Ames, IA 50011-2046
Phone: 515-294-6675
Fax: 515-294-4715
Website: http://
www.extension.iastate.edu/finances

Jump$tart Coalition

919 18ᵗʰ Street, N.W., 3ʳᵈ Floor
Washington, DC 20006
Toll-Free: 888-45-EDUCATE
(453-282283)
Fax: 202-223-0321
Website: http://
www.jumpstartcoalition.org
E-mail: info@jumpstartcoalition.org

Nasdaq

One Liberty Plaza
165 Broadway
New York, NY 10006
Phone: 212-401-8700
Website: http://www.nasdaq.com

National Association of Real Estate Investment Trusts

1875 I Street, N.W., Suite 600
Washington DC 20006
Toll-Free: 800-3-NAREIT
(362-7348)
Phone: 202-739-9400
Fax: 202-739-9401
Website: http://www.reit.com
E-mail: info@nareit.com

National Council on Economic Education

1140 Avenue of the Americas
New York, NY 10036
Toll-Free: 800-338-1192
Phone: 212-730-7007
Fax: 212-730-1793
Website: http://www.ncee.net
E-mail: sales@ncee.net

National Endowment for Financial Education (NEFE)

5299 DTC Boulevard, Suite 1300
Greenwood Village, CO 80111
Phone: 303-741-6333
Website: http://www.nefe.org

National Futures Association
300 South Riverside Plaza
Suite 1800
Chicago, IL 60606
Toll free: 800-621-3570 (outside IL)
Phone: 312-781-1300
Fax: 312-781-1467
Website: http://www.nfa.futures.org
E-mail:
information@nfa.futures.org

Native Financial Education Coalition
National Endowment for Financial Education (NEFE)
910 5th Street, Suite 101
Rapid City, SD 57701
Phone: 605-342-3770
Fax: 605-342-3771
Website: http://www.nfec.info

New York Stock Exchange, Inc.
11 Wall Street
New York, NY 10005
Phone: 212-656-3000
Website: http://www.nyse.com

North American Securities Administrators Association, Inc.
750 First Street, N.E., Suite 1140
Washington, DC 20002
Phone: 202-737-0900
Fax: 202-783-3571
Website: http://www.nasaa.org
E-mail: info@nasaa.org

Pink Sheets, LLC
304 Hudson Street, 2nd Floor
New York, NY 10013
Phone: 212-896-4400
Fax: 212-868-3848
Website: http://
www.pinksheets.com
E-mail: info@pinkotc.com

Securities Industry and Financial Markets Association Foundation for Investor Education
120 Broadway, 35th Floor
New York, NY 10271-0080
Phone: 212-313-1200
Fax: 212-313-1301
Website: http://www.sifma.org.org

SmartMoney
1755 Broadway, 2nd Floor
New York, NY 10019
Website: http://
www.smartmoney.com

Toronto Stock Exchange
P.O. Box 450
130 King Street West, 3rd Floor
Toronto, ON M5X 1J2
Canada
Toll-Free: 888-873-8392
Phone: 416-947-4670
Website: http://www.tse.com
E-mail: info@tsx.com

USAA Educational Foundation

9800 Fredericksburg Road
San Antonio, TX 78288-0026
Phone: 800-531-6196
Fax: 210-498-9590
Website: http://
www.usaaedfoundation.org
E-mail: site.feedback@usaa.com

U.S. Commodity Futures Trading Commission

3 Lafayette Centre
1155 21st Street, N.W.
Washington, DC 20581
Phone: 202-418-5000
Fax: 202-418-5521
TTY: 202-418-5514
Website: http://www.cftc.gov
E-mail: Questions@cftc.gov

U.S. Department of the Treasury

1500 Pennsylvania Avenue, N.W.
Washington, DC 20220
Phone: 202-622-2000
Fax: 202-622-6415
Website: http://www.treasury.gov;
http://www.treas.gov

U.S. Securities and Exchange Commission

100 F Street, N.E.
Washington, DC 20549-0213
Toll-Free: 800-SEC-0330 (732-0330)
Phone: 202-551-6551
Fax: 202-772-9295
Investor Information: http://
www.sec.gov/investor.shtml

Wi$eUp

JFK Federal Building
Government Center, Room 525 A
Boston, MA 02203
Toll-Free: 800-827-5335
Phone: 617-565-1988
Website: http://
wiseupwomen.tamu.edu
E-mail:
wiseupwomen@wiseupwomen.org

Help And Protection For Savers And Investors

Alliance Against Fraud in Telemarketing and Electronic Commerce

National Consumers League
1701 K Street, N.W., Suite 1200
Washington, DC 20006
Phone: 202-835-3323
Fax: 202-835-0747
Website: http://www.fraud.org/
aaft/aaftinfo.htm
E-mail: info@nclnet.org

Coalition Against Insurance Fraud

1012 14th Street N.W., Suite 200
Washington, DC 20005
Phone: 202-393-7330
Website: http://
www.InsuranceFraud.org
E-mail: info@insurancefraud.org

Comptroller of the Currency

Office of the Ombudsman
Customer Assistance Group
1301 McKinney Street, Suite 3450
Houston, TX 77010
Toll-Free: 800-613-6743
Fax: 713-336-4301
Website: http://www.occ.treas.gov

Consumer Federation of America

1620 I Street, N.W., Suite 200
Washington, DC 20006
Phone: 202-387-6121
Fax: 202-265-7989
Website: http://
www.consumerfed.org

Federal Financial Institutions Examination Council

3501 Fairfax Drive, Room D8073a
Arlington, VA 22226
Website: http://www.ffiec.gov

Federal Reserve System Board of Governors

20th and C Streets, N.W.
Washington, DC 20551
Website: http://
www.federalreserve.gov

Federal Trade Commission

Consumer Response Center
600 Pennsylvania Avenue, N.W.
Washington, DC 20580
Toll-Free: 877-FTC-HELP
(877-382-4357)
TDD/TTY: 866-653-4261
Website: http://www.ftc.gov

Financial Industry Regulatory Authority

1735 K Street
Washington, DC 20006
Phone: 301-590-6500
Website: http://www.finra.org

Municipal Securities Rulemaking Board

1900 Duke Street, Suite 600
Alexandria, VA 22314
Phone: 703-797-6600
Website: http://www.msrb.org

National Association of Insurance Commissioners

2301 McGee Street, Suite 800
Kansas City, MO 64108-2662
Phone: 816-842-3600
Fax: 816-783-8175
Website: http://www.naic.org

National Credit Union Administration

Consumer Complaints Specialist
1775 Duke Street
Alexandria, VA 22314
Phone: 703-518-6300
Website: http://www.ncua.gov

National Fraud Information Center/Internet Fraud Watch

1701 K Street, N.W., Suite 1200
Washington, DC 20006
Toll-Free: 800-876-7060
TDD/TTY: 202-835-0778
Fax: 202-835-0767
Website: http://www.fraud.org

Securities Investor Protection Corporation

805 15th Street, N.W., Suite 800
Washington, DC 20005-2215
Phone: 202-371-8300
Fax: 202-371-6728
Website: http://www.sipc.org
E-mail: asksipc@sipc.org

U.S. Department of the Treasury

Office of Thrift Supervision
1700 G Street, N.W.
Washington, DC 20552
Toll-Free: 800-842-6929
Website: http://www.ots.treas.gov

U.S. Securities and Exchange Commission

100 F Street, N.E.
Washington, DC 20549-0213
Toll-Free: 800-SEC-0330
(732-0330)
Phone: 202-551-6551
Fax: 202-772-9295
Complaints: http://www.sec.gov/
complaint.shtml

Chapter 41

Additional Reading About Savings And Investing

Teen-Friendly Finance Books

Cash and Credit Information for Teens:
Tips For A Successful Financial Life, Including Facts About Paychecks,
Taxes, Budgets, Banks, Contracts, Major Purchases, and Everyday
Spending Habits
Edited by Karen Bellenir (Omnigraphics, 2009)

College Financing Information For Teens:
Tips For A Successful Financial Life, Including Facts About Planning,
Saving, and Paying for Post–Secondary Education, With Information
About College Savings Plans, Scholarships, Grants, Loans, Military
Service, And More
Edited by Karen Bellenir (Omnigraphics, 2008)

Complete Idiot's Guide To Money For Teens
By Susan Shelly (Penguin, 2001)

Debt Information for Teens:
Tips For A Successful Financial Life, Including Facts About Money,
Interest Rates, Loans, Credit Cards, Finance Charges, Predatory
Lending Practices, Preventing And Resolving Debt-Related Problems,
And More
Edited by Karen Bellenir (Omnigraphics, 2007)

Motley Fool Investment Guide For Teens:
8 Steps to Having More Money Than Your Parents
Ever Dreamed Of
By David Gardner and Tom Gardner (Simon & Schuster, 2002)

Rich Dad, Poor Dad for Teens:
The Secrets About Money That You Don't Learn In School
By Robert T. Kiyosaki (Little, Brown, 2004)

Straight Talk About Money
By Marion Rendon and Rachel Kranz (Facts on File, 1992)

Street Wise: A Guide For Teen Investors
By Janet Bamford (Bloomberg Press, 2000)

Teen Guide To Personal Financial Management
By Marjolijn Bijlefeld and Sharon K Zoumbaris
(Greenwood Publishing, 2000)

Teenvestor:
The Practical Investment Guide For Teens
And Their Parents
By Emmanuel Modu and Andrea Walker (Penguin Group, 2002)

20 $ecrets To Money And Independence:
The DollarDiva's Guide To Life
By Joline Godfrey (St. Martin's Press, 2000)

Wall Street Wizard:
Sound Ideas From A Savvy Teen Investor
By Jay Liebowitz; (Simon & Schuster, 2000)

Online Investment Games

Investopedia Simulator
Website: http://simulator.investopedia.com

It All Adds Up
Developed by National Council on Economic Education
Website: http://www.italladdsup.org

Planet Orange
Sponsored by Ing Direct
Website: http://www.orangekids.com

Stock Market Game
Foundation for Investor Education
Website: http://www.smg2000.org

Virtual Stock Exchange
Produced by MarketWatch, Inc.
Website: http://www.virtualstockexchange.com

Online Financial Journals and Publications

Barron's Online
Website: http://online.barrons.com

Business Week
Website: http://www.businessweek.com

Forbes
Website: http://www.forbes.com

Investor's Business Daily
Website: http://www.investors.com

Kiplinger Personal Finance Magazine
Website: http://www.kiplinger.com

SmartMoney
Website: http://www.smartmoney.com/mag

Wall Street Journal
Website: http://www.wsj.com

YoungMoney
Website: http://www.youngmoney.com

Other Web-Based Sources Of Additional Information

CNN Money
Website: http://money.cnn.com

Federal Reserve Education
Website: http://www.federalreserveeducation.org

Financial Planning Association
Website: http://www.fpaforfinancialplanning.org

Financial Planning Toolkit™
CCH Financial Planning, a Wolters Kluwer business
Website: http://www.finance.cch.com

Gainskeeper
Wolters Kluwer Financial Services
Website: http://www.gainskeeper.com

Investing for Your Future
Rutgers Cooperative Extension
Website: http://www.investing.rutgers.edu

Investing Online Resource Center
North American Securities Administrators Association
http://www.investingonline.org

Investopedia
Website: http://www.investopedia.com

Investor Protection Trust
Website: http://www.investorprotection.org

Investor Words
Website: http://www.investorwords.com

Investorguide.com
Website: http://www.investorguide.com

Investor's Business Daily—Learning Center
Website: http://www.investors.com/learn

Investor's Clearinghouse:
Alliance for Investor Education
http://www.investoreducation.org

Managing Your Money
Public Broadcasting Service (PBS)
Website: http://www.pbs.org/newshour/on2/budget.html

Market Watch
Website: http://www.marketwatch.com

MoneyWi$e
Website: http://www.money-wise.org

MotleyFool.com
Website: http://www.fool.com

My Bread:
NEFE High School Financial Planning Program
National endowment for Financial Education
Website: http://hsfpp.nefe.org/students

MyMoney
U.S. Financial Literacy and Education Commission
Website: http://www.mymoney.gov

Online Publications for Investors
U.S. Securities and Exchange Commission (SEC)
Investor Education: http://www.sec.gov/investor/pubs.shtml

Teenvestor.com
Website: http://www.teenvestor.com

Treasury Direct
U.S. Department of the Treasury
Website: http://www.treasurydirect.gov

Young Investor
Columbia Management
Website: http://www.younginvestor.com

Young Investors Network
Citi, Smith Barney
Website: http://www.smithbarney.com/yin

Index

Index

Page numbers that appear in *Italics* refer to illustrations. Page numbers that have a small 'n' after the page number refer to information shown as Notes at the beginning of each chapter. Page numbers that appear in **Bold** refer to information contained in boxes on that page (except Notes information at the beginning of each chapter).